PENGUIN BOOKS
THE BLACK ECONOMY IN INDIA

Arun Kumar teaches Economics at the Centre for Economic Studies &
Planning, Jawaharlal Nehru University (JNU), New Delhi. He has
Masters degrees in Physics from Delhi University and Princeton
University, USA and a doctorate in Economics from the JNU. His
areas of special interest are Public Finance and Public Policy and
Growth Theory.

He has coordinated the work of producing Alternative Budgets for
1993-94 and 1994-95 and demonstrated that alternative policies are
feasible based on the nation's own resources. Earlier he was at the
National Institute of Public Finance and Policy and worked on the
Report on the Black Economy in India. He has written extensively on
the subject in the last 18 years.

THE BLACK ECONOMY
IN INDIA

Arun Kumar

PENGUIN BOOKS

Penguin Books India (P) Ltd., 11 Community Centre, Panchsheel Park, New Delhi 110 017, India
Penguin Books Ltd., 27 Wrights Lane, London W8 5TZ, UK
Penguin Putnam Inc., 375 Hudson Street, New York, NY 10014, USA
Penguin Books Australia Ltd., Ringwood, Victoria, Australia
Penguin Books Canada Ltd., 10 Alcorn Avenue, Suite 300, Toronto, Ontario ŷM4Vŷ3B2, Canada
Penguin Books (NZ) Ltd., 182-190 Wairau Road, Auckland 10, New Zealand

First published by Penguin Books India 1999

Copyright © Arun Kumar 1999

10 9 8 7 6 5 4 3 2 1

Typeset in Times Roman by Digital Technologies and Printing Solutions, New Delhi

Printed at Chaman Offset Printers, New Delhi

This book is dedicated to the memory of my father,
Late Prof. Asha Ram,
whose implicit and explicit support to me
in my experimentation with ideas has made this book possible.

Contents

Contents

Preface

This book has been in the making for a long time. Since the late seventies I have been thinking on this subject. When I returned from the USA in 1976, I found my parents had not planned for a house on their retirement. So, in consultation with a friend, I thought of investing money into real estate. I was rapidly introduced to the world of black money. Speculation in real estate in the late seventies was rapidly driving up its prices.

I built a model of how to speculate in real estate and made some money. This required dabbling in black incomes and I was uncomfortable with the illegality. Even though I declared my full income in the tax return, I realized that illegality led to other problems in society. The lure of making money made one tolerate illegality, an ill which is causing breakdown of policy and weakening social structures. By early 1980, I decided that this activity was not for me.

I was introduced to other aspects of the black economy—in industry, the share market, gold, public finance and policy. Soon I became convinced that it was a macro phenomenon and that it was the principal cause of India's economic problems.

This partly explains my bias in this book. All writings in social sciences have an underlying bias and it is useful to be aware of an author's inclination. I believe that the black economy is eating away at the innards of Indian society. I thought it sufficiently important to write on the subject both at the academic and the popular levels so as to bring this ignored subject into focus of economic discussion. After more than thirty articles, I realized that I need to put together an overall perspective on the subject which is only possible through a book. An article is always written in a limited context and the reader is always left with doubts about other aspects of the problem. In writing this book, I have further developed the ideas in the various articles (listed in the bibliography) I have written from time to time. This has produced a complex structure whose logic has been presented in the Introduction.

The title of the book contains the word `black'. I am not happy with its use since it has racial connotation—black is bad and white is good. This term is being used only because people are familiar with the `black economy'. There is a need to find more appropriate term for it.

Writing a book like this poses several problems. First, the black economy is an under researched area so a lot of research is needed to say something significant. Secondly, those involved in it are interested in hiding rather than revealing facts. Finally, how does one confirm what an individual narrates or what is reported? For instance, in interviews, it was revealed that a key investigating agency had evidence of Rs 1 crore being paid by a businessman to a well-known top politician but those close to the latter flatly denied it. The official from the investigating agency also mentioned that there was repeated interference from the head of the agency and finally he was transferred out. In another interview, a former top functionary in the government revealed that the intelligence agencies had placed before the political leadership the details of who received the funds in the Bofors case. He reported that the leaders reacted to this out of fear and even implied that there may be a threat to their lives if they acted on the information. Others denied all this.

The book steers clear of such anecdotal accounts of the subject. Juicy bits of information revealed in the interviews, like, that the benami property of one top mafia man was around Rs 60,000 crore was not used since there was no way of getting confirmation.

At times, officers with a reputation for honesty were chary of talking. Some good friends straight-away said they did not know of anyone who would talk on the subject. There was another set who agreed to talk but never did. A retired head of police working in a research outfit said `come any time' but every time I called him up he said `next week'. Other friends in the police after twenty to thirty calls still did not oblige. One charitable explanation could be that they did not know much. An honest officer accepted that the corrupt ones changed the topic of conversation as soon as he walked in.

Nonetheless, this book represents the joint effort of a large number of people who talked to me in confidence. Given the nature of the subject, no names are mentioned. The book in a sense is a documentation of an important aspect of our times; one which has in some sense become a key aspect of our social existence. This is not to argue that honesty does not exist in our society but only to point to how marginalized it has become.

I was a member of team at National Institute of Public Finance and Policy (NIPFP) which studied the black economy for the Central Board of Direct Taxes (CBDT) and published a report on the subject in 1985. I had strong disagreements with the analysis being put out but these were not taken into account. Since then it has been in my mind that one day I will write an analytical account of the subject so that economists begin to see how critical the black economy is to their analysis. In drafting the Alternative Budget for 1993 and 1994, I showed how this could be done. What emerged from these exercises was in sharp contrast to the policies being pursued by the government. It reinforced the idea that the black economy cannot be ignored if a complete understanding of the Indian economy is the aim of the analysts.

Everyone thinks they are an expert on the black economy since it is so widespread that it touches, directly or indirectly, the life of all citizens. Only a minority directly benefits from it while most are its victims. Unfortunately, most commentators see the black economy is seen as episodes and not as a system—not as an interlinked and interconnected whole with widespread consequences for all, including their own welfare. This view needs correction if social action is to be taken.

For these reasons, this book is not anecdotal but analytical. An attempt has been made to use the material at hand and the results of interviews conducted to understand the overall pattern. In other words, I have tried one tried to see the unity in the diverse phenomena to draw lessons for the system as a whole.

Analysis requires a method. The title of this book suggests its subject matter is only economics. However, economics is a part of social sciences. Unfortunately, modern social sciences treats different subjects as distinct — history, sociology, politics and economics. This division is itself an analytical device but one which creates problems for gaining a broader understanding of society. In economics itself, there is so much specialization that few have an overview of the subject and often, the specialist loses track of his subject.

The black economy is not only an economic phenomenon but also has political, social and historical dimensions. What occurs at one point of time effects the subsequent events. Society has a collective memory based on its experiences and this effects future actions. What one society may take for granted another may reject outright. A foreign student at JNU noticed that most Third World students tended to go to the kerb market to change their foreign exchange into rupees while the students from the advanced nations went automatically to the banks. This is social conditioning.

Society is ever changing. That which has happened is not automatically repeated. Learning from its past, society is capable of changing itself. What appears insurmountable often has changed and very quickly and this introduces a large element of uncertainty in any analysis.

Analysis of the past can only be a guide to future action but cannot predict it. In social sciences an analysis yields judgments —there is no one unique path laid out. The outcome of an analysis is linked to one's vision of society. In other words, there is a large element of subjectivity in any analysis. Typically, for most problems there is no single or simple answer to a problem.

Experience is critical in social sciences both to posit the assumptions and to interpret results. It is the former which helps distinguish between the important and the unimportant. Experience helps decide how significant a result is. Yet, in today's rapidly changing world, experience is at a discount. The here and now has come to dominate and has led to a narrowing of the vision of society and man and atomization of entities both in space and time.

The narrow view of the subject, uncertainty of the future and the perspective in which the present dominates all else are intimately connected with the persistence of the black economy. It is within this broad sweep that the analysis of the black economy has been carried out. It is not treated merely as a topic in economics, but discussed in the widest possible context. The narrowly technical arguments are critiqued since they are influential and serve as points of departure.

For instance, a commonly held view is that the black economy makes things happen, that is, makes society dynamic. In a narrow sense this is true. But the real dynamism is in ideas and if they cease to matter because those proposing them are discredited then society is the loser. Whether it is an outcome of cynical manipulation by some elites or recycling of ideas from advanced nations, it kills dynamism and creates dependency. For instance, if an idea is proposed, it is asked `where else has this been tried?' or what does the USA do in this context?' As if no new idea can be tried out in India first.

When Queen Elizabeth came to India in 1997 she commented that there is terrible poverty and filth all around in Delhi. None need point it out since it is so obvious. We felt bad for a few days but then continued as before. This is loss of dynamism.

As a nation/civilization have we given up? Are we now no more than a geographical entity where? After all, life continues even in Kosovo or Afghanistan but at an extremely low level of social achievement. This book is not written to point fingers but to document a reality and to indicate how much of the nation's potential is wasted as a result of the existence of the black economy. It is possible to change this if we get our act together and then we as a nation will begin to count.

Given the wide canvass the book covers, it addresses issues at several levels—from the purely theoretical to the descriptive. There are a few technical portions which require familiarity with some tools and terminology. Most of the technical terms used are explained in a glossary of technical terms to help the non-specialists.

While the book tries to present the matter in simple terms some people may like to skip certain theoretical sections in a first reading. This does not disturb the flow of the argument. Later, if a reader so desires, she/he can return to the sections skipped to gain a deeper understanding of the subject.

The theoretical sections are in the middle of Chapters 2 and 3 and Chapter 4 is largely theoretical. The detailed descriptive or empirical or the very theoretical portions in the form of equations have been put in Appendices so as not to disturb the flow of reading.

The book takes the view that everyone can understand theory, if it is simply presented and without jargon. Analogy with traffic circulation, something most are familiar with, is used in each of the chapters to make things understandable. There is nothing like 'theory is not applicable' or 'theory and practice do not mix'—that is bad/wrong theory. In social sciences, theory is about the real world. In fact, the stand point of this book is that all those who ignored the black economy in the analysis of the Indian reality were doing bad theory and coming up with the wrong answers to the problems of the Indian society. The book takes the view that things are bad but a solution exists provided we confront the situation and for that we need to know the truth.

I must thank all those who readily agreed to talk to me about matters that are not usually made public. They ran a certain risk in talking but without their help this book would not have become what it is. I must thank my students over the years who attended my lectures in Public Finance and questioned me and helped me to sharpen my understanding of the subject. I must thank Saumen Chattopadhyay, Nirupam Mehrotra and Partha Sarkar for assistance with data and for discussions. Thanks are due to Jayendu Krishna who acted as a Research Assistant during the entire period the book was written. In the end, I must mention Kamini Mahadevan, my editor at Penguin who helped me put the book together and was patient with the delays and the glitches that came up.

Arun Kumar
Centre for Economic Studies and Planning
Jawaharlal Nehru University
July 1999

1

Introduction

What is known to exist but is not visible is surrounded by mystery. It excites the imagination and people spin yarns about it. The subterranean nature of the black economy makes it difficult to get a clear picture of it, though there are many images which are popular. Often it is believed that the black economy is all about bribes. Certainly bribes are an important component but they are a small part of the total picture. Bribes are seen by some to be speed money—money given to get work done quickly. It is supposed to promote efficiency. But that is a bit like a sale where prices are raised and then slashed. The black economy is supposed to promote employment but so does smuggling and drug trafficking. Some argue, it promotes economic efficiency. But then, however fast a runner someone may be, without a map of a labyrinth, she/he may not be able to get out of it.

It is also popularly believed that the black economy is a result of a lack of economic freedom or the absence of free markets or of high taxes or of disequilibrium between demand and supply in the market, say of foreign exchange. But unregulated markets like the stock markets have been the biggest conduits of circulation of black incomes and a highly taxed economy, like Sweden has had a tiny black economy. Thus, the reasons for the phenomenon of black economy are much more complex than what may appear to be the case at first sight.

Since each person is guided by her/his own experience, there are many views of what it is. The laymen with limited experience of the economy may take a narrow view. The businessmen may be excused for taking a partisan view of the subject since they think it benefits them. But what of the economists? Most have ignored this subject and act as if it does not matter. This is partly a result of the weakness of theory and linked to it a lack of understanding of the institutional factors of the Indian economy.

Economists have not even clearly defined what black incomes are. Consequently, there is confusion on what the size of the black economy is and widely varying figures are available in the literature. It is not even clear that analysts are talking of the same entity. Similarly, since analysts differ on what the causes of black income generation are there is no clarity on the remedies.

THE BLACK ECONOMY AND THE CITIZEN

The black economy in India is all-pervasive, affecting the day-to-day life of common people. Be it the purchase of a house or a pin, they have to pay a higher price either due to corruption or due to poor quality or due to a black premium. The loss of money is not the only cost to the common man since there are also associated delays, harassment and tension. While most citizens are its victims, suffering from its consequences in a variety of ways, a tiny minority (around 3% of the population) is its principal beneficiary. This minority enriches itself and accumulates wealth far beyond what it can do legally. The 'havala' and the 'gwala' episodes forcefully illustrate this.

Though accurate figures are not available, the black economy as a percentage of the national income (GDP) is supposed to have grown from about 3% in the mid-fifties to 7% by the end-sixties to 20% by 1981, to around 35% by 1990-91 and 40% by 1995-96.

Given its significant size, it is little wonder that the citizen's life is affected at every step by the black economy. Whether it is the education of a child for which a capitation fee has to be paid or it is the visit to a doctor who follows unethical practices to make an extra buck or the courts where various kinds of malpractice prevail or the police which extorts money for cases or the electricity, water and telephone departments which harass the citizen to make a fast buck, the list is endless.

It is not just the public sector but also the private sector that is involved in this harassment. Whether it is the landlord harassing the tenant for higher rent or the builder, broker and developer who cheat the public in the real estate market or the trader who sells adulterated stuff (food and medicines) or the restaurant owner who provides sub-standard food, the public has little relief. Then there is the mafia or the dadas who operate in slums and make life difficult for the citizen. A poor family migrating to a city with no assets is an easy prey for the land sharks. In connivance with the police and the local politicians, they get these immigrants to encroach on land and which pushes them into the grip of the local toughs who then get the family involved in drugs, prostitution, gambling, bootlegging, contract killing, and petty crime. The youth become easy victims to the scheming of the smugglers, the terrorist groups and the mafia in the urban slums because of the difficulty of obtaining decent (legal) jobs and frustration of their rising expectations.

In fact, more and more of police has not meant that law and order has improved. The reason is not only greater strife and criminalization in society but the nexus that has allegedly formed between the criminals and the police force. Increasingly, problems are sought to be settled through muscle power. This simultaneously weakens the state and encourages criminalization.

Many, specially amongst the well off, are involved in some illegality and have stopped taking a stand on social issues. The crack has widened into a breach. Principles have become relative —anything can be justified by a little twist. This and tne proliferation of the black economy has had a deep impact on youth which expects quick and easy money.

The burgeoning random violence, terrorism, sense of deprivation and criminalization in society are all linked to the black economy and have affected the lives of citizens.

The Macroeconomic Policy Failure

The pattern of problems encountered by the citizen suggest that there is a common thread running through them. If this is so, the causes of these problems are not specific but macroeconomic and systemic. But if the share of the black economy in national income has been growing, is that not something to be happy about since it implies a higher growth rate in the economy than the 'Hindu rate of growth'?

One of the biggest failures of the last three decades is that of planning. This can be linked to the growing black economy. Tax collection is inadequate, creating a shortage of resources, funds are siphoned off from allocations and from profits so that projects fail. Financial planning and time-schedules go haywire. The surplus needed for reinvestment into other projects does not materialize so that public sector becomes dependent on the budget and on subsidies. According to one estimate, the public sector lost Rs 30,000 crores through such corruption in 1990-91. In effect, but for the thriving black economy, the rate of profit of the public sector would have been at least 30% and not the 5% reported

The public sector has been privatized through the black economy. Its privatization under the New Economic Policies will only change the set of profit-earners—politicians and bureaucrats will get a smaller share of it. It is not that greater efficiency will follow but a redistribution of incomes is likely and the social role of the public sector will be altogether eliminated. Capital is looking for a way of increasing its share in society and not necessarily for a way of improving social welfare.

Generally, it is believed that black incomes are spent and much employment is generated. But this is not obvious since it depends on where expenditures take place. It is also not true that all the black incomes are consumed. Since black incomes tend to be large, a high proportion of them are saved. But then, why is there a shortage of savings in the economy? Is there a lot of associated waste of investment resources? A major part of black investment goes into real estate, gold, flight of capital, illegal activities, etc. The citizen regards these as savings, so why is there a shortage of them? The answer lies in understanding their impact on employment and the rate of growth. The paradox is, that India is seeking funds from international agencies for primary education, primary health, slum housing, whereas none of this requires anything to be imported. Does this not reflect a shortage of resources?

If the size of the black economy is 40% of GDP, today the loss of direct tax revenue at the present rates of taxes would amount to at least Rs 2,00,000 crore. The fiscal crisis and the balance-of-payments the country faces become natural corollaries. The rising debt burden and the consequent increase in the interest burden on the budget are also linked to inadequate tax collection.

How poor is the country and how short of resources for development to deal with its economic problems is often asked. Only macro analysis can provide answer and help understand the policy failure so evident in India.

The various policy failures (both macro and micro) have led to demands for the retreat of the State. Is policy failure worse than market failure so that leaving matters to the markets is more desirable? Is this true and if so, does it take into account the relationship of failure of policy with the black economy? Without understanding this, should the State abdicate its responsibility to society?

Rajiv Gandhi in 1989 suggested that out of every rupee allotted for rural development only fifteen paisa reached the field. This trickle can only thwart development. If one rupee is required for development and only fifteen paisa becomes available then the work would remain incomplete or it would require an investment of seven rupees. In the former case development would be stalled while in the latter case, development would be far too expensive and, therefore, remain limited. Either way then development would be limited.

The Usual is the Unusual and the Unusual the Usual

Hardly anything happens in India the way it should. Take the example of electricity. First, power plants break down or generate far less than they are capable of. Secondly, a huge percentage of what they generate, is lost in transmission and distribution—much of it stolen. What is supplied to the consumer is of the wrong voltage and frequency so that equipment breaks down. It is only by accident that one gets 220 volts of electricity; generally it is between 170 volts to 250 volts. State Electricity Boards are supposed to run at a profit but due to the black economy make huge losses. This example can be multiplied. What should happen does not and that which should not, happens.

Milk should be pure but chalk powder and urea are mixed in it. Mustard oil is adulterated causing dropsy. It is difficult to find unadulterated foodstuffs. Weights are fixed to give the consumer less. Most petrol pumps deliver 5 to 10% less petrol by volume and it is contaminated. With some exceptions, professionals—teachers, doctors, chartered accountants, lawyers, architects, etc.—are committed less to perfection and more to making money by any means. This has created a mindset in which the citizen expects things to go wrong as a matter of routine and acts accordingly, through channels which are outside the system. This is the starting point of the black phenomenon.

In how many places can an honest citizen fight and carry on his normal activities? The system and those running it are discredited. There is a loss of trust all around and rise in tensions. The rundown nature of the systems makes things go wrong more often than not. It is often hard to pinpoint the causes and therefore remedies are difficult at best. People become fatalistic and begin to believe in luck, astrology and God rather than in effort to achieve perfection.

Waste and Sub-optimality: Digging Holes and Filling Them

High and rising transaction costs follow for everyone. For business, the waste involved may be in transportation, procurement of materials, sale of products, necessity of buying influence for continuing projects, in doctoring accounts and maintaining expensive lawyers, employing liaison officers to develop bureaucratic and political contacts, in breakdown due to poor quality services (like, electricity, and roads). The cost of doing business rises and so does overcapitalization of projects. In the net, businessmen lose due to slow growth and waste even though they gain through the black incomes they generate.

For citizens there are rising costs (time and money) of getting work done, like extra health costs due to impure water supply, additional expenditures incurred due to poor law and order and poor standard of products available which need constant repair or attention. Even those individuals who gain through earning black incomes lose through the collective inefficiencies of the system.

Most of the unproductive activities result in generation of easy money and this has an impact on the work ethic. The idea that incomes should be related to the work effort stands devalued. Further, to obtain bribes, individuals do not work in the routine way. A salary is treated as pocket money while work is supposed to be done on receiving an illegal gratification. The spread of such practices widens the circle in which work is not done as a routine and inefficiency follows.

The professional class does not work as it should. Many teachers do not teach properly at school so that the students take private tuition from them. Many doctors prolong illness to get extra fees, chartered accountants sometimes sign on inaccurate accounts. As a result, attention to detail is often missing and the quality of work is poor. It is not so much that Indian sportsmen lack the killer instinct but that they do not have the finish that is needed to be world beaters. The system neither picks them early nor does it train them well; neither for technique nor for discipline. Talent comes up accidentally and not by design. The work culture is poor even amongst the elite even though they tend to blame the non-elite for this and other ills of the country.

Consequently, there is much waste in society attributable to the black economy. Many rich folk like to pay in cash to circulate their black incomes or some businessmen deliberately make their cheques bounce. As a result, the use of cheques has not spread and a lot more cash is needed by the economy. Similar sub-optimality prevails in most black economy activities. In other words, for a given effort, far less is achieved or the effort put in is less than required and the best is not attained. One can think of 'digging holes and filling them'. Everyone is active but very little is accomplished.

SIZE AND MEASUREMENT

If the black economy is to be taken into account in analysis, one needs to know its size and where it is important. How good are the statistics on the black economy? Obviously, no one reports these figures so that indirect methods are needed to measure its size. What are these methods?

One could ask, is it possible to simply use the white economy to represent the goings on in the black economy as well? Only if the two parts behave similarly. On the face of it, the two economies work differently, their practices are not the same so this is not a good idea. But there is no one place where one can learn about all these differences. This requires an extensive effort.

One could also ignore the black economy if it was small. But the size of the scams and their numbers are constantly growing as can be seen from the appendix to this chapter. Are there other indications of what is happening to its size? Indeed, yes as the book discusses.

Is there one good estimate of the size of the black economy that may be used in data work? There are so many widely varying estimates. But do they measure the same thing? If yes, why do they differ so much. Most estimates do not begin with a clear definition of the black economy. Given this lack of clarity, one is comparing oranges and apples when comparing the different estimates. Some methods have been termed 'scientific' but on scrutiny they are found to be deeply flawed, yielding a size by assumption. The size of the missing income added in these methods turns out to be the size of the black economy.

Before measuring, black incomes need to be defined. What all should be included in the definition? Are bribes black incomes? Are undeclared capital gains in real estate and share market to be included? (None of these should be included in the definition.) How should the purchase of gold and other smuggled goods be treated? What about the completely illegal activities, like drug trafficking and prostitution? Should one add everything that escapes taxes or only those incomes which bear a relationship to production?

Clearly, what is significant about the black economy is how much production is being missed out when the white economy is erroneously taken to be the total economy. In other words, if the black economy represents the national effort that is not captured in the national income, then as it fades away, what would be the size of the economy? This is a complicated issue since many black incomes do get included in the national income so that they are already counted. Similarly, some white incomes get excluded because of methodological deficiencies.

Apart from these theoretical difficulties, there are practical ones. How to define the businessman's income? Think of the small time business person next door who runs her/his office from the home, calls her car the company car and her servant the company peon, etc. In the evenings when the family goes for a meal at an expensive restaurant, the expenditure is shown as entertainment expense. How to account for all this?

A senior bureaucrat relative or friend may see as his privilege the use of his office staff and car for private family matters. The attached servants' quarters would enable various services to be obtained free of cost. A view has to be taken whether these activities with shades of illegality are black or white. Worse, these are hard to quantify.

Our major industries deny that they generate any black incomes. Yet, international agencies (including the IMF) report that Indians have stashed away a few lakh crores of rupees in secret bank accounts abroad. MNCs use transfer pricing to take out a part of their profits and pay top managers salaries in foreign exchange. How to account for all this?

Based on the examples discussed, the black economy is defined as the totality of economic activities in which black incomes are generated. Black incomes are defined as factor incomes which should have been reported to income-tax authorities but are not. In this, illegal activities are included but not transfers.

Causes

If the above discussion is correct, something needs to be done to control the black economy in India. But before that can be attempted, one needs to know why has it come into existence. Once the cause is identified, a remedy may be possible. Since there seems to be an underlying unity in the various manifestations of the black economy, the causes must also be systemic.

In the popular perception, high tax rates and the controls in the economy are taken to be responsible for the generation of black incomes. But does a teacher who does not teach well so that he can get tuitions think of these factors? Is a policeman collecting hafta propelled to do so by tax rates or controls? Why has the size of the black economy grown from around 10% in 1971 when the income-tax rate was as high as 97.5% to the current size of at least 40% when the highest rate is down to 30%? Further, since 1991, in spite of the dismantling of all kinds of controls, why has the size grown? The number of scams and their size have also grown.

Many government reports have dealt with various aspects of the black economy and have proposed hundreds of technical solutions. Some of them have also been tried but there has been no dent on illegality. Only laws have got more complex. Clearly, the problem is not a technical or a simple one.

Primarily, the black economy involves illegality, to earn extra profits or to retain them. When those who can afford to pay taxes to run society do not pay them and the social structure is subverted through the defiance of the rule of law, then other tax collectors emerge—like, the mafia today in the major metropolitan centres.

Adam Smith argued that while pursuing one's own self interest one may create social good—the invisible hand. However, it is also true that in pursuing one's narrow interest, in the short run, one may create social ills and in the long term harm one's own self-interest and that of society. The paradox is that those who gain the most from the growing black economy, the elite, are the biggest losers in the process.

The payment of black money in land transactions, encroachment on land, payment of bribes, evasion of taxes, misuse of public property, the misappropriation of public funds, and the like, are all illegal activities. Usually a chain of illegality is set up and forces even honest citizens to keep quiet. Those who have given a bribe do not stand up against corruption since they feel that others may also have had trying circumstances. The voices against the black economy weaken even amongst those who are its victims and the biggest losers from it.

These trends induce in the individual a widespread feeling of dissatisfaction with society and a helplessness. Social norms matter less and less. The individual draws support from other structures, like wider family, caste or community. The elite form a network to facilitate each other's work. Whether it is a telephone connection, a visit to a specialist in a public hospital or a train reservation, a contact is needed. There is a fragmentation of society.

Alienation of individuals and fragmentation of society along with breakdown of institutions leads to a sharpening of conflict in society. The primary conflict in a capitalist society is between labour and capital. They fight over their shares in the national cake. As the cake grows in size, each gets more but they are not satisfied since they want a share of the growing cake. It is a zero sum game and the conflict is sharp.

In India, the situation is much more complex since there is no neat division between capital and labour. There are other conflicts as well. There is an unorganized sector which can always be squeezed. There is agriculture which is a mixed bag. There is the conflict in the market place where the weak lose out. A new realization dawned amongst the elites in the sixties that they can overcome their weakness in the market through manipulation of policies, if they have the numbers. This added a new dimension to the conflict and has made it even sharper.

Thus, stakes in policy and the political process are very high. The political process needs to be kept in control to achieve unstated goals. Control over power gives the elite the freedom to make economic gains over and above what they can legally make. This is the source of growing illegality and the black economy. As democracy is subverted, people lose faith in it and it becomes easier to carry forward the process. They know, the systems are not going to deliver so they look for other mechanisms to get something from them. They vote for their caste, community or regional Robin Hoods.

A vicious circle occurs of a) conflict over the cake, b) need to control government policies or subvert them, c) the need to be in power to do so and d) the subversion of democracy. Through this process illegality and the black economy grow.

Since the New Economic Policies are deeply undemocratic, there is a further marginalizing of the vast majority of the population. New actors in the conflict have been added in the shape of the MNCs and international finance capital. National capital used to making easy gains through the black economy is now at a disadvantage and is trying to squeeze the other groups harder. Fragmentation of society and conflict over policies has become more acute. With a weak state and a freer business environment, illegality is now easier so that the black economy has continued to grow.

In brief, the black economy is a consequence of a vicious cycle of a crumbling social structure and growing conflict. The black economy in turn undermines social functioning and makes society less civilized by reducing the individual's faith in collective functioning. It undermines the sense of social justice, alienates individuals and engenders the feeling of each one for themselves—which ends with 'might is right'. It represents the narrowing of the social horizons of the social elite in the country and a truncation of democracy.

The private sector has exploited the weakness of the Indian state and of democracy to indulge in primitive accumulation of capital by any means. The black economy makes public profits into private profits. These accrue to the corrupt businessmen, politicians and the bureaucrats. Favourite suppliers and distributors give a cut to the politicians and the bureaucrats. Recently, cases have come to light where relatives of bureaucrats and politicians have opened firms to siphon out such profits.

To successfully bend rules, the vested interests need to not only subvert the politics but also the bureaucracy. A nexus has emerged amongst the businessmen, the bureaucracy and the politicians. *This is the triad.* The bureaucracy, a relic of the British rule, was always a part of the elite structure. It has not been difficult for it to change its role in post-independence India since it has hardly had a commitment to democracy.

Black Economy and Analysis

Some intellectuals have got coopted into the system. Mostly, they have ended up justifying and rationalizing the growing black economy. Many have argued that black economy and corruption exist everywhere in the world—as if that justifies its existence in India too.

Worse, there is a theory which justifies the existence of the black economy as a rational behaviour of optimizing individuals. In this framework, the black economy (say smuggling) is supposed to make the economy more 'efficient'—read, working of the market. These arguments based on static analysis and using a micro-theoretic framework treat society as an n-fold replication of the behaviour of an individual But is not society often greater/different than the sum of its individual parts? Philosophically, the fallacy of composition comes in the way of building the macro from the micro, by multiplying the micro behaviour n-fold.

Such analysis leads to the prescription that the State must retreat and the market must be allowed its fullest play even if it fails and equity remains a problem which markets cannot deal with. These theories justify the preservation of status quo and identify the interest of those who have market power as the interest of society. In its neo-liberal version, it provides a reason for the State to reduce its obligation to the individual and specially to the deprived in society.

Analysts who have used the fact of a growing black economy to discredit state intervention in the economy and policy failure to attack the pro-poor orientation (at least on paper) of policies as populism, they invert the logic of the black economy. Rather than see the rising share of the black economy and the consequent rise in the share of property incomes as the cause of policy failure, they depict state intervention as the cause of the black economy and economic failure. The international trends since the seventies —namely, the rise of Reaganism and Thatcherism, the decline of the Soviet system and the growing dominance of the IMF and the World Bank over the Third World—have been pushing this line of thinking.

Economists who analyse the black economy in micro terms, usually resort to optimization under given constraints and focus on individual behaviour. Income is taken to be given and its dependence on expenditures and output is ignored. This argument is fundamentally flawed.

Leo Hubberman, in his lucid book *Man's Worldly Goods*, showed that the State emerged in Europe as a need of business to conduct trade. Today, it is needed to enforce the laws by which citizens deal with each other in a collective way. Many other functions are assigned to the State by the citizens or are performed by it on behalf of them on the premise that it can perform them better than the individuals and can thereby improve the welfare of the society. Hence a modern society requires a State for a variety of purposes and this requires means of financing these functions.

Ultimately, each society has to decide the extent of state intervention in the economy. But even at a minimum, in a complex modern society, these requirements are large. A civilized society, realizing the advantages of the State carrying out many of the activities, may tend to a maximalist State but even in the normal course, just to set the parameters of a functional society, the State has to be fairly large (as in the advanced nations). The need for finance then is large and which can be raised most efficiently through direct taxes. Such taxes are also preferable since they promote a sense of equity in society.

In India the retreat of the state is a critical element of the New Economic Policies (NEP): liberalization and reform. However, what has happened is that the restraint exercised by the state on capital to keep its greed in check has been diluted and parts of the black economy are in the process of being legalized. In the process, the state has given up its attempt at more optimal utilization of national resources for the wider good. Illegal activities are being redefined as legal activities. Earlier, the import of gold, silver, electronic items, etc., was called smuggling. Now the import of these items is legal. Holding foreign exchange outside the economy was considered illegal but not any more. The black money held inside and outside India is being given a variety of amnesty, tax concessions and tax holidays. Ill-gotten wealth from the past is being legalized through 'voluntary disclosures'. The actions of law-breakers have been legalized.

In brief, the functioning of the black economy which has caused widespread policy failures has led to the discrediting of the notion of state intervention in the economy for the wider good of all. This has not only discredited the State but led to a further boost to the black economy and to a sub-optimality. The loss of the capacity of the State to push through an agenda has resulted in the erosion of the national will, ad hocism and a situation which seems to be unmanageable going out of control.

Remedies

The prerequisite to any remedy is the existence of a national will. But with the decline of politics and the breakdown of institutions, this has become a rare commodity.

In India, systemic solutions are needed. The triad needs to be dismantled. For this democracy needs to be strengthened and this requires electoral reform. Will state funding of elections work? These and other suggestions need to be evaluated. The experiences of fourteen senior politicians with elections have been presented so as to provide a background to this discussion. How much do they spend and can the State finance such expenditure? How are elections hijacked? These issues come out clearly.

The black economy has hit at the very roots of civilized society in India. It has adversely affected the long-term prospects of the elite groups themselves—those who have spawned it for their short-run gains. It has not even improved their short-run prospects since they also lose in the short run. The growing black economy has led to policy failure and strengthened capital relative to labour. But contradictions have forced the system to take steps which boomeranged into the current crisis compelling Indian capital to yield gains to international capital. The latter are strong enough to to make Indian capital concede much more than is necessary. This is specially so since national capital as the prime mover of the black economy in the last fifty years had weakened itself technologically and financially and has convinced itself that the nation lacks resources. This notion that the nation is short of resources has been internalized by other sections of the society, like the politicians. Hence indigenous alternatives are ruled out of hand. For any solution proposed, they ask, 'where else has it been tried?' This is the root cause of poverty in India.

The poor in India are at the receiving end of this process either way. Marketization whether of the global or indigenous variety marginalizes the poor further. The black economy has been playing this role in India and its legitimization will worsen the situation for the poor.

While society implies the coming together of individuals, forging it is a continuing process. Its progress depends how well society functions to achieve its goals. A civilized society is one which functions purely at the voluntary level (without coercion) based on a consensus about its goals. Becoming civilized is also a process. This requires individuals to feel a part of society and not be alienated from it in any way; the black economy impacts both these adversely.

2

Defining the Black Economy

The definitions of the black economy which are generally in use are either vague or not very meaningful. They either refer to some aspect of the problem (and not the whole of it), or they identify it as completely different animals. There is then a need to define the black economy.

To take an analogy from road traffic. What may be a violation of law in one country may be the rule in another—for instance, in a country with left side driving, driving on the right side would be an offense. As traffic grows and specially the fast moving variety, zebra crossings, lane driving, flyovers, etc., become necessary and the nature of violations changes. Likewise, the black economy changes over time and differs from one region to another.

The black economy is not an abstract entity. An understanding of it can be obtained by observing institutions and the key activities where it is important, like in business, the police, income-tax department, real estate, havala, gold market, the financial market and the public sector. Some of these activities have also attracted public attention recently for one reason or the other.

Of course, the black economy thrives in virtually all the sectors of the economy (some of which are briefly described in the appendices) and a complete listing is impossible. However, even from the activities mentioned above one can learn enough to obtain a theoretical understanding of the macro-economic features of the black economy and to define its key variables, investments, savings, exports, imports and consumption. This is crucial to a definition of the black economy and spelling out what is included and excluded from it.

DIFFERENCES WITH THE DEVELOPED WORLD

The black economy is a worldwide phenomenon—to a greater or lesser extent. Table II.1 gives the size of the black economy in select economies of the world around 1980. The difference is not just numerical but significant in qualitative terms, specially, between the developing countries and the advanced nations. For instance, in India, it affects all aspects of life but that is not so in the advanced nations. Offering the traffic policeman a bribe for a traffic violation is normal practice here. Tax inspectors or officials checking industrial pollution or sanitary conditions in restaurants routinely have fixed monthly pay-offs. Such occurrences would be the exception in the advanced nations.

Various names are used almost synonymously to refer to the black economy: parallel economy, black money, black incomes, unaccounted economy, illegal economy and irregular economy. As in many other fields of knowledge, these terms have originated in the West and there they refer to different aspects of the economy. However, these terms are often confusing or inappropriate when used in the context of the Indian economy.

To call the black economy a parallel economy is inappropriate. It suggests that the white and the black economies are independent of each other and never meet, like the railway tracks. In the western economies, illegal activities, like, prostitution, mafia and drugs and irregular or informal activities constituting the black economy are largely independent of the activities in the white economy, hence the use of the term, parallel economy. In the Indian economy, often white and black incomes are generated simultaneously in the legal activities. The two parts of the economy are intertwined and are not parallel.

Consider the sale of real estate, a legal activity, a part of the capital gains generated in the transaction are not declared. Similarly, in the manufacturing sector, a part of the production is not disclosed. When over-invoicing and under-invoicing are resorted to in contracts and in international trade, black and white incomes are simultaneously generated. In the rich nations, people may not report their incomes from secondary sources and this then becomes black income but in India, such incomes mostly fall below the taxable limit, hence they can not be termed as black.

The level of social organisation is higher in the western economies than in India. Most activities are legal and incomes from them are reported to tax authorities. Prostitution, gambling, bootlegging (in an earlier period) and smuggling are illegal activities. Incomes from these activities are not declared for tax purposes and hence constitute the black economy. That is why it is also called the illegal economy.

In India, illegal incomes are earned from legal activities also. For instance, in the manufacturing sector, to make extra profits, a part of the production is not shown in the books. Thus an illegal act becomes a part of a legal activity. Since most activities have both legal and illegal income components, using illegality to define the black economy would make almost the whole economy black which would not be correct. Hence, the term illegal economy would not be synonymous with the black economy in the Indian context.

In the developed world, most people are employed in the regular or the organized sector of the economy and have a taxable income. There exists an irregular economy in which people do a second job (or a third) in their spare time but do not report these additional incomes in their tax returns. There is also a growing trend of mutual exchange of labour services which also belongs to this economy. Hence, from amongst the legal activities, the irregular or the informal sector is the major source of black income generation in the developed world. Since the mid-1970s, with unemployment growing in these economies, the trend of taking odd jobs has increased, not just for a second job but even for simply earning a livelihood.

In the Indian economy, the unorganized sector employs a major portion of the work force (93%). These people are all around, in homes as domestics, in small establishments, in agriculture as landless labourers and so on. Most of them earn incomes below the taxable limit. Even if these incomes were reported, no tax would have paid. Hence, incomes in the irregular economy would not all be black in India and identifying the black economy with this term would be inappropriate.

To call the black economy unaccounted is also misleading. In western economies, as information is better organized, accounting of the national income is almost complete and accurate as far as the legal economy is concerned. In the Indian economy, information is sparsely available even for the legal activities. For instance, in respect of the private sector and especially in its unorganized components—say, incomes originating in trade, hotels and restaurants and construction— data are inadequate. Consequently, government estimates of incomes originating in these sectors are rather crude. Incomplete accounting of national income in India therefore is not only due to the existence of the black economy (because people hide their income) but also because data are incomplete. One cannot then take the part of the economy which is missed out in the national income accounts (unaccounted) as black economy.

Finally, the black economy in India leads to inefficiency in the system unlike in the developed world. The time wasted in non-working telephones, payment of municipal bills, delays in banks, slow movement of materials for industry or trade, etc., raises transaction costs all around. This leads to low productivity, poor quality of goods and services and non-competitiveness of exports (in spite of low wages). This inefficiency is a part and parcel of the existence of the black economy since people pay extra for any work where additional costs and hassles are involved.

FUNCTIONING OF THE BLACK ECONOMY: A FEW EXAMPLES

Understanding Speculation in Real Estate in Delhi

In 1995-96, 27 million individuals in the country were employed in the organized sectors (including in the government). The average income of this group was Rs. 6500 per month (Table VII.1). There are others in business and professions who may have average incomes similar to or larger than this group (Table VII.2). But their numbers are much smaller if tax data are to be believed. Thus, not more than a few million households in the country can afford to pay the rents implied in the present day prices of land in the major urban centres.

Flats in South Delhi priced at upwards of Rs 10 lakhs imply a rent of Rs 10,000 per month. The market (purchase or rental) for such flats can only be amongst those who have savings of Rs 10 lakhs or more or who have current incomes to pay such rents. Either way it requires a family income of at least Rs 15,000 per month. Such households would not number more than a few lakh in Delhi. All of them would have to be living in South Delhi for such high-priced properties to be supported there. Clearly, this is not the case. The implication is that in South Delhi, real estate has been bought up as investment for making capital gains. (In 1995-96, advertisements used to announce the willingness to buy any property in specified localities of Delhi.)

However, those who sell today are usually not in a position to buy a similar property a few years later unless they can add to their savings even faster. This is difficult, since real estate prices have been rising faster than that of other assets. People can of course sell a higher value property and move to one of lesser value.

Those finding the opportunity cost of their property high (and since renting out is not an easy option), tend to sell and use the money to generate income for current consumption. Such people can also purchase a new smaller property whose unit price is high. Thus, those who today own real estate are also the ones who can afford the high prices. However, if what is sold is not held back for speculation by the buyer then it would generate more of accommodation rather than less. There would have to be many more individuals with high incomes to purchase such high priced property for the price to remain high.

This mechanism alone should generate more of supply than demand, if speculation is curbed. Prices ought to decline unless some artificial demand is generated at the prevailing high prices. Some of this demand can come from foreigners and private sector companies. But, there are just not enough Indians with such high incomes to afford to live in such high-priced properties. Also, there is no great flood of foreigners into India.

It may be argued that individuals do not necessarily sell their property because its opportunity cost is high. They also look at its convenience. If they have stayed in a particular neighbourhood, they do not like to be dislocated. This is indeed true but it only slows down the rate at which landed property comes into the market. It does not stop this process. For instance, older people decide to shift to smaller towns or to their home towns after retirement. Sale also occurs at the time of death when the estate duty had to be paid. Now of course with the abolition of the estate duty this process has slowed down. Also, with greater mobility in the job market more people are moving about and buying and selling real estate.

Basically, at some level, the opportunity cost calculation comes into force and high-priced properties enter the real estate market and are parcelled out into smaller ones. However, the prices of even the smaller parcels are high enough to be affordable only by a few. Thus, rapid price rise in real estate is sustainable only if demand is created artificially through speculative activity.

Prices of real estate have declined when the speculators have not been able to hold on to property since too much of it has come into the market or because funds have been diverted out of the property market. This has happened many a time. For example since 1995, during 1990-92 and during 1981-83. In Delhi and Bombay, a very rapid rise in property prices had been witnessed prior to these periods.

Real Estate and Share Markets

The real estate markets in India where land or constructed property changes hands are conduits for the investment of black savings and for the generation of black incomes. Real estate is susceptible to speculation showing wild swings in prices and has strong links with the informal money markets. Transactions range between those that are entirely in white to ones completely in black—no clear norm (black to white rate) exists all over the country even though people often mention a ratio of 40:60.

Why is real estate an ideal conduit for circulating black incomes? The reason is that it is hard to value it. Hence, in a property transaction, if a certain value is declared by the buyer/ seller, it is tough for anyone else to prove that the price paid was different. The product is also heterogeneous, so that a flat on the ground floor has a different price as compared to one in the basement or two floors higher. The price of a plot in a colony varies depending on whether it faces a park or a main road or is in a cornei or is rectangular, etc. Depending on the material used, the cost of construction of a flat may vary from Rs. 300 to Rs. 1,000 per square foot.

The ability to undervalue real estate makes it an ideal investment for black savings. The demand for it comes both from those having black and white savings.

The trends in the real estate market are governed by growing demand; a result of the rising pressure on prime land in urban areas. The buyer transfers her/his savings to the seller and in return gets the real estate. There is little production or value addition (only to the extent of the brokerage paid which is usually 2% of the total value of the transaction). As discussed later, this causes a drag on the productive activities in the economy.

Ownership of land bestows on its owner a monopoly of a non- reproducible (not produced by human effort) asset. By virtue of this monopoly, the owner of the property is able to extract a return called 'rent'. The rent payable is linked to the economic potential of the property and goes up as its associated infrastructure develops. If the relative scarcity of developed land increases, the property is able to command a higher rent; at times it is higher than return from economic activity involving human effort. The higher the return available, the more desirable the investment becomes and the more it attracts funds. This leads to speculation as explained below.

The relative scarcity of developed land is a result of the investment pattern in society and it critically depends on the policy of the government since development of infrastructure is largely in its hands. If resources are concentrated on developing infrastructure in limited areas then not only the desirability of developed land in relation to other less developed land goes up but its scarcity is accentuated.

The economic potential of developed land goes up rapidly and leads to an upsurge in prices of such land. This pulls up the price of neighboring less developed land also and imparts a one way push to prices of real estate in urban areas. The benefit from this social development accrues to the individuals who own the land.

If the price of an asset rises continuously, it becomes desirable to invest in it for a profit (whether it is used or not). This increases the demand for the asset above that dictated by economic activity and leads to a further rise in its price. In such a situation, the motive for investment is not the income from the economic activity associated with it but the expected capital gains from it. Much of the investment in real estate is of this nature. Investors desire it more for the expected rise in its price rather than the rental income. The higher the expected capital gains the more the investment and the more the price rise.

That is why in a city like Delhi the rental income from residential property has been around 4% of the market value and yet funds pour into real estate. The expectation is that the capital gains would be around 25% per annum. In most areas, land prices have risen by more than 100 times in 20 years (roughly 25% per annum) between 1975 and 1995. Thus, including capital gains the return becomes about 30% per annum which is much higher than in almost any other investment. This return is nearly effortless since nothing much needs to be done (except holding on to property). Often property is kept locked up since rent constitutes a small part of the return and is not worth the risk.

From another angle, a high land value implies a high rent; a drain on the economic activity carried out on a given premises. This reduces the desirability of that activity itself as compared to investment in real estate. For instance, if one wishes to open a shop in a building, the high rent may deter such a step and the capital may simply be used to buy more real estate. Investment then gets diverted from productive economic activities to an unproductive activity, namely, speculating on the rise in price of real estate. This does not contribute to welfare of society.

If we now look at the secondary share market it is found that investments are also made largely with a view to obtaining capital appreciation. The earning power of a share is related to the profitability of the company issuing it. The expected capital gain on shares is related to the future earning capacity and the growth of the reserves of the company. Both these are determined by the profitability of the company. Policy plays an important role in determining profitability.

With the expected rise in a company's future incomes, the current price of the share rises. This possibility of a capital gain is then the source of speculation in share markets. Again, the reason for people investing in shares is capital gain rather than the expected dividend paid out by the company. Typically, on the market value of a blue chip share, the expected dividend gives a rate of return of 3% or 4%.

Therefore, the investment booms in real estate and shares markets are based largely on considerations of expected capital gains. This makes the two markets volatile. Whereas the swings in the stock market are both ways, in the case of real estate, the fall has usually been less than the rise. This is because the former is dependent on the level of economic activity in the country which goes through ups and downs (Earlier the failure of the monsoons was a major reason).

In the case of the real estate market, the link is not with the productive capacity of the economy in the short run but with the capacity to coerce out a larger share of incomes from economic activities. In fact, earlier, in times of economic crisis, real estate prices used to rise even faster. Investments flowed into hoarding those commodities which were in short supply and whose prices were expected to rise. This generated inflation and black incomes. A major portion of the black profits from speculation were invested in real estate so that it came in the grip of a vicious circle of investment and price rise.

Speculative funds from a declining stock market, looking for more lucrative investment have switched to real estate. Prior to 1991, when the stock market used to decline, the property market would rise. The rise in the one accentuated the fall in the other.

These trends were so powerful that even the government was not able to counter these tendencies. For instance, in April 1988, even a large intervention by the financial institutions failed to lift the stock markets whereas those days, even a rumour that the financial institutions are likely to enter the markets used to be enough to send the market zooming up. However, post-1993 all this has changed, now the markets depend on the actions of the FIIs based on their international perceptions. So, speculation continues but on a different basis.

The interesting aspect of real estate transactions and secondary share markets is that they are guided by capital gains. But this is unrelated to production and simply results in transfer of assets from one entity to another. Such activities may be characterized as unproductive.

Should the government not control the undesirable trend of funds shifting from productive into unproductive activities? After all, this tendency on the one hand dampens the investment climate and slows down the rate of growth in the economy, and on the other hand, it makes the access to land for the genuinely needy more difficult (at least in the urban areas). The crisis is serious on both fronts.

In brief, it is seen that a) the share market and the real estate market are interlinked b) they have been conduits for circulating black incomes and c) they constitute transfer activities generating capital gains and unproductive investments. These characteristics are also associated with other activities in the black economy.

Havala

The term havala refers to an informal banking channel (international) which runs along side the legal one which may be defined as having the sanction from the country's financial authorities. It can be used to transfer funds from or into the country or into the country. There are always people abroad, say the non-resident Indians (NRIs), who would like to send funds into the country. There are others who want to send their funds outside the country for activities which are not legally allowed; for example, earlier for taking a vacation, a child's education or for purchasing property abroad. The havala route connects the two. Those wanting to send funds abroad, get foreign exchange and those desirous of sending money to India get rupee funds here and get a premium for it too.

There are various intelligence agencies in India which collect information and keep tabs on illegality—both within the country and outside. There is also information flowing in from international agencies. It is believed that the world trade in drugs in the early nineties exceeded that in petroleum products—estimated to be over $500 billion. This was about twice India's GDP then. According to one estimate, in 1990, drug traffickers in India earned a staggering profit of Rs 20,000 crore from drug smuggling and it accrued to them in foreign exchange. A part of the proceeds needed to return to India through the havala or the smuggling route since they were required to continue the business.

Drug profits have been used to finance terrorism in the South, the North-East, Punjab and Kashmir. This is called narco-terrorism. In fact, the havala case came to light when a terrorist was caught with havala funds. Further investigation revealed the names of others. Funds are also used to finance films, purchase of political influence, etc. Pay off to politicians are made in India and abroad, in foreign bank accounts, to front companies, relatives, among others.

Since havala is not under the scrutiny of any government agency, illegal transactions are facilitated. One can use it to import goods illegally, say, smuggling of gold. If capital is to be taken abroad, called 'flight of capital', the havala route may be used. It is estimated that the country has lost through gold smuggling and its import (after 1992) an estimated $150 billion since independence. The estimates for flight of capital are unreliable but it could be anything upwards of $ 100 billion by now. (See appendix 2.7 on illegal international trade.)

Havala is the international component of a vast and flourishing informal credit market in India. Like the havala, it is outside the purview of government's (RBI and the Ministry of Finance) policies and provides businessmen with liquidity for both legal and illegal businesses. It enables businessmen to escape official scrutiny, for example, from tax men. When the RBI tightens the credit screws or tries to slow down the increase in money supply, these informal credit channels provide businesses the liquidity they need.

Small businesses having difficulty in obtaining credit from banks depend on the informal markets for liquidity and so do the illegal businesses. The share markets, builders and others use it to obtain funds. However, the informal credit markets are not involved entirely in illegal activities. For instance, they finance trade.

The activities of foreign firms in India have increased over time and in may of the deals struck by them a cut is paid through Indian middlemen. These funds are channeled through the havala route either to be taken out of the country or brought back when needed (like, for elections). The Jain Havala case provides an example of this.

In brief, funds routed through the havala channel are not only illegal but also violate foreign exchange regulations and tax laws of the country. This activity results in leakage of capital from the economy and causes problems for balance of payments. It also results in growing criminalization and capturing of businesses by illegal money.

The Economics of Gold

Gold production in the country has been negligible so that the demand for gold is met through importation (till 1992, smuggling) of gold. Till 1992, when inflow of gold into the country was banned it could only be brought in illegally through smuggling. This spawned illegality. Even though gold can be legally imported now by paying a nominal duty, smuggling has continued. Couriers bringing in gold without declaring it are periodically intercepted. The inflow of gold which was 190 tons in 1990-91 has increased to 815 tons in 1998, a 400% increase.

When gold is purchased abroad for dispatch to India, the person doing so parts with foreign exchange (howsoever, obtained) and knows that on the sale of gold in India she/he will get rupees. In effect, foreign exchange is converted into rupee funds outside the official channels. When the official channels are used to bring in funds from abroad, foreign exchange is deposited with the RBI which then releases rupee funds to the seller of foreign exchange. The foreign exchange tendered to the RBI goes to increase the country's reserves and the rupee funds released boost the money supply in the economy.

Gold is brought into India not only because it is profitable to do so but also because funds can be transferred to the country without questions being asked. Those earning incomes abroad through drug trafficking, under-invoicing of exports or over-invoicing of imports can use this route to transfer their funds back into the country. Non-resident Indians also use this route.

Gold has many uses, like, for jewellery and industrial uses (like in electronics components). However, in India these demands are not too large and much of the jewellery is made out of recycled gold—the family ornaments are converted into something else. In brief, demand for consumption is a small part of the total demand for gold.

People buy gold because it has a high unit value and it does not spoil. It has the ideal characteristic for being a store of value. It has traditionally been a good hedge against inflation. Over long periods, the value of gold has appreciated so that it gives a return. It is easily accepted by all and so is highly liquid, like money. Hence it has been considered a desirable asset into which Indians have put a significant part of their savings, especially the black ones, other nations have not shown such a high preference for gold so that India is now the largest importer of gold.

Those having large black savings hold a part of their assets in the form of primary gold (gold held as ingots called biscuits and bricks because of its convenience). As discussed in the next chapter, those with substantial black incomes, and, therefore, savings are no more than 3% of country's households, numbering about 6 million families or 30 million persons. Only these people are likely to have substantial holdings of gold, on an average Rs 13 lakhs per household assuming they possess the entire gold in the country. The annual import of 800 tons of gold would imply an average annual purchase of 133 grams per such family (4 grams per family for all families).

An asset is held when return on it is attractive. Since gold is imported, its value in India is linked to the dollar value of gold.

Hence a devaluation of the rupee vis-à-vis the dollar raises the price of gold in India. As inflation takes place in India, the value of the rupee falls in relation to the dollar and the value of gold appreciates. Thus, when a devaluation is expected or when the rate of inflation rises, holding gold becomes desirable.

Further, with inflation, while real wages decline and the demand for gold from wage earners falls, this is more than compensated by the rise in the demand from businessmen whose incomes rise with inflation. Thus, demand rises during inflation and the price of gold increases even faster so that it becomes even more desirable to hold.

The gold price differential between the international and the Bombay markets has been an important determinant of the inflow of gold. In the past it led to smuggling. Even now, it spurs the sending of gold by the NRIs since the differential means a profit. With the cost of bringing in gold reduced after its import was legalized, even though the differential has decreased, a larger amount of gold is coming into the country.

Even though more of gold has come in legally, the black economy has grown. Those who indulge in this activity are really the big sharks who were earlier involved in smuggling. They have continued their activity but with much lower risk. Their couriers shuttle in and out carrying gold legally and as contraband. Since holding primary gold is legal, it is difficult to catch smuggled gold. Sale of gold brought in has generated enormous liquidity in India for these people and has led to an increase in speculative activity, criminalization, interference in politics and to the generation of more black incomes.

Some argue that gold flowing into the country brings in wealth so it should be considered a positive thing. This is not true. First, when gold is brought into the country, foreign exchange is lost. If this had come into the country instead of gold, it would have accrued to the RBI and enhanced the country's reserves and improved the BOP situation. Secondly, privately held gold does not help the BOP. In 1991, when the country faced a default in debt payment to the IMF, this gold was not available to the government to meet its international obligations. Thirdly, some argue that foreign exchange would have also not come if gold had not been allowed to be brought in. But this is not true.

Fourthly, purchase of gold by an Indian in India is only a transfer activity. Savings of the purchaser are transferred to the seller of gold who is the importer or smuggler. This is siphoned out of the country. Hence, purchase of gold results in loss of savings to the national economy. Finally, gold is not a productive asset since only a part of it is converted into jewellery and its making charges constitute only a tiny fraction of its value. To the extent gold is imported for export of jewellery, there is no net import of gold and neither leads to loss of savings nor to unproductive activity. What is being referred to here is the gold which stays back in the country. In brief, the gold economy is linked not only to the black economy but to international and national illegal activities, to leakage of savings from the national economy and to unproductive activities.

The Financial Scam

The country faced a financial scandal of an unprecedented magnitude in 1992. Even though the Janakiraman Committee set up by the RBI estimated that the sum involved in the scam was over Rs 3,000 crores, the final tally remains a matter of conjecture. The entire financial sector of the economy was under a cloud. Fears have been expressed that a cover-up took place to protect the system. Be that as it may, the country needs to draw lessons from the scam and set its financial sector in order.

In popular perception, the scam relates to the share market but it must be understood that its ramifications were much wider, involving the entire financial sector—the RBI, banks, mutual funds, PSU bonds and government securities. Money made fraudulently by a few may have specifically been used in the share market but could as easily have been siphoned out into other speculative activities, like real estate or gold or foreign exchange.

Corruption and inefficiency, it was proved, are not the preserve of the public sector. Individuals are equally capable of subverting systems in the private sector to make a personal profit. Standard Chartered Bank, ANZ Grindlays and the Bank of Karad (all private banks) were the worst culprits and victims of fraud in the scam.

Public or private sector ownership did not make for any difference because the black economy is rampant in both and it was the real reason for the scam. This came through clearly. Further, the black economy works through the subversion of the law. The BRs were working smoothly as mechanisms of transfer of government securities amongst banks until some officials in connivance with the share-brokers decided that they could get away with irregularities. How could Bank of Karad with an equity base of less than Rs 1 crore, issue BRs worth more than Rs 1,000 crores? How did Standard Chartered accept BRs worth more than Rs 200 crores from this bank? Was there a quid pro quo promised in terms of future accommodation?

The link between liberalization and the scam needs to be understood. Irregularities in government securities transactions were pointed out by the RBI in July 1991. Yet, these transactions increased after July 1991. This is where policy enters the picture. The scam was not just the result of any specific policy in the liberalization package introduced in July 1991; the policy as a whole enabled the scam to take place on such a large scale and prevented it from being detected early enough. The rising share prices were considered to be 'good' for the economy. The Finance Minister stated in Parliament that he would not lose sleep over this price rise. Indeed, as is clear now the free markets were functioning but fraudulently. What the policy makers refused to consider was that resources were going into an unproductive activity and that could do long term damage to the economy. The policy makers' logic was that to maintain growth in the economy, in spite of cuts in public sector investments and government expenditures (since 1991), there was need for increase in private investments. A buoyant secondary share market is supposed to spur investment in the primary markets. It was hoped that this rising profitability in the secondary market might encourage flow of foreign exchange from the NRIs and foreign mutual and pension funds.

What this line of argument ignored was that the Indian stock market has been prone to malpractice (See appendix on the stock market) and if encouraged it could get out of hand. Indian industrialists indulge in insider trading not only to raise the price of their shares but also to bolster their own control over their companies, to ward off the threat of takeovers. In the liberalized free market environment, takeovers were expected to be easy. Smugglers and other NRIs (possibly as fronts for others) were reported to be sending in money and could easily take over companies. It has been suggested for some years that smugglers have been trying to buy out legal businesses to gain legitimacy. This is dangerous for the country.

It was not just the smugglers who were threatening takeovers, other Indians were also getting into the act. Even the Tata companies felt threatened. In any case, in a rising market, it made sense for the industrialists to buy shares rather than raise fresh equity for new projects. New projects take at least a few years to yield a profit. The share market was yielding much more than that in a few months time.

Floating new equity for new projects (rather than raising money for speculation in the share markets) was bad business since it would have led to dilution of control. Not only would industrialists have to buy own equity but also the Rights shares, otherwise the control would weaken. Fly-by-night operators hoodwinked the public and raised money for further speculation. There was a parallel for all this in the previous share market boom in the mid-eighties. Then, as after 1992, primary investment suffered and industrial recession deepened in spite of the concessions given by the government.

Banks' Profitability

Liberalization meant that commercial banks came under pressure to improve their profitability. Simultaneously, they had to face uncertainty in interest rates and the SLR requirements were enforced more strictly to keep money supply under control. The former coupled with the latter two has meant that banks were forced to do a lot more trading in government securities. Increase in interest rates on government securities meant a capital loss on the holdings of old securities. Therefore, they needed to be sold before the increased rates were announced.

The need for higher profitability and compliance with requirements of SLR meant that idle funds had to be circulated more rapidly. Brokers played an important role in this. To boost profitability, funds were diverted by banks into the rising stock market. Funds were channeled to brokers through foreign banks which had no problem in trading in the share markets through brokers. In fact, even mutual funds were routing their funds through the foreign banks. The foreign banks were obviously playing on the margins between the rates they had to pay and what they could get in the share markets. This is how brokers, like, Harshad Mehta became important and could have access to thousands of crores of banking funds. Initially, when the scam story broke, Mr. Mehta could clear his liability of Rs 600 crores to the SBI in a matter of days; indicating his clout.

Policy encouraged setting up of mutual funds to channel capital into the share market. Since the mutual funds promised higher returns, the market had to be made to go up and the policy maker facilitated it. The market read this as a signal that the government would not allow the market to fall. This suited bulls, like, Mr. Mehta. They not only got funds through the mutual funds, but were assured of success.

In other words, the government fell into a trap of sustaining a rising share market and a rising price-earning (P/E) ratio which was making the market increasingly unstable. The policy maker knew all this but was unable to/did not take corrective steps.

The share market became the mechanism for a few people in the know to make a lot of money at the expense of a lot of gullible middle class investors. Some analysts suggested that a lack of computerization was the reason for the scam. This argument does not hold water. In the advanced nations where all manner of computerization exists, markets are manipulated and scams occur. Computerization does not prevent frauds.

To conclude, it is evident from the above, how a reduction in controls and regulations by itself is not enough to reduce illegality. In fact, an atmosphere of permissiveness may be used by businesses to indulge in more illegality.

Public Sector and Black Economy

The Different Types of Black Incomes

Due to the black economy national production is incorrectly estimated. One part of it is under-estimated while another part is over-estimated. For instance, when cuts are taken on purchases and sales, the true output is understated since input costs are raised and the revenue realized less than it actually is; black incomes are generated. On the contrary, when a public servant does not do the work she/he is supposed to do her/his salary which is taken to be the contribution to national output overstates the output. For instance, a bank officer who does not reach office at the appointed time and then disappears for tea during public dealing hours is performing less work than assigned (and what she/he is paid for). However, these do not constitute black incomes.

The work of an income-tax officer incorrectly assessing income to harass a tax-payer so that she/he could extract a bribe is overstated. This is linked to the black economy and suggests that personnel of regulatory authorities who create work to harass the public in order to extract a bribe are those, a part of whose output should be counted as black incomes.

Not just regulatory work but the work of say, a teacher or a doctor is also overstated when they do not perform their work in the public domain but do it privately. Teachers resort to tuition and doctors to treating patients privately or recommending tests that have to be done privately. Likewise is the work of the policeman who is busy collecting hafta on the beat rather than overseeing law and order. Society suffers on three counts as a result of these activities.

First, the work which should be performed is not done so that essential social functions remain unfulfilled and result in losses. For instance, environmental pollution that should have been checked is not.

Secondly, the public sector is discredited and there is a demand for its disbanding. People become cynical and resigned to their fate and belief in collective activity suffers. Social action, essential for a civilized existence does not occur.

Finally, costs to society rise. That which should not happen happens and that which should does not happen so that society bears unnecessary additional costs. Since things keep going wrong, a permanent sense of crisis pervades and since administration becomes ineffective only ad hoc steps are taken to meet contingencies. Prevention is not feasible and costs of cure rise. The plague episode in Surat or the outbreak of gastro-intestinal diseases in large parts of the country or the rapid spread of asthma, AIDS and TB illustrate this.

There is another category of activity which amounts to misuse of public sector facilities, like the Minister using official transport for personal and party work, furnishing his own house at state expense, taking his family on vacation at the expense of some public sector concern, etc. This is all illegal, and therefore black but not overstatement of the output since work is actually performed.

What is the net effect of all this on the true output of the country? If the definition of the contribution of a service to the national output is the value of the salaries then public services are counted (though they are inefficient and raise social costs). However, public sector output is understated and needs to be recalculated to get the true contribution of the public sector to GDP.

The Middleman

To make corruption feasible in public life, 'middlemen' have emerged. Corruption creates uncertainty in transactions since it is an informal activity where norms are unclear. Middlemen smoothen the process of corruption by serving the needs of both the public, specially the moneyed and those in power—the politician and the bureaucrat. Those in authority do not have to sully their hands directly and minimize risk of detection and scandal. The middlemen dare not squeal for that would deprive them of their vocation since no one else would trust them in the future. Those in power can, therefore, rely on these people, the way they cannot on an average citizen who after offering a bribe may create a public scandal.

The middleman has a vested interest in the system not working smoothly and being opaque. The public believes that money needs to be paid even when no illegality is involved—whether it is for grant of licenses or for obtaining work under the Employment Guarantee Schemes (for the rural poor). Whether true or not, the public perception is that corruption has become universal and no work is done in the routine way. If nothing, the official is not found at her/his seat or will raise spurious objections since rules are never clearly stated. This fear forces many of the public to approach the middleman for getting even routine work, like, filing income-tax returns, getting property registered, paying electricity bills or getting water meters repaired, etc. Businesses do not mind employing middlemen once they rationalize payments to middlemen as service charges and get tax exemption on the bribe since it is a cost to them.

It is also true that the public does not know what the bribe should be for a given work, while the middleman, aware of the system on a daily basis, knows the rates prevailing at any given time. The middleman who has regular contact with the officials or the politician may also develop social contact and gives gifts at festivals and at social occasions. All this results in economies of scale for the middleman so that she/he has to pay a smaller bribe than what the public may have to pay.

The middleman also promises to be able to bend the rules for the client so that it appears as if the individual also derives a benefit from his service. The income-tax to be paid or property tax assessed becomes less than required by the law so that there is a saving for the client. The government, and, therefore, society loses while the official, the middleman and the individual share this loss. This three way sharing of the loot brings law into contempt and makes the citizen accept illegality all around her/him.

FROM THE SPECIFIC TO THE LARGER PICTURE

The examples of black activities described in the previous sections are only the tip of the iceberg but they help develop an understanding of many similar activities; malpractices in a few other activities are described in the appendices. What emerges from these descriptions is that illegality in each of the activities is not one of a kind but there is a common thread running through them. In fact, they are a part of a system and influenced by it. Understanding the specificity of a malpractice does not explain why it continues and what is its overall implication. A different understanding emerges when each activity is understood as a part of a macroeconomic system.

For instance, it is only from the macro system that one can study the impact of the black economy on say, the budget deficit or investment in the economy or the balance of payments. Consequently, one can figure out the impact of the black economy on employment, prices, growth of the economy, etc. (See Chapters 4 and 6)

Budget Deficit and the Public Sector

The budget deficit is the difference between the government's expenditures and revenues. The impact of the black economy on the budget deficit is both because expenditures are inflated and revenues are understated. For instance, when contracts are awarded, expenditures are higher due to pay off to politicians and bureaucrats and because they allow super profits to businessmen. Fictitious expenditures are claimed. Revenues are lower because tax collections are less than what they could have been. Even non-tax revenues are affected. For instance, the profits of the public sector are lower since some of them may be siphoned out. As a result, their contribution (to the Internal and Extra Budgetary Resources) to finance the public investments programme gets reduced and their dividend to the government (the budget) is less than it could be.

Consider two important expenditures. Subsidies, a major item of budgetary expenditure, are partly misappropriated by the propertied. Like, traders diverting grain from public distribution or FCI paying more for poor quality grain. Subsidized public services cornered by those in power are also transfers to the propertied. Expenditures on subsidies get inflated or misappropriated.

The rapid rise in the interest burden on the budget is a result of the black economy. White liquidity is preferred over black liquidity due to its greater flexibility of use and lower risk. Consequently, the return on black investments have to be higher than on white investments. Further, the rate of return available on black activities become higher by the tax saved so that the post tax rates of return on black activities turn out to be much higher than on white activities. Among the white activities, the interest rates offered by the government provide the floor rate of return for the economy as a whole.

With an increasing share of the black economy, a disequilibrium arises. The white rates of return tend to rise as demand for funds from the state grows and this leads to a sympathetic rise in the black rates of return. To preempt funds from flowing into the black economy so that the state can fulfill its requirements, the state has had to offer higher returns on funds it borrows. This raises the floor of rates of return available in the economy. The effect is a rising share of profits in the national income and a profit inflation. It also implies that over time, the cost of borrowing to the state and the interest burden rise.

The state has been forced to pre-empt banking resources by increasing the SLR and imposing social sector obligations on the banks. To maintain a semblance of profitability of the banking sector, the government had to allow banks to charge a higher rate of interest from non-priority clients and this further raised the floor rates.

The effect of the black economy on the budget is that instead of showing a primary fiscal surplus there is a deficit. Profits of the private sector rise by the amount of transfers from the public sector and swell undeclared profits. As shown in Chapter 4, no rise in demand is associated with such transfers even though the fiscal deficit rises. (However prices may rise due to increases in costs.)

Black Investments

Private investments, call them, I_p, need to be split up between a black and a white component, I_{pb} and I_{pw}. It is not that the black component comes necessarily out of black incomes and the white one from the white incomes only. For instance, savings from black incomes go into bank and post office accounts which channel them into white investments. While I_{pw} is reasonably well known and presented in the NAS, the other term needs to be modeled. I_{pb} may be classified into seven broad categories.

1. Under-invoiced inventories (including cash holdings)
2. Over-invoiced and under-invoiced plant and equipment
3. Informal sector activities, including trade, films, production, etc
4. Illegal holding of precious metals, gems and jewellery
5. Flight of capital for investments abroad
6. Transfer activities (like, secondary share market and real estate) and buying of influence (bribes for work, legal or illegal)
7. Illegal activities (like, smuggling, drugs, prostitution and crime)

Nature of Transfer Activities

Flows into real estate (not construction), secondary share market, and the like, where assets simply change hands, constitute transfers and do not result in production. They result in large transactions but little value addition (which is brokerage in these cases). There is little employment generation in the process.

To the extent that some of these transfers may be to those who have small incomes, say, old people, widows and small farmers who sell these properties, they lead to an increase in consumption, lowering the savings propensity in the economy. However, the bulk of these transfers are to other propertied who then have to make another decision to invest the proceeds. This holds for both the black and the white components of these transfers. As long as these investments circulate in transfer activities, like, say, from one property to another, the savings remain immobilized, lowering the income velocity of money. At some stage they may link up with productive investments but until then they lower the profile of investments and increase liquidity.

Given the overall macro black resources and the prevailing practices in the black economy, black savings (including the ones transferred) flow into each of the remaining six black investment channels. Some of these channels result in leakage of savings from the economy and require conversion into foreign exchange either through exports or through cornering private capital inflows (through havala). In the case of the havala transaction, rupee proceeds are paid within the economy and the transfer continues or consumption rises while savings leak out abroad.

Investment in precious metals, gems and jewellery is also like a transfer activity. A leakage of savings takes place when precious metals and gems are brought into the country or when there is flight of capital. The country also loses foreign exchange in both the cases and this affects the BOP. However, there is a minor difference between the two cases. When precious metals or gems which are smuggled in are held, assets are purchased in the economy but savings are lost to the economy. In the case of flight of capital, the national economy loses savings but Indians still own the savings abroad. In the two cases, even though the same havala channel is used, in the former case, the chain of transactions is longer due to the transfer of goods (which are simultaneously assets).

In effect, the transfer activities of the black economy either lead to larger consumption or savings leak out of the economy or they are invested in a white or some other black activity. Investment in other black activities gets counted under those heads. The tendency of investing black savings in the white economy cannot be large (otherwise they need not have been generated as black). As argued a little later, consumption out of these incomes would also not be large so that the major avenue left would be leakage from the national economy. To conclude, black savings when invested in transfer activities discussed above and which are not counted in the national income account lead to transfers from one black investment to another till they largely leak out of the national economy. The leakage of savings corresponding to these transfers requires surplus on the current account so that foreign exchange is earned to enable the leakages to occur. However, these leakages involve illegal activities.

Manipulation of Inventories

When inventories (stock of unsold goods) increase, they amount to unrealized profits. By valuing them lower or not disclosing their full extent, the total profits are reduced. In the books, the income of the firm is the revenue from sales while the total cost of manufacture for the year includes the cost of manufacture of unsold goods, the inventory increase. The additional cost must be deducted from the costs to obtain the cost of manufacture of the output sold.

If the cost of inventory increase is underestimated then the costs attributable to the output sold would be higher and the book profits lower. Similarly, when the inventories decline, it would pay to reverse the process and reduce the profits. Since sales are larger than the output, revenue is higher by the amount the inventories decumulate. Now, by overvaluing the inventories, the cost of these inventories would be inflated and the overall profit reduced.

In this mechanism, the black income, since tax is being evaded, is retained in the firm and accumulates as a stock. This may be skimmed off by the management through financial jugglery. For instance, credit may be taken on the basis of the market valuation of the stocks. Fictitious sales may be shown (running down book inventories). Correspondingly, the debtor's column in the balance sheet would show a rise and the cash flow of the company shows a deterioration. But this is only a financial device and does not convert black into white.

Another method for under-valuation is through the stamping of incorrect prices on the products. Take the example of certain textiles and cigarettes both of which have a high excise duty component. There is under-invoicing of bills and subsequent collection of the balance in cash from the wholesale dealer. Often under-valuation is resorted to through the system of offering discounts or through the sales of so-called 'seconds' or 'scrap'.

Other Investment Channels

Increase in under-invoiced inventories are undeclared investments, that is, investment through the black channel. Increase in cash holdings are likely to be a small part of the total. On the contrary, over-invoiced plant and equipment implies a lower real investment; in fact, negative black investments. Under-invoiced investments, like, undeclared investment in construction, imply that the actual investments are larger by this amount. An important component of this investment is the flow of incomes from illegal activities (like, drugs). Finally, undeclared investments and investment of black savings in informal sector implies that white private investments rise as unfulfilled projects get funded and working capital becomes available. Investments in illegal activities also raise the level of investment in the economy. (For more detailed treatment of each of these aspects, see Kumar, 1999.)

In brief, only a part of what are understood as black investments constitute real investments in the national economy. It is this component which raises the level of output. The total investment in the true economy is then larger than the declared investments both because the size of the economy is larger and also because of the higher savings propensity out of black incomes. However, it is smaller than what it could be because of the transfer activities, illegal activities and the leakage of savings from the national economy.

The white investments have more interlinkages in the economy associated with them as compared to the black investments. Further, a part of the output from white investments is not declared and generates black incomes while black investments mostly generate black incomes but due to leakages, have a small multiplier.

The External Sector

As pointed out earlier, due to smuggling in of gold, silver, gems, electronics goods and due to flight of capital abroad, the national economy loses foreign exchange. The foreign exchange for these activities is raised through a) the havala route which taps the Indians abroad wanting to send remittances back to India, b) exporters and importers indulging in under- and over-invoicing, respectively and c) drug smugglers whose profits accrue abroad and who want to transfer funds to India.

Out of the incomes of Indian nationals working outside, a part is invested there itself. This is an unavoidable loss of savings and should not be counted as part of the black economy savings. Another part, which Indian nationals want to send to their families or businesses in India comes through the havala channel. If a businessman needs funds outside the country he takes them there from the havala operator and pays the operator's Indian counterpart from his rupee funds in India. The rupees are then paid to those who were to receive the foreign funds. This involves leakage of savings of those sending their funds outside. Those receiving funds in India may save a part of it and consume the rest. This is no different from what such individuals would have done had they received the funds through the official channels. This leaves the savings-investment pattern of the black economy unchanged and as captured in the remaining six channels.

The third part of the earnings outside may be used to smuggle in goods. Precious metals and gems are largely smuggled in to be held as assets, they represent a transfer of savings out of the economy and are like a capital account transaction. Smuggling of other goods increases consumption in the economy at the expense of savings.

Indian nationals holding assets abroad, purchased from savings siphoned out of India, earn a return on them. This should have accrued to the Indian economy through invisibles. These proceeds are lost to the national economy and result in lower official remittances and a larger official current account deficit.

In brief, there are four kinds of effects on the national economy due to the black transactions in the external sector. First, is the implication for foreign exchange reserves and money supply. Remittances which do not flow into the country through official channels means that foreign exchange does not accrue to the RBI and corresponding funds are not released in the economy. Secondly, for national savings. Not only is the flow of savings of Indians abroad reduced but savings in the national economy either leak out through this route or are lowered through increased consumption. Thirdly, for the current account. Exports are larger by the extent of under-invoicing while imports are larger by the extent of smuggling and under-invoicing but smaller by the extent of over invoicing. In the net, the true deficit in the trade account (not counting drug traffic) is lower than indicated by official data and current account of the true economy shoulds be in surplus (Table II.2). Finally, private holdings of assets abroad or gold held in the country does not help the official reserves or the BOP situation.

Given the above, the true current account deficit consists of a black and a white component with the latter reflected in the official data and the former the remaining part. The economy's BOP situation continues to be reflected by the official data with its growing dependence on inflow of capital (FDI, FII) through official channels.

Consumption of the Rich: The Black Component

Wage and salary incomes are well defined except the managerial salaries, a part which are paid in cash and are not reported to the tax authorities. It is the incomes of the owners of businesses and those who are self-employed, like doctors, lawyers, chartered accountants, etc., which are ill-defined. Their income is calculated by deducting costs from the total revenue (collections) they get—the net income is taxable.

The total collection of a private doctor (or of other businessmen and professionals) is not her/his income since out of that she/he may have to pay the salary of a receptionist or assistant, rent for the premises, consumables, depreciation of equipment, etc. All these costs are not income for the doctor and are to be deducted from his total revenues. But costs are not well defined and this enables the misreporting of personal expenses as business expenses.

Consumption of the well-off, is out of both black and white incomes. It is generally believed that the consumption propensity (the fraction of the income consumed) out of the former is larger than out of the latter and also more import intensive. But it is found that the consumption propensity of people out of their black income is much smaller than that of the wage earners whose income is mostly white income or lies below the tax limit and who earn much less.

The savings propensity out of black incomes is smaller than that of the property earners as a class because, as pointed out earlier, there are transfer activities associated with them. The transfers result in some incomes being redistributed to those with smaller incomes. However, most of the transfers are also highly concentrated so they would have a high savings propensity. In brief, savings are made by property owners out of their white and black incomes and by the wage and salary earners out of their incomes. The saving propensity out of these three components is in a declining order. Inspite of an increase in consumption of the rich, an increase in the share of black incomes causes the savings propensity to rise. (Kumar, 1995).

Expenditures from black incomes are on items like consumer durables, housing, entertainment, children's education abroad and foreign holidays. What is spent abroad is clearly import intensive but there is also an increased demand for imported goods in the national economy. Earlier, this demand led to increased smuggling activity. Post-1991, since import restrictions have been fewer, smuggling may have declined but legal imports have expanded faster than the nominal GDP. Indirectly also, imports rise, say, to meet an increased demand for energy as luxury consumption rises.

The goods consumed using black incomes do not necessarily originate in the black economy. Also, white incomes may be used to purchase goods or services produced in the black economy. It is enough to recognize that the consumption propensity of the well off would have a value larger than that implied by the white economy alone. Also, the consumption out of black incomes is supposed to take place more quickly than out of white incomes.

Is the slow growth of the economy then a result of low savings, i.e., lack of resources in the economy? A consequence of the growing incomes in the hands of the property owners should be a rise in the savings propensity in the economy and this should have made more resources available for development. Official statistics indicate a decline in the savings rate in the eighties. The reasons for this perhaps lie in a) the consumption pattern of the people whose share of incomes is rising and b) in the inadequacy of data. The surplus earners demand luxury goods which when unavailable in the economy have spawned smuggling and leakage of savings. What this points to is a wasteful use of scarce resources rather than a shortage of resources. Slow growth also wastes resources by leaving them idle or by not producing them.

In brief, the above discussion suggests that there are several factors which cause the savings propensity to decline. The substantial black component of the property incomes should have caused it to rise but such savings are underestimated.

DEFINING BLACK INCOMES

The description of the black economy in India so far can be used to derive at a definition of it. All the activities in which black incomes are generated must be included. The existing literature suggests several ways of doing this but a clear picture is still missing.

S.B. Gupta (1992) emphasized that the violation of state laws is the source of black income. Earlier Kabra had like Gupta emphasized the political economy approach. However, this idea is only a partial indirect definition since black incomes are also generated in the private sector, independent of the state.

Kabra also defined what he called 'simple' and 'compound' black incomes. 'Simple' black incomes refer to incomes from legitimate activities on which taxes are evaded. 'Compound' black incomes refer both to incomes generated in illegal and hidden activities (called gray area activities where white and black incomes are simultaneously generated). S.B. Gupta terms these as reportable and unreportable black incomes. The latter are incomes that cannot be reported for tax purposes because they are earned through illegal activities. The former are incomes earned in legal activities but not reported to tax authorities.

Here the problem arises that any probable links between these suggested categories of incomes and national incomes accounting are not pursued, and hence there is ambiguity in regard to the exact definition of black incomes. Gupta adds up all the incomes that are evading taxes. But what if the same income evades several taxes? Would it not cause an overestimation of the size of the black economy?

This raises an important definitional issue. Namely, is it the income which is evading taxes that is to be counted as black income or is it the amount of each tax evaded; or is it that each time a tax is evaded out of a given income, that income is to be counted as black income (again and again)?

Niklos Kaldor in 1956 provided an intuitive analysis about black incomes which may help arrive at an acceptable definition. This idea was further developed by the author in 1988 and 1993. Kaldor suggested that black incomes are generated from what are called property incomes in the National Accounting System (NAS). These are called factor incomes and tax evasion is based on them. In this definition, there is no multiple counting of black incomes since each income upon which any taxes are evaded is counted only once.

Within the framework of NAS, black incomes are property incomes— profits, interest and rent. Transfers are made out of these in the form of bribes, etc., but these are not to be counted since they only cause redistribution. This is not to say that they are unimportant. They are important because of their impact on consumption, savings and investment. Consider why bribes are not to be counted in the black economy. If bribes were not illegal, they would have been a cost for earning the income and hence been deducted in the calculation of the income on which tax is to be calculated. It would have been taken to be income only once in the hand of the bribe taker. In the scheme used here they are counted once in the hands of the bribe giver. If they are also taken to be income in the hands of the one receiving the bribe, there would be double counting.

Take another case, that gold smuggling. It was illegal earlier and is now legal. Would the gross revenue of the smuggler, the insurance paid, the bribes given and wages paid be counted separately as black incomes? Now that this activity is legal, the net profit would be taxed in the hand of the importer (the former smuggler) and wages in the hand of the courier. Here, the net profit includes the former bribe and insurance which are (hopefully) not required. Thus, the gross profit should be counted only once and not several times.

Thus, it is hard to accept (as S.B. Gupta has attempted) in a global measure, the addition of the various figures, like, evasion of corporation tax, excise duties, customs duties and sales taxes to income tax evasion. It amounts to counting the same income as black several times over.

An estimate was made by the National Institute of Public Finance and Policy (NIPFP) in 1985. It also adds estimates of black incomes in different activities without taking care that there may be multiple counting. The NIPFP estimate is based on the definition that black incomes are 'incomes which are taxable but are not reported to the tax authorities' (p. 10). This is a tax man's definition. Apart from the problem of multiple counting, it does not discriminate between whether the economic activity in which the black income is generated is legal or illegal and by definition leaves out all incomes generated in illegal activities which lie below the taxable limit.

The definition does not concern itself with whether production (and, therefore, national income) is underestimated. This could be either on account of deficiency of data or due to tax evasion and these aspects need to be separated. Finally, certain incomes that get counted as black in the NIPFP total, like, capital gains, are transfers between individuals and not linked to production and national income.

Some studies such as by Cagan (1958) and others following from it define black incomes as factor incomes which should have been but are not captured by national accounts statistics primarily on account of taxes and/or regulations (see Tanzi, 1982: p.70). The US tax authority, IRS, took the view that black incomes are those on which taxes are not paid. Molefsky adopted an intermediate position which combined the above two definitions (Tanzi, 1982: p.47). Contini identifies the problem very differently as market for "irregular labour services" (Tanzi, 1982: p.201).

Different authors seem to implicitly adopt the definition appropriate to the problem at hand. For instance, the definition used by IRS (given above) is important from the point of view of budgetary resources but is not of much use for estimating the true production in the country. The NIPFP definition is a similar one since the study was conducted for the Central Board of Direct Taxes.

There is also a political dimension to choosing the question to be studied and the definition to be adopted. For instance, if black economy is only a matter of statistical illusion, i.e., a result of faulty methods of estimating national income or of inadequate and incomplete data, etc., then no hard decisions are necessary. Purely administrative measures and streamlining of procedures can be considered to be adequate responses to the black economy. However, if the problem is viewed as a structural one, wide-ranging political changes may be called for.

National Accounts Statistics and Black Incomes

It may appear that black incomes are not counted in the national accounts because they are not reported to the government. This is not true for two reasons. First, the white GDP may capture some aspects of the black economy as well. For instance, as already discussed, in some cases, say when the quality of the mark is poorer than in the specifications, the contribution of the public sector to the national accounts includes the cuts received by various people. It is accounted for in this way and need not be added separately. In contrast, bribes paid by the private sector for getting work done are not counted since they are paid out of black incomes already generated through some economic activity. They should have been counted in that activity but are not. Consequently, that difference between white and black incomes is not between that which is counted or not counted in the NAS.

Secondly, a part of the incomes are missed out from the NAS due to methodological reasons and absence of reliable data. This is not only due to deliberate falsification of data to generate black incomes—a point to be elaborated in the next chapter.

Both wage incomes from illegal activities and unaccounted business incomes which lie below the taxable limit should not be considered as black incomes if tax revenue is a criterion. Typically organized sector wages would fall in the tax net and are reported by employers automatically. Unorganized sector wages usually fall below the taxable limit. Hence it is the non-wage and non-salary incomes (property incomes) that evade taxes.

Other Aspects of the Definition

Often black incomes are referred to as black money. This is not the appropriate term to use since it connotes currency held under the pillow. It signifies immobilized currency and deposits.

But, it needs to be remembered that money is a store of value and a medium of exchange and not useful in itself. It circulates incomes and moves from one hand to the other in exchange. This can take place faster or slower depending on what the velocity of circulation is. If economic activity is slow, money also circulates slowly.

Money which is kept as a store of value is only one of the assets in the portfolio of savers. It is chosen it over other options due to its liquidity and future use possibility. It enables its holder to quickly invest in other assets when an opportunity presents itself. Usually, only a tiny fraction of the savings of the nation are held in the form of money. Similarly, black savings can be held in many forms with money as one form. Since this is only a small part of the total black savings, use of the term black money to signify the black economy is inappropriate.

It is also inappropriate since the concern here is with the annual black income generation and not the immobilized stock of money held by those operating in the black economy. The former signifies a flow and the latter a stock.

Finally, there is some printing of illegal currency and its circulation. This may also be referred to as black money since it does not have official sanction. But from all indications, such activity is not yet large in comparison to the total size of the annual black income generation in India.

At times, the black economy is also referred to as corruption. However, as already discussed, bribes, pay-off and cuts are mere transfer of incomes. These do not relate to production of goods and services. Estimating them and adding them to the total for black income generation would amount to double counting. Anyhow, they constitute a fraction (an important one) of the black economy and cannot, therefore, signify the whole.

Definition of Black Incomes: Undeclared Profits

Gross profits are made up of white and black profits. White profits are the ones declared for tax purposes. No taxes are paid out of black gross profits since they are undeclared. As already seen these are generated in several ways. Abstracting from details, the following methods are used for generating black incomes.

First, by inflating costs in the books through showing higher expenditures. For instance, personal expenditures are shown as business expenses. Over-invoicing of purchases and falsification of employment data (muster rolls) are also used. Second, gross revenue is understated in the accounts through under-invoicing sales, by misdeclaring the price or output or both. The output may either not be shown or declared as 'seconds' or shown as waste. The actual cost of production of this undeclared output is loaded on to that of the declared output. Third, there are illegal activities where the entire output is black. For instance, in the case of smuggling, prostitution, drugs, gambling, etc. From these black activities a part of the profits accrue outside India.

Out of the black gross profits undeclared interest and rent are also paid. In partnership firms, undeclared dividend are also paid out of these profits. Since profit, interest, rent and dividend are referred to as property incomes, one can argue that *black incomes are property incomes* (See Kaldor (1956) and Kumar (1988b)). In completely illegal activities, there is no question of declaring wages so that these should constitute black incomes. However, in the rest of the economy, wages are inflated so that there would be a tendency for the under-reporting of wages to cancel out. Finally, most wages, even the illegal ones would tend to fall below the taxable limit so that would not need to be reported, hence not black. Anyhow, as a first approximation, it may be assumed that in the economy as a whole, wages are not underestimated.

The definition that is the easiest to work with in the Indian economy would be—incomes that ought to have been declared for tax purposes but were not. Here, a whole set of incomes from petty bribes, corruption and the like, would be included but that component of these activities which falls below the taxable limit would be left out. Incomes from capital gains and illegal activities would be included. This definition would be analytically incorrect and results in double counting.

Considering the above arguments, the focus of any definition of black income has to be on *factor incomes and elimination of double counting.* Evasion of multiple taxes from a given factor income has to be eliminated. Out of the gross profits, either income or corporate taxes are to be paid so that evasion of these taxes constitute black incomes. Theoretically, even illegal incomes should be reported to the tax authorities. So even they should be included in the definition.

Black incomes may be defined as factor incomes, property incomes, which should be reported to the tax authorities but are not. Transfer incomes are not to be counted as black incomes. Since tax evasion is also illegal, other forms of illegality should also be included in the definition. This definition it should be noted, covers evasion of all other taxes, like, excise and sales taxes since evasion of these taxes involves declaring only a part of the true output, hence evasion of incomes.

The implication of this definition is that as black incomes are revealed, the amount of tax collected will rise by a higher percentage than the amount of incomes revealed—from the same income several taxes are evaded. With the older definition, tax collection would rise by a smaller percentage since for each tax there is a separate black income.

Finally, since black incomes are factor incomes, they measure economic activity. Some of these are socially useful (like, undeclared production) but missed out from consideration of analysis or policy-making. These activities result in considerable amount of social waste and this needs to be curbed.

Social bads also get included (like, prostitution or drugs) in the definition but these activities need to be discouraged. In brief, the black economy represents that economic activity with which some degree (ranging from zero to hundred per cent) of illegality is associated. Since this involves a considerable amount of waste of social effort, society is less well off than implied by the work put in.

3

Measuring the Black Economy

Is the black economy a significant proportion of the total economy? If not, why worry about it? Is it concentrated in some sectors of the economy or even if it is small in magnitude does it have a strong impact on certain activities, and therefore, needs to be studied? Before discussing how to measure its size, it is useful to understand how important the black economy is.

Think of road traffic. If only a few break traffic rules then this may be ignored. But, even if violations are not too many on an average but are more concentrated in some areas or specific to certain forms of transport this would have to be noted and acted on. Abuse of traffic rules are not voluntarily reported and only that which the police record (a fraction of the total) gets known. The police, even if assumed to be honest, cannot catch all traffic violators. Hence, the infringement of traffic laws has to be estimated by various means. This is exactly the case with measuring the size of the black economy.

SOME MAGNITUDES

The size of the black economy is usually reported as a percentage of the reported GDP at market prices. In the literature, several measures are available and whichever one is used, the size of the black economy turns out to be significant. The NIPFP Report (1985), estimated the size of the black economy (not counting smuggling and illegal activities) to be 20% of the white economy for 1980-81. Gupta (1992) pointing to errors in this estimate corrected it to 42% of GDP for 1980-81 and 51% for 1987-88. The 'Monetarist' estimate yielded a figure of 47% for 1978-79.

These widely varying estimates obtained from different methods are not comparable because of various definitional and methodological inconsistencies. Most critically, due to lack of definitional clarity, there is double and multiple counting and transfer incomes are clubbed together with factor incomes. Correcting for these infirmities, a figure of 30% for 1990-91 and 40% for 1995-96 seems more plausible (See section 'A rough estimate').

This implies that the black economy was by 1990-91 larger than the primary or the secondary sectors. Its effect on any analysis of the Indian economy, namely the growth of output or of the demand (especially, consumption) patterns could not be ignored.

It is sometimes argued that the white economy can be treated as a proxy for the total economy, consisting of the black and the white components. But this is possible only if the black economy affects everything in the economy in the same manner. On available indications this would be an incorrect assumption since different aspects of the economy are affected to varying degrees by the black economy. Hence the black economy therefore needs to be explicitly introduced in the analysis and cannot be assumed to be represented by the white economy. This has major implications for analysis and policy.

Likewise, with regard to the external sector, the magnitudes of the black economy in relation to the official data are very significant. For instance, while official exports in 1990-91 were $ 18 billion, 170 tons of gold valued at $ 2.2 billion or Rs 6,000 crores at the then current domestic prices was smuggled in. In 1990-91, there was an estimated flight of capital of $ 5 billion and smuggling of other items (silver, electronics goods and synthetics) of at least another $ 1.5 billion. This was financed through two sources the havala channels and the profits from drug-trafficking as discussed in the previous chapter.

Further, savings held abroad (in foreign exchange) by Indians was said to be at least $ 100 billion. Interest earned on this would have been at least $6 billion (annually). Adding up all this, the country lost in 1990-91, foreign exchange of at least $15 billion, not counting drug traffic earnings. This amount would be equal to 80% of the official exports. If this loss had not occurred, in

1990-91, the country would have had a current account surplus and not a deficit of $9.7 billion. Any discussion on the country's BOP difficulties clearly needs to take into account the black economy and the leakages from it.

National Income Accounts and the Black Economy

Most analysts ignore the black economy. This is so either because they have not developed the required analytical framework and/or because they argue that the data is not available (or is unreliable). But this misses the point that even the statistical basis of data on the white economy is often only a little more firm than that relating to the black economy.

The implications of under-estimation of the size of the economy and specially of the service sectors for calculating the growth rate of the economy since at least the seventies has been serious as it has resulted in misconceptions about the trends prevalent in the economy.

The economy is divided into the primary, the secondary and the tertiary sectors. These are further divided into nine sectors. The contribution of each of these sectors to output are estimated by different methods and are affected differently by the black economy. In certain sectors, the method used for estimation does not utilize tax-reported data. Hence, existence of the black economy does not affect the determination of the size of these sectors. Agriculture and construction fall in this category. The contribution of certain other sectors to the NAS is incorrect not because of the existence of the black economy but due to a lack of reliable data sources, for example, in the unorganized sectors.

An indication of the errors in the white estimates may be made from the former finance minister's statement that excise duty evasion maybe of the order of 40% (Budget Speech 1993). Since excise duties are mostly paid by the organized manufacturing sector, this statement implies that the official production data from this sector are in error by 40%. After all, data reported to the excise department is the data provided to the income-tax department and the Annual Survey of Industries (ASI) and these are the ones used in the National Income

Accounts. But, this is the sector the data of which is supposed to be most reliable. Thus, the uncertainty in the data from other sectors, especially from the unorganized sectors (with substantial self-employment) and more so in the case of the tertiary sector is likely to be even more than 40%.

Given that the margins of error in the various components of GDP may be large, how much faith should an analyst have on the GDP data from the National Accounts? It is surprising that though the degree of uncertainty is large in each of the components of the GDP, yet the sum of these components is used as if it is precise. Further, even though it is the existence of the substantial black economy which creates the errors in the data on the white economy, few analysts make the attempt to rectify this defect.

The National Account Statistics (NAS) reveal only a part of the economy and there is a reality beyond it which may be referred to as the true picture. The debate on the growth rate of the economy refers only to the revealed picture.

The problem of estimating the true growth rates of any sector are at two levels. First, there are deficiencies in the methodology and in the data base available for estimation. Second, independently, there are problems arising from deliberate suppression of information by economic agents for generating black incomes. These cause under-estimation of both the size and the growth rate of the national income and its components. If there are problems of under-estimating the size of any sector, they are the greatest in the tertiary sector as discussed below.

In brief, two points emerge regarding the use of data from the black economy. First, the degree of uncertainty in the data for the black economy is certainly higher than that for the white economy but that is a quantitative matter and cannot be the reason for excluding the black economy from theoretical analysis. Secondly, the uncertainty in the data for the white economy relates in a large measure to the existence of the black economy. As discussed below, the black economy is concentrated in the services sector and as argued in the previous chapter, black incomes are of property incomes. Both these facts are important from the point of view of measurement of the size of the black economy.

Black Economy, Services and Surplus: The Trinity

The growth of the black economy and the services sectors in India were not taken seriously till the eighties. Even now the real significance of these trends is not fully appreciated. The former has been anecdotally commented on because of its negative consequences on not only the economy but more generally on the political and the social fabric of the country. Its role in controlling elections and consequently the politicians and the political process, in fostering corruption and the consequent inefficiency and the decline of the various institutions of our society has been causing grave concern.

The growth of the services sector in the economy (Table III.1) has produced a mixed response. On the one hand, it has given the growth rate of the economy a buoyancy which the traditional primary and the secondary sectors could not do. On the other hand, it is viewed as the growth of an unproductive sector. Whatever be the judgment, it is true that since the eighties a) this sector has displaced the primary sector as the largest sector of the Indian economy and b) is growing faster than the others.

A trend less noticed but visible from the official data is that the share of factor incomes which may be classified as property incomes has been growing (See Table III.1). This growth may turn out to be even higher if calculations could take into account a) the growing black incomes and b) the share of property incomes in the category mixed income of the self-employed in the (NAS).

In the available literature, the interlinkage between these variables have been missed and each has been commented upon singly. For instance, some have talked only of the profit inflation, noting that the share of property incomes in India has been growing. The significance of this relationship has gone unnoticed because the analysts have not known how to take into account the black economy.

MEASUREMENT-RELATED ISSUES: A SURVEY OF THE LITERATURE

In India, over the last 45 years various estimates of the size of the black economy have been made. The biggest measurement exercise was mounted for the study conducted by the National Institute of Public Finance and Policy (1982-1985). It gives a 'global' estimate as well as estimates for the sugar industry and for real estate.

NIPFP Estimate

The NIPFP estimate is based on the definition that black incomes are those, 'incomes which are taxable but are not reported to the tax authorities' (p 10). The definition does not discriminate between whether the economic activity is legal or illegal. It implies that illegal incomes which lie below the taxable limit are to be left out. The definition does not concern itself with whether an income is a factor income or a transfer income. Hence the estimate is unrelated to the national income and its under-estimation.

It is unclear what exactly does the NIPFP methodology include? Two kinds of estimates are given. The first, presented in Chapter V and claiming rigour, estimates the black incomes generated in current legal activities and excludes capital gains on sale of assets. There is another total, given in Chapter XII, called the 'global estimate'. It is an amalgam of the first estimate and various other guesstimates.

The guesstimates include undeclared capital gains on sale of immovable assets, black incomes generated in exports and imports, fixed capital formation in the private corporate sector and public sector, smuggling of gold and finally import licenses and imported goods. A number of problems arise here, like the inclusion of capital gains which are transfer incomes and as explained earlier should not be included in national income accounts.

The problem with the global estimate is the degree of reliability that can be placed on the final figures given. For instance, if it was assumed, following the data collected for Delhi, that only 50% of the value of documents registered in Book I corresponded to the sale of immovable property, under the Indian

Registration Act, 1908, the black income estimated from this item would be in error by 50%. Similarly, the black to white ratio assumed is 2:3; if the yardstick adopted was 2:1 as may be the case for smaller value property, the error would be enormous. Clearly, most of the estimates are highly sensitive to the assumptions and at times it is not clear why a certain assumption was chosen.

For 1975-76, the estimate of black incomes from legal activities yields, with considerable accuracy', a figure of Rs 3,741 crore. In the global estimate for 1975-76, the figure added to this 'accurate' figure is Rs 6,200 crore. Thus, guesstimates dominate the global estimates.

However, this in itself may not be entirely objectionable. The more important drawback of the whole exercise is that it is unclear as to what are the various components of black incomes which get included in the supposedly rigorous estimate. In other words, if one does not know whether or not some of the sectors of the economy are getting excluded then one would not be able to identify and add the missing elements alone and may end up double counting some of the components.

The NIPFP 'rigorous estimate' is based on the National Council of Applied Economic Research (NCAER) survey conducted in 1975-76. This was supposed to capture all incomes including business and other activities (like, bribes). Hence all incomes, black and white, legal and illegal should have been captured to give the true income distribution in the country. But if only some incomes were reported to NCAER and not others, then it was necessary to know which ones were being reported. If the assumption is that people were reporting some of the black incomes (otherwise the method does not make sense) to the NCAER survey and the white incomes were being fully reported, then the NCAER total should have been higher than the NAS total and not lower since the official national income data does not take into account the illegal incomes.

The NCAER survey total of income was 44.4 % less than the official total so that one cannot even assume that all the white incomes were reported to NCAER and it is even less likely that black incomes were reported. The distribution of income in the country obtained from it cannot be accepted as representing the true income distribution. For instance, it is not clear from the survey that illegal foreign trade is missed out and should be added later in the global estimate. If what is excluded in the survey was well defined then one could add what is missed out by taking recourse to independent surveys.

In brief, the NIPFP estimate is not really 'scientific', whether one considers the narrow or the global estimates. It should be treated on par with other estimates which are guesstimates. Above all its lack of definitional clarity regarding black incomes makes it non-comparable with other estimates.

S.B. Gupta critically evaluated the NIPFP estimate and agreed with the criticism that it contains '. . . an unknown degree of bias'. Curiously, without establishing this bias and reassessing the NIPFP estimate he goes on to use it as a base for his own estimate. Further, he adds many more items of black income generation to the NIPFP estimate so that the chances of double counting in his estimate are even greater. For instance, he has added the evasion of various taxes, like, corporate tax and excise duties. As discussed in the previous chapter this leads to multiple counting of black incomes.

Some other omissions in Gupta's estimate may be mentioned. The mistake in the NIPFP study about adding black premium on real estate is repeated. Leakages from the public sector could have been estimated since they are significant and reported in several studies. The size of the public sector in the national economy is significant so that this is an important source of black income generation which is missed out.

METHODS TO ESTIMATE THE SIZE

It is evident that there is no foolproof way of estimation available. The reason is that the black economy exists in the shadows and no one reports their black incomes. One cannot simply add up reported figures so that estimation has to be done through indirect ways. These are really in the nature of guesstimates.

The analyst has to be like a detective, gleaning from the clues left behind who the thief may be. Since the shadowy black economy is integrated with the white economy (and is not parallel to it) it leaves traces in the white economy. These traces are used to estimate the size of the black economy. Several methods have been developed for doing so and four of them are discussed below. It must be remembered that each one of them has problems and that the definition adopted differs across methods. Within each method there are several ways of estimating the size of the black economy. Here only the method is discussed and not the details of measurement which differ from model to model.

The Input-Output Method

This method uses a well-known truth that you cannot get something out of nothing. There has to be an input to produce (say, using machines) an output. Sugar-cane is converted into sugar by the sugar mill or various inputs and seeds are used to produce a crop. The output obtained from an input depends on the available technology. Since each output requires several inputs, there is a separate input to output ratio for each of the inputs and these are technologically defined. For instance, if to produce 1 ton of sugar, the factory uses 10 tons of sugar-cane and 100 man hours, then the ratio is 10 for sugar-cane and 100 man hour/ton for labour.

If the input-output ratio is known with respect to one of the inputs, then the output can be estimated. So, if in the above example, it is given that 200 million tons of sugar-cane was crushed by the mills, then one can conclude that 20 million tons of sugar would have been produced. The true output is estimated using the quantity of an input and when compared to what the mills report, say 19 million tons, it can be gathered that the undeclared output of sugar must be 1 million ton.

In brief, the method consists of using the output-input ratio (c) along with the actual amount of that input (I) to calculate the true output ($X' = I.c$) and when this is compared with the declared output (X), then the amount of undeclared output ($X'-X$) can be estimated.

This method is deceptively simple. How does one obtain c and I to get X'? Even if the correct I is known, c can only be obtained by dividing the declared output X by I. But this will give a wrong c (c') so that (c'.I) will only give X and not X'. Hence, evasion would not get detected.

Further, as technology changes, c changes so that a value of c obtained at a point of time will not be applicable at a later date. For instance, if in the sixties a computer of a given capacity needed a few kilowatts of energy to run, today a similar computer needs only a few watts of energy. Thus, c is hard to get unless technology can be taken to remain unchanged.

Some have used this method for calculating the size of the black economy on the assumption that energy is used in all production so that an output-input ratio with respect to energy can be used to calculate the true output. Since a bulk of the energy is generated in the public sector, it was assumed that the input is accurately known. But the output-input ratio has changed dramatically in the last fifty years. It was assumed that over time this ratio has changed in a defined manner so that it can be obtained for any year. This is sheer guesswork.

Energy as an input is also not well defined; use of one form is being substituted by others, like bio-organic materials (cow dung) and non-commercial sources (animals) are being replaced by commercial sources (kerosene, electricity and coal). Each source of energy has its own efficiency of use so that both I and c are poorly defined. Finally, even for the commercial energy sources, there is lot of theft, so what is sold and what is actually used are different amounts.

In an economy the production pattern also changes which in turn changes the input output ratio. For instance, as the tertiary sector, concentrated in the cities, grows at the expense of the primary sector, energy intensity of production rises. Urban areas are more energy intensive since transport and other infrastructure are required on a much larger scale.

While the output-input ratio is difficult to obtain for the economy as a whole, it is easier to get for an industry. Technology and inputs are far better defined. Such a method was tried with some success in the case of sugar industry in India for the period

1960 to 1978. But even in this case severe difficulties were encountered.

The Survey Approach

As the name suggests, this method is based on using sample surveys. For instance, one can survey the consumption pattern of a representative population and then project from it the total consumption of the country. This can be compared with the data for the reported production of consumption goods to find out the amount which goes unreported. One could also use an income survey but this is inherently unreliable since as seen in the case of the NCAER survey, perhaps even all the white incomes are not reported. The interviewers are worried about being caught by the income-tax authorities if they reveal their true incomes. With consumption data this problem is somewhat less.

In India the National Sample Survey Organization (NSSO) undertakes consumption surveys and classifies the population according to consumption classes. But, this cannot be used to get the income distribution. The reason is that those in the lower income category resort to consumption loans and consume more than they earn. Those in the upper income categories are inadequately covered in the survey. Further, consumption as a proportion of income declines as the income level rises. The consumption of upper income groups is not only not captured in the survey but as one moves up the income ladder it represents their income less and less.

These surveys can serve the limited purpose of finding out the practices that prevail in each of the sectors and from that one may make an estimate of the extent of illegality prevalent in the various sectors. In some countries, surveys have been conducted to find out how many people have second or third jobs or are involved in mutual help. Specific surveys like these are different from those which involve asking people about their illegal activities. Unless the person is comfortable with the surveyor, it is unlikely that the information given would be honest. Impersonal questionnaires cannot be a substitute since people can hardly be expected to commit things to writing.

Recently, surveys have been used to develop corruption indices. Nations have been ranked according to perceptions of businessmen. Based on an elaborate procedure, an index is prepared to compare corruption across nations and over time.

However, basic questions remain unanswered by these surveys. It is assumed that corruption exists in the public sector (the government, police and judiciary) while it exists in the private sector as well. The surveys used are largely confined to the top echelons of managers and businessmen and often from the transnational firms. Such surveys would be biased and not yield correct results. Corruption has a country specificity which cannot be easily captured in an index. Those interviewed may be talking about different things across nations so that comparisons may be difficult, if not impossible. Finally, individuals are not comfortable talking about their own illegality. Ultimately, in constructing the index, many judgments may be implicitly involved so that one arrives at a guess sanctified by a 'scientific methodology', as pointed out earlier in the case of the NIPFP estimate.

The Monetarist Method

This is an important trace method and is akin to the input-output method. The idea is that in a modern economy, money is needed for every transaction. A good passes from the seller to the buyer and money passes in the opposite direction. Money is not just cash but also what is held in banks or the credit limits given by banks.

Money moves from transaction to transaction and goes around several times each year. It is the totality of the annual transactions which result in the generation of national income. Thus, money circulates the incomes in an economy. How fast or slow it circulates incomes is called the velocity of circulation of money. Money itself is not eaten, only its circulation can be faster or slower. When people are uncertain, they may hold money and not circulate it so that the velocity of circulation declines and at other times, the velocity may rise.

Currency entirely issued by the Reserve Bank of India (a small amount of counterfeit currency also exists) circulates through the banking channels and results in the money supply in the economy. This is rather well documented by the RBI. Hence the input is known and the velocity of circulation is the output-input ratio. The two together should yield the estimate of the true total income generated in the economy.

Money is needed to circulate incomes in both the black and the white economies. Since white incomes are known, it is felt, it should be possible to find out how much money is needed to circulate these incomes. The difference between this amount and that in circulation—the balance amount of money in the economy—can be taken to be circulating the black incomes. Applying the velocity of circulation to this figure would then yield the size of the black economy.

This sounds simple, but it is deceptive. Drastic assumptions are required at each stage. How much money is required to circulate white incomes? Money has no colour; that which circulates the black economy also circulates the white one. Indirect ways have been devised to estimate the amount of money used to circulate the white economy. For instance, in one model, by looking at the market practices, an estimate has been made of how many times coins and currency notes of different denominations move in one year. This enables the estimation of the total income circulated annually. A comparison of this with the incomes captured in the NAS then gives the incomes not captured. This is taken to be the black income generated.

Usually, using sophisticated equations, the demand for money is estimated. One of the factors included in this equation is a proxy for the size of the black economy so that the amount of money needed to circulate the black economy is obtained. If the velocity of circulation is applied to this figure the size of the black economy gets determined. However, the velocity of circulation required which is the relevant variable for the black economy is not known.

The velocity of circulation depends on the institutional factors in an economy. Hence it is likely to be different between the white and the black economies. For instance, individuals consume more out of their black incomes than out of white incomes. But transactions in the black economy require a more circuitous route and extra costs so the velocity of transaction may be more than in the white economy.

A common fallacy is that all black transactions take place in cash. However, banking channels and post-office accounts are routinely used to park funds and circulate them so it is not just cash that is used in the black economy. What is true is that due to lack of trust and the need to keep transactions away from official eyes, there is greater circulation of cash in the black economy than in the white economy. It may then appear that the velocity of circulation should be higher. However, because people may like to be more liquid in the black economy and indulge in more of speculative activities, sometimes the velocity may shoot up and at other times come down.

In other words, with the institutional practices not well known, it is difficult to say what the assumption about the velocity of circulation in the black economy should be. Usually, it is assumed to be the same as in the white economy—a big assumption. Besides, there are some basic problems with the idea of a constant velocity of circulation over a long period of time. Often the income generated is a small part of the total transaction, say, in the purchase of gold or real estate or shares. In these cases, income is only a few per cent of the value of transaction. The rest is all transfers as discussed earlier. Since the volume of such activities has increased enormously, the velocity of circulation has also correspondingly changed. The velocity of circulation assumed to be a constant in monetarist models cannot therefore be justified.

It is also assumed that the NAS income total is the white income but this is not correct since some black incomes are also captured in the NAS. An error creeps into the equations used to estimate the demand for money. Finally, all incomes which may not be captured in the NAS cannot be treated as black incomes. A large percentage of them may be below the taxable limit, like incomes from the unorganized sector.

In brief, the monetarist method is not only based on unrealistic assumptions but is flawed. It estimates the total amount of transactions in the economy and compares that figure with the NAS. Thus, it is a measure of unaccounted incomes and not necessarily black incomes; often constitues double counting. It was this method which gave a figure of 47% in 1978 for India's black economy.

The Fiscal Approach Method

This method recognizes that an economy consists of several sectors and each one of them has its own institutional practices. This also applies to the black economy. A separate method needs to be adopted for each sector, to calculate its contribution to the black economy. Here, the size of it is the sum of the contribution from each of the sectors.

Kaldor who initiated this method in the mid-fifties, calculated the black incomes generated in each of the thirteen sectors of NAS. He assumed that no black incomes are generated from the wage and salary component. For the remaining part of each of the sectors he applied ratios which gave the amount of black income generated in that sector. What ratios did he apply? He asked around and based these ratios on informed judgment. There was a large element of guess involved.

Other models using this method have divided the economy into legal and illegal sectors. It may be assumed that all incomes generated from the legal sector and which lie above the taxable limit should pay income tax. Black incomes from the legal sector are those incomes which evade income tax. To this can be added the figures of incomes generated in each of the illegal activities to get what is called a global (total) estimate.

The most elaborate such exercise was mounted by the NIPFP. Here the difficulty lies in getting the correct income distribution in the economy, that is, how many people earn how much. Unfortunately, surveys do not reveal this information as already discussed so that assumptions have to be made. The estimate then depends on the assumptions made.

S.B. Gupta revised the NIPFP estimate without rectifying the mistakes he himself pointed out and added what he thought was missed out by the NIPFP team.

Sonali Basu in 1996 revised these figures by correcting the bias in the NIPFP estimate and subtracting those elements which amounted to double counting in S.B. Gupta's estimate. If capital gains are also excluded from the estimate, the size of the black economy turns out to be about 25% of GDP for 1980-81. For 1987-88, the last year for which Gupta gave an estimate (51%), the figure turns out to be about 30%. As will be evident in the next section a conservative estimate of the size of the black economy, including illegal activities, may be taken to be about 40% of the white economy in 1995.

The above discussion suggests that a) there is no definitional clarity in the various methods available b) many questionable assumptions have been used in each of the methods c) at best one can get guesstimates of the size of the black economy, and d) a lot more research on the institutional details about the black economy is required.

Given the definitional differences amongst the estimates, comparing one estimate with the other is like comparing oranges and apples. If there are as many significant assumptions in one method as in the other, there does not seem not much to choose from. However, the fiscal approach has an edge since it is the method which recognizes that different methods may have to be adopted to study each of the sectors since the institutional details differ. Further, it allows the use of the analytically correct definition of black incomes, suggested in the previous chapter.

The monetarist approach tries to identify all transactions where money is used and which are missed out by the NAS. Thus, all incomes, including those below the taxable limit, which are missed out from the white economy are treated as black. Further, since the white economy is taken to be the accounted national income, the portion of national income not accounted for by deficiency of data and methodology also becomes black. Finally, those incomes which are black and included in NAS are missed out.

In the fiscal approach, these errors do not arise. One need include only the incomes above the taxable limit. The NAS total of incomes is not required to be used as the controlling total. Thus, a priori, one may expect that the estimate of black incomes based on the monetarist approach would be higher than the one obtained from the fiscal approach for at least three reasons. First, the monetarist measure would be higher by the extent of black incomes below the taxable limit and the underestimation of national incomes both due to the methodological reasons and problems in data. Secondly, there would be an unspecified discrepancy between the two due to under-reporting of incomes for tax purposes. Thirdly, the estimate would be higher because it captures transactions which do not directly correspond to factor incomes (but are transfers). Finally, the monetarist estimate would be lower by the extent of inclusion of black incomes in NAS. However, this last element is not likely to be large.

A ROUGH ESTIMATE OF THE SIZE OF BLACK ECONOMY IN 1995

In the previous sections it has been argued that all the available methods for estimating the size of the black economy in India have major lacunae. To overcome these problems, there is a need for fresh surveys based on the prevailing practices in the black economy. This is a herculian task.

What is attempted here is to use the figure obtained by Sonali Basu for 1980-81 as the base for estimation (Basu, 1996). In this study, the estimate for the black economy is obtained by correcting the figures obtained by S.B. Gupta and by the NIPFP. The total obtained by Sonali Basu is further corrected to remove the few remaining infirmities—namely, multiple addition and addition of transfer incomes. This corrected figure for 1980-81 is used as a base for projecting the figure to 1995-96, the last year for which the NAS data were available.

Basu assumed that agriculture can be used to find the bias in the NCAER survey and correct it. She got a figure of 10% for tax evasion in legal activities with a possible error of 6%. Nothing else, other than incomes in illegal activities need be added to this figure. Assume that illegal activities were another 5% of GDP so that the size of the black economy for 1980-81 could be taken to be 15% of GDP. This is half the figure of 32 to 34% that she got.

To blow up this figure for 1995-96, it is recognized that there are a few sectors where no (or negligible amount of) black incomes are generated. These are agriculture and public administration. In the latter, the salaries paid are the contribution to the NAS. In the former, crop cutting experiments are used, so contribution to NAS should be fully accounted. Thus, the black economy is taken to be concentrated in the rest of the economy which was 57% in 1980-81 and 68% in 1995-96 (See Table III.2). Further, it is assumed that the behaviour in the organized sector can be dtistinguished from that in the unorganized sector of the economy. Finally, it was assumed that the black economy differs in its functioning in the organized sector between the public and the private sectors.

Using the studies available for the late seventies and the early eighties, for 1980-81, evasion in the public sector may be assumed to be 4% of its value added and in the organized private sector to be 12%. In the private sector it would have been more in the tertiary than in the secondary sector but the average was taken to be 12%. This implied that in the unorganized sector (the residual) the size of the black economy was 26%. Again, it would be more in the tertiary sector than in the secondary sector.

In 1995-96, it was assumed that black incomes in the public sector rose to 6% while those in the organized private sector rose to 40% (as stated by the finance minister in 1993). Thus the share of the black economy rose in the organized sectors by roughly 300%. Assuming that it increased by the same factor in the unorganized sector, the figure for black incomes in this sector came to 74%. The average for the legal sectors of the economy obtained using these three figures turns out to be 32%. If activity in the illegal sectors is taken to rise from 5% of GDP (not counting wages) in 1980-81 to 8% in 1995-96, the black incomes can be taken to be 40% of GDP.

The figures for the legal and the illegal sectors would have been higher but for two factors. First, the legalization of certain activities after 1991. Like, the legalization of gold flow. Black premia on foreign exchange had declined and the smuggling of other goods declined with easing of imports. For these reasons, the illegal sector was taken to be 8% and not 10% of GDP.

Secondly, the corporate sector declared a part of its undeclared output in that year to improve its balance sheet profitability. Hence the figure for 1992-93 given by the Finance Minister was taken as such and not increased. These decreases were not taken to be larger since misuse of trade to generate black incomes increased with the opening up of trade. Further, other forms of illegalities proliferated with the easing of controls and regulations.

It must be emphasized that this is a very crude estimate. To obtain a better estimate a major national effort needs to be mounted.

Services and Goods in the Private Sector

The share of black incomes varies widely amongst the different sectors of the economy. Table II.2 shows that in 1990-91 it was 5% in the primary, 25% in the secondary and 70% in the tertiary sector. This calculation did not take into account the differences that arise due to the existence of the unorganized sector or the public sector. Accounting for the differences due to the unorganizecd sectors would be difficult but the public sector can be incorporated more easily.

In the public sector, output suppression is likely to be small as discussed earlier. The contribution of this sector to the black economy is largely through transfer incomes which are not to be counted. The black incomes are mostly the result of the operations in the private sector. Two important factors need to be taken into account. First, the share of public sector in the GDP has risen from 14.9% in 1970-71 to 19.8% in 1980-81 to 26.3 in 1990-91 and 26.7% in 1995-96. Second, the contribution of the public sector to each of the sub-sectors is vastly different.

The implication of the first point is that a growing relative size of the black economy is to be explained along with a declining proportion of the private sector in the economy. Even more critically, there are sectors where almost the entire output is from the public sector. For example, for 1995-96, Table III.3 shows that this is true for mining and quarrying, electricity, gas and water supply, public administration and defence and railways and communications. The contribution is substantial for banking and insurance (69%) and for other services (43%).

In agriculture, the contribution of the public sector was 2.9% in 1995-96. In other words, the contribution in this sector is mostly from the private sector. Here, as already discussed, there is no output suppression for reasons of black income generation. In brief, there is little output suppression from 52% of GDP, contributed by the public sector and agriculture. In effect, 32% of GDP is generated as black income out of 48% of GDP.

In the primary sector, there is output suppression in the non-agriculture part. Even from the public sector, there is theft, etc., so there would be some output suppression. For instance, there is theft of electricity but this is at the stage of distribution and not generation so that the output is correctly reported.

Manufacturing and construction accounted for 28.3% of the GDP in 1995-96. Of this, the contribution of the public sector was 23%. The private sector contribution to this activity is substantial, accounting for 21.7% of the GDP. If 40% of this output is assumed to be evaded, the contribution to the black economy would be 8.7% of the GDP. The figure of 40% is an average of the evasion in the organized and he unorganized parts of this sector. It would be obviously less in the former and more in the latter (Table III.2).

In brief, from the material-producing sectors (the primary and the secondary) and the public sector, the contribution of the black economy to the GDP would be 1% from non-agriculture primary sector, 8.7% from the secondary private sector and 1.6% from the public sector, a total of 11.3% of GDP.

The rest of the economy is the non-material goods sector (42.2% of the GDP), broadly categorized as the services sector. The share of the public sector in this sector was 28.3% so that the contribution of the private services sector to the GDP was 30.2%. This was associated with a contribution of 20.7% of the GDP to the black economy. It follows that the proportion of black in this sector was 68.5%. This coincides with the general impression that the proportion of black here is the highest of the three sectors.

Most of the illegal activities are concentrated in the tertiary sector so that another 8% of GDP comes from them. If this figure is added, the share of black incomes in the tertiary sector becomes 95%.

One implication of the above is that a mere suppression of material output of 11.3% of GDP is driving a black economy of 40% of GDP. NAS data suggest that in the eighties and the nineties, the growth in the public and the tertiary sectors has been rapid. But it is not that the latter is the cause of the former as often believed. While in the public sector, the growth in the material goods sector has been more rapid, in the private sector it is the growth of the tertiary sector (though roughly the same as in the public sector) which has been more rapid.

In brief, NAS shows that while in the public sector the share of the material goods has risen, in the rest of the economy it is the share of the tertiary sector which has risen. If the black economy is also taken into account, the divergence is even greater given its concentration in the tertiary and the unorganized sectors. It is clear that the growth of the services sector is not only (or just) because of the expansion of government.

BLACK ECONOMY CONCENTRATED IN THE THREE PER CENT

Gupta (1992) noted that black incomes are concentrated 'in the uppermost decile of the population . . . this decile represents the rich and the upper class in India . . .' (p 145). How credible is this figure? There are two different ways of figuring this out. First, by looking at the numbers involved in various activities where substantial black incomes are generated. Second, by analysing the consumption pattern in the economy.

Assume that in the public sector 50% earn some black incomes. That is 9.5 million. If out of this number, 20% earn significant amounts, they would number 3.8 million.

In the private corporate sector say 10% are in the managerial cadres of whom half may make significant black incomes. That is 4 lakh.

There are approximately 29 lakh firms. Assume there is one owner per firm. Those firms with partnerships and those where one owner owns many firms will hopefully cancel out. The general shareholders do not matter as far as siphoning out of profits is concerned.

Some professionals, like, doctors, lawyers, engineers, consultants, stock and property brokers, private tutors, from entertainment world and CAs earn substantial black incomes. Assume that 75% of them get counted in the public or the organized private sector or are honest. The balance may be taken to be self-employed and evading taxes and may number 5 lakh.

Assume, that high income earners in illegal activities are in the same proportion as in the legal GDP. 8% of GDP is illegal. So, such people would be 3% of 8/140 of work force of 350 million. Hence 6 lakh individuals.

Assume that there are another 1 million entrepreneurs from the unorganized sector who earn significant black incomes. These may be transporters, hoteliers, artists, those from agriculture who divert their income and show it as agricultural income, those involved in lotteries, etc. The total number from all these groups comes to: $3.8 + 0.4 + 2.9 + 0.5 + 0.6 + 1.0 = 9.2$ million.

The primary generators of black incomes in this would be 5.4 million individuals not belonging to the public sector and the secondary ones receiving substantial transfers (in the public sector) 3.8 million. Those from the public sector who earn substantial black incomes invest their funds in enterprises, either their own or those of others. These are already counted in one form or the other in the private sector total.

In brief, there would be 5.4 million significant black income earners in the private sector and 3.8 million in the public sector. There would be many amongst these who would belong to the same family. So that these people may constitute say half this number of households. In other words, there may be about 5 million households with significant black incomes. These are also the free spenders in the economy who have expenditures similar to the middle classes in the advanced countries and the people that the MNCs may be looking for. There may be another million households which have large white incomes because of having multiple earners in the organized sector. These numbers are guesses and could be between 4 to 10 million and need to be firmed up through much more detailed exercises based on the consumption pattern of households and other supplementary data.

The use of the consumption pattern is predicated on the notion that those with 'black money' tend to live ostentatiously. If the consumption pattern of people in the country is any guide to people's wealth, then the propertied class is not very large.

The total number of families owning 4-wheeled vehicles (a symbol of luxury in India) in 1989-90 was less than 1 million. This number roughly doubled by 1995-96 and then a recession set in, in this market, both perhaps due to general recession and due to demand saturation. This number has to be arrived at by netting out multiple ownership corporate and public ownership of these vehicles (including the army) and their use in commercial applications like taxis. About 10 million households owned two wheelers (motorcycles and scooters) and CTVs.

Those with substantial incomes, black or white, are likely to have 4-wheeled vehicles. Hence, the number of families with substantial black incomes is likely to be less than 2 million since some multiple income, fixed income families with only white incomes also own such vehicles.

Asset ownership data for 1981-82 (from National Sample Survey) showed that households with assets of more than Rs 5 lakh were only 0.42% of the population. They had an average holding of Rs 7.8 lakhs which at today's prices would be about Rs 25 lakhs. The share of land and building in this was about 85%. Even if under-valuation, etc., are taken into account this also does not suggest that the black economy is concentrated in more than a few per cent of the population.

The income-tax data for 1986-87 suggested that there were only 5 million income-tax payers in the country. Of these, only 5 lakh were salaried employees. The rest belonged to the category property income. Table V.2a suggests that the number of assessees has gone up to 11.4 million in 1997. Table V.2b shows that in 1994-95 the salaried earners were 21.8% of those filing returns. Table V.3 shows that in 1997 only 14 lakh assessees fell in the higher income slabs. In effect, most of the assessees, 8.8 million had property incomes but only 1.4 million fell in the high income category; 0.15% of the population of the country. These are people who have substantial black savings and have to pay tax on the visible portion of their property.

The number of wealth tax assessees remained stagnant or declined in the seventies and the eighties. The number hovered around 1 lakh assessees. They numbered about 2.5 lakh in 1997 but paid little wealth tax. This implies that most of the propertied, even those in the high income bracket simply escaped the wealth tax net. However, those with substantial black savings would possibly have to pay some wealth tax on the white portion of their assets and it is these people who are reflected in the data. Since black incomes are property incomes, it would be safe to assume that these are the people who have a substantial share of the black economy.

Be that as it may, from the above indications it seems that the propertied who also generate substantial black incomes are no more than a few million families; perhaps, one can put an upper limit of three per cent of the families in India.

Disparity Between the Top 3% and the Bottom 40%

What would be the income ration in 1995 between those below the poverty line (40%) and the top 3% with substantial black incomes? This can be worked out.

GDP at market prices = Rs 11.2 lakh crore.

Black was 40% of GDP = Rs 4.5 lakh crore.

The population for 1995-96 = 93.42 crore.

The number of those with substantial black incomes (3%) was 2.8 crore. Assuming they have 10% of white incomes namely Rs 1.1 lakh crore and that they have the entire black incomes equal to Rs 4.5 lakh crore, their total income would be Rs 5.6 lakh crore, i.e. 50% of the white GDP and 38% of the total GDP. The top 3% then would have a per capita income of Rs 2 lakh.

The bottom 40% are at the poverty line. The poverty line was estimated to be roughly Rs 50/- per capita per month in 1973-74. The Consumer Price Index rose roughly by a factor of 6 between then and 1995-96. Hence, the per capita income of this group may be taken to be Rs 3, 500 per annum. Their total income would be Rs 1.3 lakh crore.

Consequently, the ratio of per capita income between the bottom 40% and the top 3% would be 1:57, in 1995-96.

4

The Macroeconomic Linkages

In the previous chapters, it was shown that the black economy is large and linked to every aspect of the citizens' life. The fiscal deficit, investment, consumption and balance of payments are all affected by the black economy. The macro variables play an overarching role in the economy unlike the micro ones which have a specific or a limited function. Hence the macro linkages of the black economy are critical to understanding its impact on the life of the citizen.

Here, what is a microeconomic view of the black economy may be reiterated. It argues for achieving efficiency but this does not mean what is commonly understood by the term. Efficiency refers to the best outcome that the markets can achieve irrespective of the considerations of distribution. Some argue that the black economy promotes such efficiency by enabling those things to happen which would have occurred in the market if the government had not interfered.

For instance, when the government bans the import of certain goods then smuggling enables that demand to be fulfilled, in other words, it enables that to happen which would have occurred if the market was free. Hence, smuggling is supposed to promote efficiency of the market variety. This is clearly an argument within a limited perspective and fails if one takes into account the welfare of society as a whole rather than that of the moneyed alone (who dominate the markets). This difference in perspective may be explained using the analogy of traffic.

A vehicle which gets on to a road has to exit it at some point. It circulates on the road between the entry and exit. If there is only one car on the road, it can almost do anything—it can set its own rules. As more cars enter the road, the dynamics changes and rules become necessary. If a few do not follow rules but most do, there is not much of an impact on the flow of traffic but it slows down. As more and more drivers violate traffic rules, traffic slows down and its circulation is affected. Traffic becomes chaotic. To deal with chaotic conditions, new rules come into play. Individuals obeying rules may even become an obstacle. At a crossing, when the light turns yellow if one does not speed up to cross, in India, one is liable to be hit from behind. Hence, most stop only after the light turns red. Most trucks have painted in big letters 'Blow Horn'—silence is not golden.

Individuals trying to zigzag through traffic to reach their destination quicker actually slow every one down including themselves. The individual has no idea of the overall pattern and tries to do the best in the given circumstances. A driver heading for a jammed crossing does not know that she/he is going to get stuck. He tries to manipulate the car into the available space. After a while there is no place left to maneouvere and the jam becomes impossible to untangle. When the traffic police arrive with a macro picture and redirect traffic to alternative roads and get some vehicles to back off, the jam gets untangled.

The macro enables the circulation of traffic to be observed and changed when needed. Chaotic traffic has a different pattern of circulation than smooth traffic. Individuals respond to the conditions of circulation and the prevailing rules of traffic. The system by and large determines individual behaviour. Individual motivation based on breaking the law for self-benefit, at the expense of society, not only adversely affects society but also the individual abusing the law. Individuals typically only adjust to the chaos but cannot change it by individual effort. The collective needs to act.

WHAT IS MACROECONOMIC CIRCULATION?

If society consisted of one person producing for himself, or if everyone was self-sufficient, there would be no need for exchange. There would be no macro economy. When people cooperate in production, specialization develops. Different people do different things so that no one is self-sufficient and there is a need to exchange the goods and services produced. Macro economics gains in importance and begins to govern economic phenomenon. Individuals respond to the environment they find themselves in.

In exchange, individuals transact by paying for goods and services. In a barter economy, goods are directly exchanged while in a monetized economy, money is paid for goods and services. The movement from a barter economy to a monetized economy changes the basic character of the economy. Money becomes the medium of exchange. It takes on an independent value and a financial sector emerges (and which over time grows ever bigger and dominant).

In a monetized economy when someone pays money in exchange for a good or service, the expenditure by him/her is the revenue for the seller. A flow of money incomes is set up in a direction opposite to the flow of goods and services. The macro economy deals with these opposite flows—expenditures and incomes (resulting from revenues).

Expenditures in the market constitute demand which the producers supply or fulfill. In a monetized economy, production is for meeting demand. In production and exchange, work is performed for which payments are made. These are incomes—wages and profits. It is these incomes which give the individual purchasing power and result in demand in the market. Without demand, there is no production, workers become idle and capital does not earn a profit. It is the income of one person which becomes the demand for another who then generates incomes for others and so on.

The circular flow of income and expenditure lies at the root of macroeconomic relationships. Demand is critical to this flow. The black economy affects the circular flow of incomes.

Income can be deployed in two ways, either to consume or save. Expenditure also has two channels—consumption and investment. Since in the opposing flows, incomes equal expenditure, savings must equal investments. The consumption part of the demand is automatically matched by an equal income allocated for that purpose. Thus investment plays a critical role in an economy. It results in incomes from which the requisite amount of savings are generated. Whatever be the investment decisions, matching savings are automatically generated. This is referred to as Keynesian revolution.

When the economy gets more complex, there is also a government and a foreign sector. There can also be a source of demand for the national economy. Government takes away purchasing power through taxation but pumps in demand by expenditures. If expenditures equal revenues, then there is no additional demand due to government. If expenditures exceed revenues, that is, there is a fiscal deficit, then demand is created in the economy.

Exports represent the demand from foreigners for national producers but imports reduce this demand. An export surplus creates demand for national producers.

To recapitulate, demand is generated by consumption, investment, fiscal deficit and export surplus. Consumption can be by those who earn a profit or by those who earn a wage. Though there is some mixing up of these kinds of incomes, the two categories tend to be distinct. Most of the profits are earned by those who are rich and own a lot of capital. Wage-earners typically have small savings and earn little of profits and interest so that their main income is wages. Since wage-earners save little, their consumption almost equals the income. As a first approximation one can take it that the rich earn profits and save while the workers do not save and earn wages.

With this simplification, savings equal the sum of investment by the rich, fiscal deficit of the government and the export surplus. If the consumption of these people is added to their savings, then one gets the total incomes of the rich—the post-tax profits. In brief, incomes must identically equal expenditures in the economy (since they constitute demand) and this relationship is referred to as the national income identity. It is like saying that the area of the hand looked at from both sides must be the same.

The national income identity when manipulated gives the post-tax income of the capitalists as the sum of their consumption, private sector investment, primary fiscal deficit and current account surplus.

When the black economy is introduced into this system, a part of the profits are not declared to the tax authorities so that taxes collected from profits fall and the post-tax income increases. Out of the undeclared profits, investment and consumption take place as has been described in Chapter 2. The impact of the black economy on the current account and the public sector deficit were also presented there. These when incorporated in the national income identity enable the short-run and the long-run macro implications of the black economy to be analysed.

THE LONG RUN: THE GROWING TRINITY

A critical aspect of the macro economy was depicted in Chapter 3, namely, the marked growth in the share of the services sector in the economy and in which the proportion of black incomes is the highest. As argued, black incomes are property incomes, so the share of surplus as a proportion of the output of this sector must be larger than for the material goods sectors. Consequently, with a rising share of services in GDP, the share of surplus in the national income would increase. The services sector lends itself to black income generation since a) valuation of activity is difficult and b) it has a large component of the unorganized sector in it. Often when black incomes are to be generated in other sectors, producers do so through the services sector. Say, through trade or storage or finance.

What sustains the rapid growth of the services economy? The explanation lies in the structural changes in the economy, including the role of government. It needs to be appreciated that the demand for services increases as a result of rising material goods production. There is no *necessary* contradiction between the two. Expenditures on transport, trade, storage, advertising, finance, etc., are needed to facilitate the final sale of the product.

The demand for services grows not only because of the growth of the volume of material production but also due to the increasing concentration and specialization in production. Monetization of many services which may have earlier been performed in the house, like cooking and stitching also promotes the growth of the services sector. The fight over market shares when competition increases leads to increased expenditures on advertising and other such services.

The rich also demand more services, like recreation, travel, restaurants, hotels, legal and financial advice. The faster growth of the services sector is also linked to the changes in the accounting practices in the economy. Many of the services required by the material goods sector are also produced within the material goods sector. These are based on in-house, white collar workers doing accounting, finance, marketing, advertising and so on. The in-house activities are included in the value added of that firm. But other services which are purchased by the firm are not so counted.

With specialization, the proportion of purchased services may rise and show up as an increase in the value added in the services sector instead of being counted in the material goods sector as earlier. Thus, as concentration and specialization in production takes place, even at a given level of output, not only more services, like trade, transport, etc., may be required but also proportionately more services may be purchased from outside the manufacturing set-up.

The Runaway Black Economy

It has been seen that the growing share of the property income (called surplus) the services sector and the black economy mutually depend on each other. Further, at any given point of time there are many ways of making black incomes and more are being evolved as the size of the economy (including the black component) expands. The nature of activities diversifies and more and more ways of generating and investing black incomes open up. In a sense, there is a *hysteresis*. The past is incorporated into the economy and facilitates the further operation and expansion of the black economy.

The implication is that all else remaining the same, at a given level of output, the size of the black economy would increase, and, therefore, the share of surplus in the economy and the share of services would rise. All the three would together set up a spiral of mutual growth.

Likewise, the discussion in the previous section suggests that the services sector is expanding with time, even at a given size of the economy, due to the nature of changes in technology and preferences and the monetisation of services. This would lead to an increase in the size of the black economy and the surplus in the economy.

The *gross* surplus in the economy defined as property incomes would be an increasing function of the size of the black economy. This is because (as already discussed) black incomes are property incomes.

Similarly, the earlier discussion suggests that the share of services sector would not only increase with time but also be an increasing function of the surplus because of the proportionately larger demand for services from this component. There is a substantial demand for services from black incomes.

Finally, the share of the black economy would rise with the surplus and the share of the services sector. Assuming that the functioning of the black economy has become easier, its growth with time would be rapid.

Thus, the system produces *three* mutually dependent sub-systems which can be mathematically solved. The solution can be shown to result in an explosive growth of the shares of black economy, of the surplus and of the services in the total economy. If such a dynamic continues for any length of time the entire economy would be black, all incomes would be property incomes and only services would be produced. Clearly, this would result in a crisis of deep proportions.

In fact, the crisis would manifest itself much before such a final stage is reached. As the share of black incomes rises, illegality would be so all-pervasive that society would cease to exist. As the share of surplus incomes rises, wage-earners would be squeezed out and this would cause a social crisis. The budgetary crisis would be severe. These and other consequences of the long-term dynamics are presented in Chapter 6.

THE SHORT RUN: BUDGETARY DYNAMICS OF THE BLACK ECONOMY

While the possible long-term macro consequences of the growing black economy are disastrous, the short-run ones are no better. Take for instance, tax collection and therefore, the budget deficit.

As already pointed out, the fiscal deficit of the government implies additional demand in the economy—since it constitutes an injection of demand. This results in additional employment and in profits. It sets into motion unutilized resources in the economy. However, if resources are already fully utilized, it results in inflation and only raises profits. Either way, since it raises profits, it does not go against the interest of the capitalists.

The fiscal deficit is financed either through borrowing from the market or by resort to borrowing from the Reserve Bank of India (and is almost equal to the deficit financing). Both the instruments, borrowing (B) and deficit financing, lead to an expansion of primary liquidity in the economy. The latter more than the former. Borrowing by the government leads to the creation of financial instruments which can *potentially* be used by the commercial banks to borrow from the Reserve Bank of India (through refinance). Yet, it must be remembered that as long as there are unutilized resources, potential savings exist in the economy which can be set in motion through the act of borrowing by the government. As output expands, the demand for money grows and the commensurate money supply follows. Deficit financing does the same *but* by first pumping in money supply into the economy. This is the essential difference between the two. In both cases, the circular flow of demand and incomes is set up and helps the economy grow if there are no bottlenecks.

Borrowing to spend generates demand in those specific sectors where expenditures occur. As the circular flow of income rises, money supply increases commensurate with the demand for money. Deficit financing leads to money supply expansion simultaneous with the first round demand generation and to a larger expansion of overall liquidity. This funds activities which had remained unfinanced due to the prevailing interest rates structure and the rationing of credit. The inflationary implications of this excess of liquidity are then more serious.

Activities which get funded by excess liquidity are often speculative in nature. When shortages occur, say, as with the failure of monsoon or inflation caused by other shortages, these funds are utilized for holding commodities in short supply. In this sense, borrowing by government, by not leading to excess liquidity is less inflationary.

As an alternative to these sources for raising funds for government expenditures, taxes are a superior instrument. They do not create a future obligation to pay. Amongst the taxes, reliance on direct taxes as opposed to indirect taxes has been suggested to be more desirable from the point of view of raising output (Kalecki, 1971). The latter by raising prices can reduce demand and further aggravate the deficiency in demand. The former has no such demand depressing effect.

Direct and Indirect Tax Evasion

Evasion can be of direct taxes or indirect taxes. When a tax is evaded, two things happen, the tax evader has a higher income in hand while the government's tax revenue gets reduced so that its deficit increases. Tax evasion results in higher profits to capitalists since they now have undeclared profits in addition to the declared ones. The economic implication of tax evasion is then dependent on two factors—undeclared profits and the government's deficit.

The evasion of direct taxes leads to the rise in undeclared profits at the expense of declared profits and causes a fall in tax collection. The post-tax income of the tax evaders rises and the government's budget deficit increases by this amount. Thus, while the government is forced to pump purchasing power into the economy through the increased deficit, the tax evaders who only spend a small amount of their income in increased consumption save most of it and end up reducing demand in the system. In the net, demand does not go up so that incomes remain unchanged in spite of tax evasion. So, even though the individual feels she/he has higher income due to evasion, the businessmen as a class have less incomes than they would have had if they had not resorted to tax evasion.

However, if the government keeps the deficit unchanged by reducing expenditures, the demand it pumps into the economy will remain unchanged. Since the tax evaders do not immediately generate demand from their additional incomes, overall demand falls and the gross profits decrease by the amount of tax evasion. Decline in gross profits is due to a reduction in production. Hence, if nothing else changes, an *increase in direct tax evasion will cause production to fall.*

When indirect taxes are evaded, direct taxes are not paid on the additional income. Undeclared profits rise by the *total* value of the undeclared output. The incomes in the hands of the tax evaders rise. The budget deficit rises by the amount of direct and indirect tax evaded, i.e., by an amount smaller than the amount by which the income of the capitalists rises. Hence the fall in demand is much greater than the rise in demand so that gross profits fall through a decrease in production. Firms evading indirect taxes could be expected to lower prices but this is unlikely since the object of evasion is increased profits and not lower prices. If the budget deficit is held unchanged, through reduction in government expenditures, the drop in output would be even sharper. In brief, *an increase in indirect tax evasion causes a drop in output.*

If, in the face of tax evasion (direct or indirect), indirect taxes are raised to keep the budget deficit unchanged, demand remains unchanged and so will gross profits and output. However, since indirect taxes are prime costs in production, prices will rise. Clearly, the economy faces stagflation (meaning stagnant output and inflation). *Hence, an increase in tax evasion is stagflationary even if accompanied by a rising fiscal deficit or a rising share of indirect taxes to prevent the budget deficit from rising.*

Borrowings and Deficit

As mentioned earlier, the fiscal deficit is the sum of the budget deficit and net borrowings (B). In the previous section it was seen that if government expenditures increase or remain unchanged in spite of the loss of revenue due to tax evasion, the fiscal deficit rises and creates additional markets. This causes the white profits to rise due to increase in output.

However, if in the effort to raise B, interest rates rise, total interest payments (I) rise in subsequent periods. All else remaining unchanged, the budget deficit will tend to rise by the amount of I and raise the fiscal deficit. But interest (I) is a recycling of incomes from the budget to the capitalists without a change in the output. Thus, the fiscal deficit rises without having an effect on output.

If government expenditure increases while tax revenue is held in check by the black economy, the fiscal deficit rises and has to be financed by a rising B and with a time lag an increase in I occurs. If the money borrowed does not yield the required return for payment, the debt burden mounts even if no money is needed for other purposes. This raises the fiscal deficit and creates a spectre of a debt trap, namely, borrowing more and more to pay back past debt. This eventually forces a cut back in the rate of growth of expenditures to keep the fiscal deficit in check and it affects growth.

The increased need for borrowing by the government forces it to compete with others for funds. Since lot of liquidity is sucked out by the lucrative returns available in the black economy, the government has also been forced to raise the returns it offers on its borrowings. The government's response has been to raise the rates of returns and offer tax concessions on money lent to it. The effect is that revenue is forgone and expenditures rise leading to an increase in the deficit.

It may appear that the government borrows largely from the commercial banks or the financial institutions so it is not recycling funds to individuals when it borrows. The government interest payments are going mostly to these institutions and not to private individuals. But, these institutions are borrowing from the public and paying them a high rate of interest and to stay profitable, they need to cover their costs. Or else, the government would have to subsidize their losses. One way or the other, the financial intermediaries are passing on the government payments to their depositors, those who are the savers.

The informal and the formal credit markets have links between them and this leads to the funds flowing from one to the other. To obtain funds, government is forced to pay comparable interest rates. However, the flows are not stable and this leads to government's inability to use its monetary policy for control over the financial sector. During inflationary periods the returns in the informal sector rise and the government is required to offer higher rates of interest. These do not easily revert to the old rates—a ratchet results and the cost of borrowing goes up.

All these have serious implications for the economy and these will be discussed in Chapter 6. What is clear is that the black economy forces the government to raise resources at higher and higher cost to the exchequer. The interest rates tend to rise and the budget is faced with the spectre of a debt trap. This limits the capacity of the government to intervene to the extent it ought to, to accelerate the rate of growth of the economy.

Public Sector and Deficit

As discussed in the previous chapter, the black incomes generated through the public sector lead to an increase in the fiscal deficit. Demand should rise but does not since there is an equal increase in private incomes due to a rise in undeclared profits. This is a pure transfer of profits from the public sector to the private. No expansion of the market occurs. However, if the government cuts back its other expenditures (like, investments) to check the rising deficit, then demand and profits would fall by a like amount and output would decline.

Another expenditure by the government is subsidies. Either they are provided through the budget or through the public sector. But the decrease in profits of the public sector also affects the budget. Subsidies from the budget raise the budget deficit but lower prices. If they accrue to the propertied classes then their incomes rise and output is unaffected. For instance, this is the case with export subsidies, fertiliser subsidy, subsidized services for the well off and the subsidies meant for the poor but skimmed off by the propertied. If subsides go to labour, the fiscal deficit rises and since the workers consume all of this income, the level of output increases and this also raises the profits of the capitalists.

To keep the fiscal deficit in check, government has often cut back budgetary support to the public sector and also forced it to borrow in the market (outside the budget). This device while lowering the government's fiscal deficit does not reduce the deficit of the public sector taken as a whole. The costs to the public sector rise due to higher interest charges. Consequently, either administered prices have to be raised to cover higher costs or the public sector surpluses decline and the fiscal deficit rises.

In brief, the fiscal deficit rises in response to the growing share of black economy because of a) the lower buoyancy of taxes b) illegal transfers from the public sector c) increased burden of interest payments and d) increased expenditures on subsidies, law and order, etc. Since most of them have no impact on output (as shown above), the role of fiscal deficit in increasing demand and hence raising the level of output declines with the growing share of the black economy.

Impact of Black Investments

An increase in investments (black or white) raises demand, and, therefore, profits (through an increase in output). As seen before, black investments go though seven channels. Each of these channels into which this investment goes creates a different macroeconomic impact.

1. Under-invoiced inventories lead to a rise in the level of actual investment in the economy but through the black channel. This causes a rise in undeclared profits and the level of output. However, if inventories rise at a rate faster than that of output, profitability declines and the purpose of generating black incomes is defeated so that it cannot be a very large activity. Increase in undeclared cash balances are unlikely to be significant and will cause the velocity of circulation to decrease.

2. Over-invoiced plant and equipment implies that declared investments are overstated. They are fictitious and only on paper.

In effect, black (undeclared) investment is negative and undeclared profits rise by this amount. Declared profits should be higher by the amount of over-invoicing due to the higher investments on paper. However, since it is only on paper, demand is unchanged, and black incomes are generated. Thus, white incomes are overestimated by twice the amount of over-invoicing. In brief, the true incomes must be corrected from their apparent level by twice the amount of over-invoicing. The level of real output is less than implied by the investment so that the multiplier has a negative value. This aspect is partly countered by a small amount of under-invoiced investments which increases undeclared profits.

3. Flows into the informal sector and white savings lead to an increase in investments since unfulfilled projects can be funded. Thus, gross profits and output rise. A part of these funds flow into speculative channels but this is a transfer activity so does not lead to a rise in the level of investment. As discussed earlier, it may lead to a decrease in real investment. This activity results in a positive multiplier.

4. Holdings of precious metals, etc., and flight of capital imply a leakage of savings from the economy. Investments are made outside so that output or gross profit do not rise within the national economy. However, there is an effect through the current account surplus which is dealt with separately. By itself the multiplier associated with these activities is zero.

5. Investments in transfer activities. As discussed earlier, black profits do not rise unless they lead to larger consumption or investment. But that is dependent on other aspects of the economy and taken care of separately. These activities result in an increase in the transactions velocity of money but a decrease in its income velocity. It could result in higher investments in other black channels but does not, due to the relative rates of returns being lower in those activities. The multiplier associated with it turns out to be zero.

6. Investments in illegal activities raise the level of output in the economy. Undeclared profits increase with a major part of them accruing outside the economy and promoting criminalization of society. The multiplier turns out to be positive but smaller than it could be.

In a nutshell, while the savings rate out of black incomes is likely to be much higher than that of the white economy, the investment rate is likely to be lower since many components of black investments are either transfers or leakages from the national economy. *Hence black investments tend to a) lower the rate of growth of the economy as compared to what it could have been and b) cause a worsening in the BOP.* But then why is the rate of growth of black incomes higher than that of white incomes? The reason is that the former is not generated out of black investments alone. A part of the output from white investments is not declared and results in the generation of a major chunk of the black incomes. This lowers the rate of growth of white incomes while raising that of black incomes.

The Effect on BOP

The functioning of the black economy results in a) a lower true trade deficit, b) a current account surplus rather than a deficit and c) outflow of private capital rather than an inflow. It has been pointed out that the BOP situation is reflected by the official current account deficit. The current account surplus (instead of deficit) implies higher internal demand and a *higher level of output and of gross black profits.*

Increase in black investments (in real estate, gold, gems, capital held abroad) and black consumption (consumer durables, foreign vacations, etc.) lead to *increased demand for foreign exchange, worsen the BOP situation and lead to pressures for the devaluation of the currency.*

Investments outside the national economy are matched by a rise in the current account surplus and since these are linked to illegal activities, they raise undeclared profits outside the economy with no impact on output in the economy. Hence, in comparison with a situation in which these investments had occurred in the economy, *the rate of growth of the economy and its employment potential decline*. The adverse BOP situation this creates lowers the economy's capacity to import essentials and thereby reduces its rate of growth and slows down productivity growth in the economy.

An increase in the capitalist consumption causes gross profits and output to rise. However, since its import intensity is high, it adversely effects the trade account and reduces the rise in gross profits.

In brief, the impact of the black economy on the external sector is through a) consumption of the rich, b) undeclared profits and c) the current account. These cause gross profits and output to rise but much less than if the activity was all white. The BOP situation unambiguously worsens. This poses difficulties for the white economy and slows it down. Further, since a large part of the undeclared profits associated with these activities accrue outside, no benefit results to the national economy. Finally, since a major part of this activity like, drug trafficking and smuggling, is also illegal it poses additional problems for the national economy through criminalization and increases in expenditures on law and order.

BLACK ECONOMY AND THE GROWING CRISIS SINCE THE SEVENTIES

The above analysis of the macro variables becomes meaningful only if it can better explain some of the observed trends of the Indian economy. The crisis in the Indian economy in 1991 did not materialize suddenly and had roots going back to at least the early seventies. To analyse this crisis, it is important to take into account the behaviour of the key macro variables of the Indian economy in the seventies and the eighties, and especially how the black side of them operated.

Data from the white economy indicate that the rate of growth of output fluctuated through this period. It was higher on the average after the mid-seventies. The wholesale price index fluctuated sharply during the period and the average climbed through the eighties and into the nineties. Thus, nominal GDP grew at a consistently high rate through the period. Employment generation decelerated through the eighties, specially in the organized sector. The unorganized sector data are unreliable but its share in the GDP declined. The trend in these variables depended on other macro variables, called independent variables.

The rate of growth for some of these independent variables was faster than that of the GDP. This was so for indirect taxes, borrowings of the public sector, deficit financing, fiscal deficit, subsidies, interest burden on the budget, exports and imports. The availability of consumer durables rose through the period and specially after the early eighties when many new goods hitherto unavailable were introduced into the Indian market. Certain other variables showed swings rather than a one-way movement. The ratio of trade deficit to GDP increased upto the early eighties and then declined. The ratio of direct taxes to GDP rose upto the mid-seventies and then declined. Gross domestic savings and capital formation rose through the seventies, declined upto the mid-eighties and again rose. The gap between the two however rose, indicating capital inflow from abroad.

Data from the black economy indicate a growing ratio of black economy to the white economy. Flight of capital, smuggling (of gold silver, gems, synthetics and electronics) and under-invoicing and over-invoicing of exports and imports all grew in magnitude. While gross black profits rose raising the ratio of savings to GDP, due to the leakage from the national economy, the investment ratio in the black economy was much less than that for the white economy.

Many of these trends in the white part of the independent macro variables was a consequence of the growing share of black incomes in the economy, manifested in a rise in the share of undeclared and total profits in national income and a worsening of income distribution. This along with the already discussed impact of tax evasion would create a tendency towards stagflation in the economy (if nothing else changes).

The increase in the consumption by the well-off in society and the increase in current account surplus associated with the growth of the black economy helps in boosting demand but the former is small and the latter linked to illegal activities hence with little linkage to the white economy. Higher total profits did not lead to a *corresponding* rise in investments since they leaked out of the economy or were diverted to transfer activities. The private sector which cannot on its own check the growth of the black economy found itself hamstrung in raising the rate of growth of output in the economy

Growth impulses from the private sector remained weak in spite of its rising command over the economy through the black economy. The investment process weakened in the private sector with funds diverted into unproductive channels where the rates of return were high due to tax evasion, like in the secondary share market, real estate, hoarding, etc. Rural surpluses instead of being reinvested flowed into real estate speculation, holding of gold, these are transfers with little impact on production. The black economy by diverting investments away from productive into unproductive channels slowed down the growth impetus of the private sector.

The ratio of white private investments to GDP has not grown much. While data show that the share of property income and savings in national income rose, leakages from the national economy prevented the share of white savings in the economy from rising in the eighties. As already argued, the black investments have not helped the share of investments in the economy to rise. Consequently, since the late seventies growth became critically dependent on the growing fiscal deficit which was being fueled by the rising share of the black economy.

To begin with, since interest burden was low, the primary fiscal deficit increased, boosting demand and the rate of growth of the economy. But as the black economy grew, as already discussed, the role of fiscal deficit got limited. To recapitulate, the growing share of the black economy reduced the buoyancy of direct taxes and forced increases in indirect taxes and borrowings. The interest burden on the budget rose and the primary deficit stagnated even though the fiscal deficit continued to grow and the growth impulse petered out.

The employment generation per unit of black expenditures was low except in illegal activities. Even consumption out of black incomes tended to be of the high-tech variety and capital-intensive, like in luxury tourism, hotels and restaurants, and other such professions. Consequently, the employment generation associated with the black economy has been small.

Moderate real rates of growth, coupled with declining employment coefficients of the white and the black investments led to a growing problem of un- and under-employment right through the eighties. The burden of employment generation fell on the residual unorganized sector with low paid jobs. This could not fulfill the expectations of the rising number of degree holders and manifested itself in the rising tide of social discontent and their turning towards illegal activities which the black economy was in any case promoting. *The black economy worked from both the supply and demand side to catch unemployed youth in its grip.*

The rise in the rates of return in the economy and the rising share of the indirect taxes in the economy reflected themselves in the high cost economy and a general inflationary pressure. Both these led to pressures for an increase in subsidies in the economy. Where the producers were not able to pass on cost increases as in the case of the public sector, industries with stagnant demand and the small-scale sector, there was growing sickness.

Subsidies are partly a result of the growing black economy and are of two kinds and are associated with the political compulsions of the rulers. First, subsidies are genuinely required by those (the non-propertied) whose real income generation is stagnant and their capacity to pay full cost of food, infrastructure, etc., has declined. Subsidies are required in urban areas if cities are not to breakdown because the bulk of the population cannot pay the full cost of services. Secondly, subsidies are enjoyed by the well-off sections of society who have extracted implicit subsidies (Rs 6,000 per head in Delhi in the late eighties). Subsidies for the non-propertied have also been appropriated by the propertied in many cases. This cannot be an argument for ending subsidies for the poor. Since they are required by them and if ended can result in unmanageable increase in social and political tensions. The solution to subsidies lies in checking the growth of the black economy.

The public sector has drawn large support from the budget since it is full of inefficiencies and corruption. The public sector has been used by those in power to build personal fiefdoms and this is at the root of much of the political and bureaucratic interference. It is also responsible for the demoralization of the work force of the public sector and its lack of commitment to the idea of the public sector. The budgetary subsidies to the public sector have resulted in benefits to the propertied through availability of cheap infrastructure. However, this is unsustainable since it leads to a budgetary crisis and sickness in the public sector.

Certain subsidies to the propertied appear to be legitimate. They are the result of rising costs of production as in the case of exports and fertilisers. To keep inflation in check, food price increase had to be moderated in the past which required paying subsidies for a) inputs into agriculture and b) public distribution system. All these compulsions forced the ratio of subsidies to GDP to rise. However, since a growing proportion of the subsidies were cornered by the propertied, as discussed, there was no commensurate increase in the growth of output in spite of the increase in the fiscal deficit.

In brief, the rising share of the black economy in one way or the other affected the trends in all macro variables. It explained a) the relatively slow rate of growth of the economy in the seventies and the eighties in spite of the rising ratio of fiscal deficit to GDP b) the growing budgetary crisis and the eventual petering out of the growth impulses in the economy in the late eighties c) the worsening BOP situation d) the rising costs of production and e) growing inflationary potential. These trends aggravated unemployment and along with growth in illegal activities led to growing criminalization and breakdown of cities. The private sector finding an easy route to higher profits did not need to take risks in development of technology. With public sector sickness and limitations in imports of essential technology due to BOP problems, the technological dynamism of the economy further slackened in the seventies and the eighties. The period was characterized by widespread policy failure.

NEP and the Black Economy

The New Economic Policies attempted to generate what are called 'supply side responses' in the economy. They hoped to play that role in the white economy which capitalists had been achieving through the black economy—namely, raising the share of profits in national income. With this end in view, a wide variety of concessions were granted to capital. State was supposed to retreat through privatization of the public sector, cuts in subsidies 'to get the prices right', downgrading of planning and the unshackling of the market forces. A reduction in the budgetary transfers to the non-propertied was to be implemented by cutting subsidies meant for them. Concessions, like, lowering of tariffs and taxes, and dilution of FERA were granted to foreign capital to attract technology.

A reduction in the fiscal deficit while cutting direct taxes and customs duties is the surest way to force reduction in budgetary expenditures to limit the role of the state in the economy. The *black economy was sought to be curbed by legalizing certain activities* but new opportunities seem to have opened up to generate black incomes. Quantitative restrictions on imports have been almost eliminated so that what was smuggling earlier has become importation. Tax concessions are being granted to retain national capital within the national economy and NRIs are being encouraged to bring in capital. A part of this is capital formerly taken out of the country.

These changes have converted a part of undeclared profits of industry into declared profits accruing within the national economy. Corresponding black investments abroad would decline. However, loss of foreign exchange has continued since the quantum of these legalized activities has grown. For instance the inflow of gold has increased from 190 tons in 1990 to 815 tons in 1998. Thus, the true trade account is adversely affected and profits lowered. With the cheapening of foreign goods, capitalist consumption has risen, again adversely affecting the trade deficit. In brief, the growth impulses emanating from the external sector and the public sector have weakened under the New Economic Policies.

Since tax rates have come down sharply and controls are less, some have argued that the size of the black economy would have declined. This is not borne out by a listing of the major scandals exposed in the national press between 1956 and 1996 (See appendix I.1).

What the above suggests is that the black economy measured as a share of the white economy has not diminished and most likely grown even if some activities have gone out of its ambit. The large-scale expansion of the tertiary sector in spite of a reduction in the scale of operations of the government is partly linked to increase in speculative activities which lend themselves to black income generation. A part of the growth of the economy is a result of statistical jugglry on the part of the government trying to paint a rosy picture of the New Economic Policies. Finally, a part of the growth is a consequence of the declaration of formerly undeclared output by industry.

In brief, in spite of the decline of governmental regulation and reduction in tax rates, the increases in the scale and size of corruption, the newer opportunities to businesses, increase in speculative activities and growth in the tertiary sector where the black economy is concentrated suggest that the black economy has continued to grow. Even the evidence that the buoyancy of direct tax has gone up is not an evidence of better compliance but reflec's more skewed income distribution (For a more detailed discussion see appendix 7.1). The problems originating in the black economy prior to 1991 have, therefore, continued. These are compounded by the decline in the primary fiscal deficit of public sector and the surge in imports and the decline in the true current account surplus of the external sector.

The burden of growth then falls on increasing white investments. But, this has not occurred since for much of the period since 1991 there has been excess capacity in many sectors. The decrease in black investments abroad do not automatically convert themselves to white investments. On the whole then demand has not grown in spite of the incentives. Black profits do not entirely reappear as white profits as the economy slows down. *The paradox is that an attempt to raise the share of profits in national income by giving concessions to capital can cause a fall in the level of gross profits (white plus undeclared ones).*

As already pointed out, it is not that the share of profits in the economy was not rising in the seventies and the eighties. Its further rise due to the New Economic Policies is only accentuating the problems already being faced during the earlier period—the further narrowing of markets. With slow growth in demand, and excess capacity, private investments, Indian or foreign, cannot be buoyant.

The supply side responses expected by the New Economic Policies can only occur with a time-lag provided investments rise and technology improves. If this is to be based on import of capital goods, the current account deficit will widen by an equal amount and the market size would not change. Demand would further decline if projects that could be internally set-up are based on imports. Foreign investment has affected Indian investment by posing a threat and is hardly the solution unless it comes on an unprecedented scale in spite of slowdown. But then, it would have to be export-oriented. There are few signs of this at present.

Internationalization of Indian capital occurred earlier through the black economy but now has gone a step further through the opening up of the Indian markets and the liberalization of terms and conditions for MNCs bringing in capital. However, the earlier internationalisation of Indian capital was based on illegality and criminalization so it did not help to become competitive and technologically self-sufficient. The result is, Indian capital is not ready to face competition from the MNCs and can only act as their junior partner. Consequently, a big shake-out is taking place in the Indian capital markets. MNCs initially teamed up with Indian big business (junior partners) but have been jettisoning them in the last few years. Without bringing in much capital they have controlled Indian capital through their financial clout, technology, marketing, brand names, etc.

Indian national capital by supporting the New Economic Policies has displayed short-sightedness since it did not take into account its own weaknesses. The increased share of profits in national income post-1991 has mostly accrued to MNC capital and the narrowing of the home markets has meant that indigenous capital has weakened with respect to the MNCs. Indian capital can expand at the expense of the smaller units of capital—the small and the medium sectors but this would be inadequate to counter the challenge of MNCs. The situation has been just ripe for the MNCs to absorb their junior partners—the Indian collaborators.

With slowdown in industry and rupee proceeds accruing to former smugglers, there has been a rise in speculative activity—in the foreign exchange market, secondary share market, real estate and goods in short supply. These are transfer activities but they can fuel flight of capital if a rising current account deficit on the white account leads to devaluation since that would increase the rates of return on holdings of foreign exchange and gold.

In brief, under the New Economic Policies, indications are that the size of the black economy has continued to grow in spite of the legalization of certain formerly illegal activities. This is due to the easing of the business environment and the availability of newer opportunities for not declaring profits. The pre-1991 trend of an increase in the share of profits through the black economy and internationalization of the economy has continued. Various problems encountered pre-1991 have continued and newer ones have appeared. These relate to the weakness of Indian capital and loss of direction in the public sector. Further, with opening up, Indian policy-makers have lost their capacity to solve key internal economic problems and give the economy direction. *Policy failure in key sectors is substituted by absence of policy in these areas.*

In conclusion, it is suggested that many of the features of the Indian economy, whether long term or short term ones cannot be understood unless one incorporates into the analysis the black economy. The black economy changes the pattern of circular flow of incomes in the economy and masks what is happening. For instance, employment should expand with black investments but its impact is far less than if the investments were through the white channels. India becomes a capital exporter rather than being a capital-short economy. The rate of growth is higher than that revealed by the white economy because a part of the output is not declared. The budgetary dynamics and the fortunes of the public sector are completely upset.

5

Causes of Black Income Generation

Any solution to the macroeconomic consequences of the black economy for society presupposes an identification of its causes. In this connection confusion often arises because if black incomes are found to be generated in some activity then this activity (source) itself is taken to be the cause and the solution suggested is to eliminate it (source). Say, if a tax is evaded to generate black incomes, that tax is taken to be the cause of black income generation. Obviously, if that tax is eliminated, it cannot be evaded. Can this be a solution?

Traffic police is supposed to enforce discipline on the roads. However, if it uses the law to make money, it brings the law into contempt. Bribing policemen to escape punishment for jumping a red light or for causing an accident or for encroaching on roads is a cue, specially to the well off, that abuse of the law hardly matters. The existence of rules cannot be given as a cause of their being broken.

Traffic police is insensitive to the convenience of the public and makes following rules difficult—traffic lights are placed behind electricity poles or trees, turnings are badly designed, and bus stops are poorly situated. The indifference of the law-maker and the enforcer regarding the rules makes obeying them difficult.

Traffic rules establish the right of way for all forms of traffic. Violators of rules try to take precedence over others and encroach on their rights. A conflict over the right of way develops. Those in power lord it over others, then come the trucks and buses followed by the motorized smaller vehicles, other mechanised forms of transport and finally the pedestrians. The pecking order has become more important than the rules so that social functioning is disturbed.

When those responsible for maintaining rules violate them or are indifferent to them, there is a feeling of injustice which leads to increased conflicts and difficulties in social functioning. This is also the case with the black economy. Rules or having too many of them are not the cause of violation. By eliminating roads or rules or the police, the problem is not resolved, society becomes worse off.

Scams and corruption cases are hardly ever resolved. In the Bofors case, it is clear that money was made but twelve years after it was unearthed, it is not known, formally, to this day who made the money. Businessmen, politicians, bureaucrats and the investigation agencies all know that havala channels are active in India. But, the Jain case has almost come to an end even though at least one politician admitted to having received money and colleagues of another admitted that he received funds for the party. Evidence was found that it was used to channel funds to terrorists. The state seems unconcerned about its own rot and the ruling group incapable of action in their own self interest. The cause of the existence of the black economy is at once both simple and complex, involving the entire system.

LESSONS FROM SOME SCAMS, HAVALA AND RECENT EVENTS

The chargesheets in the Jain havala case filed by the CBI showed in poor light the senior echelons of the leadership. The N. N. Vora Committee set up after the Bombay serial blasts had exposed the nexus between politicians and criminals but no names emerged.

The politicians accused in the havala case were indignant. They all claimed to be honest and argued that they are being framed for political reasons. The claim that the money was taken for the party does not make the act legal. Mr Jakhar was under a cloud in 1989 in the closing days of the Rajiv regime and was again under a cloud in the last leg of the Rao regime. He claimed there was an anti-farmer bias. All kinds of excuses were trotted out and the public expected to believe them.

Amongst those at the top of the heap—politicians, bureaucrats, businessmen, policemen and criminals—there was a camaraderie; a conspiracy of silence—like that of the mafia. Them know about each other's wrong doings but keep quiet because of their own activities. There are exceptions but even their lips are sealed.

Those in power appreciate that illegality has played a substantial part in their rise and to remain there they need to hide this fact from the public. This explains why even the best amongst them are so tolerant of the black economy, arguing that it is a world-wide phenomenon as if that is a justification.

The havala case which began in 1991 was kept on the back burner until, the Supreme Court forced the hands of CBI. The case could have been expedited, since the CBI worked under the PM. Under SC instruction, an independent authority now looks after the CBI. What does this imply? There are various intelligence agencies in India which collect information and keep tabs on illegality—both within the country and outside. But it would appear the facts collected by them are hardly used for prosecution.

The havala case showed that the system of camouflaging illegality can accidentally fail in spite of the best efforts. Those who were exposed feel indignant perhaps because they have got caught for much less than what others were guilty of. Jokes went around that the amounts mentioned were ridiculously small and that even the cooks of the accused would not accept them. It is quite possible that there was politics in selecting who all got caught but does that justify illegality? Unwittingly, the responses of the elite to the havala revelation exposes their feeling that they are above the rule of law since they are the creamy layer—Mandal in reverse.

The Joint Parliamentary Committee (JPC) set up to investigate the case, unraveled many unsavory affairs relating to some politicians, bureaucrats and brokers. Most of the fraud relating to the activities of the private businesses has still not been unveiled. For instance, the links between the politicians and businessmen, money-laundering and foreign accounts and insider-trading remain a mystery to the public. The Member Investigation, CBDT, who was in-charge of raids on Mr. Harshad Mehta was not allowed to appear before the JPC. Only after his retirement did the new incumbent appear before the JPC. The end result of such manipulations has been that the public is in the dark about how much money was involved in the scam and who actually benefited from it. Whether true or not, it believes that thousands of crores were involved.

The role of the then ruling party, the Congress party, was to try to minimize damage. The JPC report was diluted on grounds of unanimity and the reported promise that action would follow against some of the ministers. However, subsequently it used the diluted report to argue that no minister need be held responsible. Finally, action was taken only when the combined opposition took a stand and critically when the PM's position weakened in the party. It almost seemed that the actions were not meant to clarify things but to put a lid on the malaise underlying the scam.

The havala case, the financial scam and the Bofors cases are now more or less dead but highlight three important things. First, many of the politicians of various national parties are in some way involved in illegality. This was suspected by the public all along but it is now in the realm of reality. Second, the nexus is not only between the politicians and the criminals but also involves businessmen and the bureaucrats. Third, charges of corruption and illegality against the high-ups in the country seldom get proved even when taken up for investigation. The system closes in to protect itself and little thought is given to reform. These things have little to do with either tax rates or controls.

Unrepresentative Government and Foreign Influence

If those in power are allegedly compromised and part of the illegality, they cannot be expected to care about niceties like democracy and representing people's interest. In the preceding chapter, it was shown that the black economy had led to the opening up of the economy through illegal means much before 1991 and that the New Economic Policies were partly a consequence of the crisis triggered by such opening up. The weaknesses of the Indian economy consequent to the functioning of the black economy led to the granting of large-scale concessions to foreigners. The national interest neither mattered nor was the compromised elite interested in defending it.

Was there an alternative? The obvious answer was to import less since the country was importing many inessentials. Up to 1994, the option of importing less was available but was not exercised but now the advanced nations can (and have) legitimately threaten action under WTO for restricting imports.

When the choice could be exercised, the policy-makers presented a distorted picture to suit their arguments. They argued that the import squeeze resulted in industrial recession in 1991-92. But, actually there was no shortage of goods in the market—there was an excess. Demand was deficient hence the recession—not a result of shortages. Yet, the argument was used to force import liberalization.

Be that as it may, if the country needs foreign exchange for importing inessentials, the sacrifice should be made by those requiring these goods. The distinction between essentials and inessentials is because the former are needed by everyone in society and are required by general production. The latter are demanded by a few and do not affect production or prices in a basic way. The cost of these imports for a few (the 3% in India) are borne also by those who do not benefit from them.

The demand for inessentials is backed by purchasing power of the well-off sections of society. If these goods are not made available in the economy, they are smuggled in or consumed abroad and result in loss of foreign exchange. If foreign exchange is not to be lost, the well off have to voluntarily agree to forego the consumption of these goods. The government rather than persuading these people has conceded to their demand and imposed a cost on the economy as a whole.

Apart from the pressure for globalization from the Indian elite, there is pressure from international agencies, representing the interest of the advanced nations. The government is forced to concede to their pressure because of the weaknesses of the Indian elite.

The message going out is that living outside India is better than inside the country. This is doubly so since by working outside India one gets a higher value for one's labour and when one wants to bring back the savings from it one would get a preferential tax treatment. Indians who can do so would find it materially better to go abroad and return as NRIs or with MNCs. Indian businesses and those in the ruling elite who have been resorting to these routes would do so even more. Their actions have a legitimacy under NEP.

The trend of the elite in India identifying its interests with outside forces instead of the national interest would strengthen. Those who stay back in India are responsible for the running of the country and not the NRIs or the foreigners. Yet, the latter will have a disproportionate influence on policy. Indians staying back would be subject to these influences to a greater extent because of the increased legitimacy to such ideas. This would have long term consequences. Indian politics would become even more unrepresentative since it has to accommodate foreign interests.

This is already visible. National policies are being framed under pressure, with foreigners in mind. Howsoever undesirable price rise maybe from the point of view of the bulk of Indians, it is being tolerated because the policies demanded by foreign interests lead to it.

Economics is full of unintended consequences of actions taken by economic agents. With globalization and penetration of market forces and weakening of the national spirit, there would be acceleration of migration of skilled manpower from India. Migration by individuals depends on a host of factors which can be broadly grouped as social and material reasons. With the continuing deterioration in the social environment, the reasons for staying back are weaker. India cannot match the incomes available abroad and devaluation has widened the gaps so that with growing faith in the market incentive structures, the reasons for migrating are stronger.

The social reasons for staying back are the culture, the history and the social ethos. These could be the desirable features of a relatively poor India but their appeal is now surpassed by that of the market. Today, the West is the success story and its values the 'desirable' ones. In comparison to the West and its crisis-ridden social structure, India could be an alternative if it could create an environment of equity and social justice. But the black economy has undermined precisely these features and because of policy failure, makes it appear crisis-ridden and hardly an example for others.

Like the villager migrating to the town and after initial guilt settling down there, the elite is also asking, 'Why stay back in India?' The cost of the answer to this is paid by the already deprived.

In brief, the interests of the bulk of the population does not find representation. An aspect of this is the growth of illegality and the black economy which precipitated the economic crisis in the late eighties. Foreign interests have taken advantage of this crisis and the Indian elite, acting as their junior partners have gone along. This is perpetuating the crisis for the non-elite. The disenfranchisement of the vast mass of population has added to the sense of social injustice and is a contributory cause of the growth of social conflict resulting in increasing illegality and the black economy.

BLACK INCOMES: THE CAUSES

It is now evident that the cause of the black income generation lies in the social system as a whole. However, much of the literature on the subject ignores this and tries to search for narrowly economic reasons. It views the problem in a narrow framework based on individual motivation, under given circumstances and does not ask what gives rise to behaviour. The assumption is that circumstances are given and nothing much can be done about them since they are non-economic. Those who subscribe to this philosophy believe economists can only ask, what is the best that can be done under those circumstances?

The entire blame for black income generation is put on either taxes or government intervention.

High Tax Rates and Black Incomes

The very existence of a tax in a society implies that tax-payers can increase their income in hand by evading it on some part of their income. The entire income on which the tax is evaded is black income—independent of the tax rate—and is larger than the tax dodged whatever be the tax rate. The tax rate only affects the amount of tax which would have been paid. However, it is widely believed that high tax rates lead to black income generation. Is there a positive relationship between the two?

The significance of the tax rate is that it represents the benefit on every rupee of tax evaded. If the tax rate is 30% the individual saves Rs 30 for every Rs 100 of income evaded and if it is 40% the saving is Rs 40. At any tax rate, the more the income evaded, the larger the gain. Even if the tax rate is 10%, saving on an evaded income of Rs 200 is twice that on Rs 100. So that higher the income evaded the higher the benefit of evasion no matter what the tax rate is.

It is argued that tax evasion involves costs. A tax evader has to take the help of accountants and tax lawyers, maintain two sets of accounts, bribe tax officers and politicians and spend time. It is also possible that evasion may be detected and penalties imposed. Thus, tax evasion may be advantageous only if there is a net gain after all actual and potential costs of toil and trouble are deducted from the taxes saved.

It is further assumed that all these costs of evasion rise proportionately more as the amount of income evaded increases. Hence at a given tax rate, the net benefit falls as more and more incomes are evaded and at some income the net benefit becomes zero. Beyond that there is no point in evading more incomes. According to this theory, this is the 'optimum' amount of income which an individual should evade.

As the tax rate applicable on an income rises, the higher is the tax saved on the evaded income. So that with a given structure of costs of evasion, the net gains increase as the tax rate rises. The point at which the net benefit becomes zero occurs at a higher income. In brief, a higher tax rate resulting in a higher net gain from tax evasion would lead to a larger size of the black economy.

In a modern society, individuals are subject to many taxes. It is, therefore, argued that even if each individual tax is low, the multiplicity of taxes taken together leads to a high 'effective' tax rate and to greater black income generation.

But then the question arises should one use the average rate of tax or the marginal rate? While the average rate of tax is applicable to the total income (definitionally), it is the marginal rate at the highest slab the income falls in that would have to be paid on any extra disclosures an individual may decide to make. So, the marginal rate would be relevant to the argument. However, the dynamic considerations developed in Allingham and Sandmo (1972), based as they are on a stream of return from evasion, may allow average rates of tax to be used for studying tax evasion behaviour. Tanzi finds the use of average tax rates to be the better explanatory variable in his model for studying the currency to deposit ratio and hence tax evasion in the case of the US economy (Tanzi, 1982, p. 80). In other words, the literature is not clear on this point.

A simple critique of this argument was presented by Kabra (1982): if a reduction in tax rates was to lead to greater tax revenue then at a given level of income, the tax-payers would be paying more taxes and have less income and so be worse-off. They would then prefer the status quo with its high tax rates and not clamour for lowering of tax rates—but individuals do not have to pay more tax, they need only declare more of their black incomes while paying the same tax—, the black economy would decline in size and this could have a snowball effect as newer channels of evasion and investment in black are not evolved. The argument needs to be viewed in a dynamic context and not set in a static one.

In this analysis those who are successful in completely evading taxes are not accommodated. A lowering of tax rates may draw some of these successful dodgers into the net so that, at least theoretically, tax revenues may go up despite lower tax rates and reduced payments by those already paying taxes. However, this is most unlikely since once in the tax net, previous accounts may also be opened up or the option of dodging in the future may be closed.

This suggests that the relationship between tax rates and tax evasion is not clear cut. Singh (1973) concludes on purely theoretical grounds that effective implementation may reduce tax evasion but lowering tax rates hardly guarantees it. On empirical grounds, much the same conclusion is reached in the case of Sweden by Hansson (Tanzi, 1982, p. 237). Finally, as discussed later, the relationship between tax rates and evasion may be non-reversible due to cumulative effects of a growing black economy. Thus, a reduction in the tax rates may not reduce the size of the black economy.

The 'optimization' argument [say, in Allingham and Sandmo (1972) or Singh (1973)] discussed above may be rejected purely on logical grounds since it is based on unrealistic assumptions and constraints which do not hold in reality.

Income taxes are usually progressive so that for a large range of incomes, the effective tax rate keeps on increasing as incomes rise so that the benefit of evasion rises. Hence the argument hinges strongly on the costs rising faster than the benefits of tax evasion. But why should costs rise at all or sharply?

For those not in high income slabs, the costs of evasion are small since the income-tax department is hardly interested in detecting such incomes. Then there is a category of tax payers who pay what they must because of tax deduction at source. They usually try to evade tax on everything else they may earn. For another category, who belong to the unorganized sector, where the income tax department has no reach, tax rate is immaterial. They are completely outside the tax net and have no cost of evasion.

Only at reasonably high levels of income from the organized sector, detection becomes meaningful for the income-tax department and the costs of evasion may come into play. For such entities, individuals and businesses, costs of evasion become important. They employ accountants, lawyers, middlemen, etc. However, businesses and rich individuals in any case employ accountants and lawyers for their normal work so the additional costs are not too great. Further, for their routine work, such people have contacts with bureaucrats and politicians and these often turn into social relationships which helps reduce the cost of evasion. Lavish parties and marriages are socially accepted and are not objects of investigation. Tax raids can be politically managed or advance information obtained through the bureaucracy so that they become ineffective. Penalties can be nullified even if evaded income is detected. Appeals can be filed and judgments delayed through various devices.

It is unclear that there are significant costs of evasion for the well-off sections and if anything, there are possibly scale economies in evasion. That is, the higher the income, the lower the cost of evasion for each rupee evaded. If this is so, there would be no point of 'optimum' evasion or black income generation.

Even if an optimum exists, it may be far out on the income scale so that almost no one may reach it. For most of the rich the tax rate may be immaterial. In the circumstances, lowering tax rates will only result in loss of revenue and not an improvement in compliance.

However, the most important objection to this hypothesis is the one based on macroeconomic arguments. The optimum amount of tax evasion is based on the micro understanding that individuals act so as to maximize their income under given constraints. Everything else is held fixed. There is a representative individual whose income is held fixed while she/he decides on how much income to evade given the representative constraints. This behaviour is multiplied 'n' times to get the behaviour of society.

But, in the previous chapter, it was shown that tax evasion affects the income of the tax evader (over and above what is obtained through evasion) so that income cannot be taken to be held fixed. When tax is evaded by a class and other things are held unchanged, government's revenue falls so that to hold deficit unchanged, expenditures have to be curtailed. As demand falls, incomes go down. It was shown that gross incomes for the entire class fall exactly by the amount of tax evasion and net incomes remain unchanged.

In other words, when the individual's behaviour is aggregated to that of society, things cannot be held constant as they can be for one individual. Since one is trying to explain the social behaviour by modeling an individual, there is no escaping the consequence of adding things up. This happens because incomes are cycled through the economy. Incomes and expenditures are interlinked. Tax evasion changes the pattern of circulation of incomes and expenditures (distribution changes) so that things cannot be held constant even for the sake of the argument. This undermines the very basis of the high tax rate hypothesis.

The question arises, if costs of evasion are unimportant, why does anyone pay any taxes? There are many reasons for it. For the fixed income group, tax is deducted at source. Public companies have to declare a dividend if they have to raise money from the public so they have to show some profits, etc. Many of the incomes in the economy are interlinked, and, therefore get captured in the tax net. The point to note is that none of these factors have a link with the tax rate.

Theories of taxation suggest that taxes are levied either on the basis of the 'benefits received principle' or the 'ability to pay'. Broadly speaking, since the poor have had little control over policy and the country has at best had negligible trickle-down, the benefits received by the poor have been negligible. Thus, applying the first principle, taxes should be paid by the rich. Yet, through indirect taxes, a substantial portion of the taxes are sought to be collected from the poor.

On the 'ability to pay' criterion, taxes ought to be paid by the better-off sections of society. To start taxation of personal incomes at 700% of the per capita income makes the base of taxation very narrow. This problem is further aggravated by the large number of concessions available to the tax-payers. In brief, taxes should be collected from the well-off sections but they are the ones who avoid paying a part of it both through legal and illegalments.

Those who argue that high tax rates cause evasion not find support in theory but have built up a climate for this idea because of their vested interest in getting taxes lowered; the well off are the biggest beneficiaries of reduction in tax rates. The fixed income earners are the ones who are unable to evade taxes and they resent paying taxes and demand their reduction. What they do not realize is that they have to pay heavy indirect taxes whose incidence on the rich is small due to their low consumption propensity. The evidence on direct and indirect taxes and real estate taxation is revealing.

Direct Taxes: the Evidence
The data on taxes paid by individual assessees are hard to come by and are available with a considerable time lags. Such data are available from the All India Income Tax Statistics (AIITS) and the report of CAG. Looking at Table V.1 it is seen that for the year 1991-92, only 1.58 lakh individuals had an assessed income of over Rs 1 lakh. These people constituted 3.5% of the total individual tax-payers. They paid 40% of the taxes on returned income which constituted 17% of the incomes, and paid an average tax rate of 35%. However, given the deductions, the returned income was typically less than the actual income.

In 1998-99, when the highest tax rate was 30% at an income of Rs 1.5 lakh and above, along with usual deductions, an assessee fell in this tax slab only if her/his income was close to Rs 2 lakh. This figure did not take into account PF and PPF interest income and income from dividends. The latter could be in lakhs. Tax liability could be lowered by another Rs 16,000 by making deposits. Assuming an income of Rs 1 lakh from dividends, PF and PPF, on a gross income of Rs 3 lakh one could be paying a tax of Rs 3,000/-. This was so, provided there was no income from capital gains. Hence at Rs 3 lakh of income one could be paying 1% of income as tax. If in the above case there was only Rs 50,000 of income from dividend and interest (from PF and PPF), one could have just paid Rs 18,000 of tax which is still 6% of the gross income. The more the share of property income, the less the tax.

Rs 3 lakh was 20 times the per capita income in 1998-99. If the data for 1991-92 is any guide and if those earning Rs 1 lakh or more in 1991-92 were taken to be in this category, of the total number of ten million assessees (Table V.2), hardly a few per cent would fall in this category. Table V.3 also supports such a conclusion. Hence, even if 6% is considered to be a high average tax rate, hardly 3% of the tax payers in 1997-98 paid this. For those with property income, the average tax may not be in the 30% (the tax rate theoretically applicable on incomes above Rs 1.5 lakh) range even for incomes above Rs 10 lakh. That is about 60 times the per capita income.

A similar situation prevailed in the mid-eighties when the tax rates were much higher. According to income-tax rates then applicable, the highest marginal tax rate of 60 per cent was applicable to incomes above Rs 1 lakh with an average tax of 40 per cent. High tax rates became applicable only at levels of income which were more than 40 times the per capita income (which, at the then current prices, was around Rs. 2,200).

Three conclusions may be drawn from these figures. First, the tax rates applicable to individual tax payers are far from extortionary except for a few lakh individuals. Secondly, if average tax rates of 30-40% are considered extortionary they have been applicable only at levels of income which are more than 40 times the per capita income. Lastly, there are so many loopholes and deductions that are deliberately provided that the actual tax rates are very low for over 95% of the tax payers.

Further, by various legal means, people falling in top brackets of tax rates split up their incomes to reduce their tax liability and lower the average tax rates they pay. For instance, at current rates of taxes, business income of Rs. 18 lakh split up into six equal parts between the husband, wife, three children and an HUF account, would result in a tax liability of Rs. 1.08 lakh instead of Rs. 5.4 lakh for a salaried person.

Those who believe that high tax rates are responsible for generation of black incomes should consider that businessmen do not even want to pay very low rates of taxes. When a presumptive tax was introduced for traders who were required to pay what would have been a two per cent rate of tax, very few obliged.

To sum up, except for a tiny minority of our population (0.005%), tax rates paid are much less than 30%. Thus, according to the theory of tax evasion, either very few Indians paying high taxes (or who would have to pay high taxes if they declared their true incomes) generate black incomes, or the costs of evasion are very low so that a significant number of Indians (a small percentage of the population) are involved in the black economy, irrespective of the tax rates applicable to them.

Other evidence to support the high tax rate hypothesis is rather thin. The highest marginal rate of income taxation has come down from 97.5% in 1970-71 to the current level of 30% in 1998-99. But black income generation has gone up and this contradicts the high-rate hypothesis. Neither data at a point of time nor over time support the contention that Indians pay a high tax rate on their declared or true incomes.

If we compare India's tax rates with the international ones, they have been moderate if per capita income is used as a measure (Table V.4 and V.5 give the data for mid-eighties when India's tax rates were much higher). In India, in 1998-99, income taxes are required to be paid on incomes of above Rs 80,000 which is 5.5 times the per capita income.

For most advanced countries, income taxes begin at a fraction of the per capita income (even student's assistantships are taxed in the USA). For many of the advanced countries, the highest marginal tax rates become applicable on incomes about 10 times the per capita income while the comparable figure for India is over 40 times. In Sweden in the mid-eighties, 84% was the highest marginal tax rate but less than 5% of its economy was black (Table II.1). There, individuals with annual incomes of over Rs 7,000 were required to pay a 20% tax rate.

Table II.1 shows that most advanced countries where taxation begins much earlier in the income scale than in India and who had comparable tax rates to India had much smaller estimated size of the black economy.

Some question such a comparison of India with the advanced countries because 50% of the per capita income in India would be Rs 7,500 while it may be around Rs 10 lakh for the advanced countries. However, the comparison is relevant since per capita income provides the yardstick for comparison between incomes of individuals in different societies. The disparities in the absolute levels of incomes depend on the productivity differences amongst the various countries but per capita incomes normalize them to the same common yardstick. Thus, across societies, comparisons have to be in terms of the per capita incomes, while within the country the comparisons can be with respect to the absolute incomes.

Table V.6 shows data on tax as a percentage of GDP and total government expenditure as a percentage of GDP for a select group of countries at various stages of development. The first reflects the total tax paid on each unit of income and the second the total size of the government which has to be financed in one form or the other. Both for 1980 and 1995, India is at the bottom. On no count is India heavily taxed compared to other countries and taxes cannot be said to be the reason for it to have a much higher size of the black economy.

Unfortunately, high tax rates are made the rationale for tax evasion by those who in any case pay little taxes. It is argued that the tax rates are high and they do not leave enough incentive for people to earn. The question is what is a high tax rate? No clear cut answer is available. What is clear is that India is not a high tax nation unless a tax rate in single digits is considered to be high.

Whether tax rates are high or low is a matter of social perception. Afterall, a tax is recycled through the economy and flows back to the tax payers in some form. If there is a consensus over policies, people will pay their taxes voluntarily otherwose not. If there is a sense of social justic, people voluntarily accept an import. This expains that in India while the highest tax rate has declined from 97.5% in 1971 to 30% in 1998, the feeling continues that the tax rates are high.

In India, irrespective of the tax rates, many simply escape the tax net. The reason is political clout, money power and tardy implementation of the laws. Repeatedly it has been demonstrated that strict implementation of the law induces compliance whereas the tax rates have little effect on evasion.

Indirect Taxes

The neglect of indirect taxes in any argument would be inappropriate since they constitute 75% of total tax revenue (85% in 1990-91). The hypothesis of high tax rates leading to a high degree of tax evasion seems to be even less plausible in the case of indirect taxes.

The reason for doubting a connection between a high rate of indirect tax and the generation of black incomes is the mechanism involved. Evasion of indirect taxes involves either the misdeclaration of the rule or the suppression of production of the associated physical goods or services. For example, if excise duty is to be evaded, a part of the production goes undisclosed; if sales tax is to be evaded, the sale of certain goods has to be suppressed. As mentioned in Chapter 2 and analyzed in Chapter 4, once a good is not reported for one tax it goes out of the reporting chain all down the line.

In the case of evasion of indirect taxes, the entire revenue from the sale of the evaded goods and not just the tax component is suppressed. Since the former is always greater than the latter, no matter what the tax rate may be, the net gain from evasion is linked not to the tax payable but to the net sales proceeds. The net gain from evasion does not accrue to any one individual but is shared at the various stages of transactions of a commodity. The gain is greater than the tax that may be payable at each of the steps. The specific case of evasion of excise duty in the sugar industry illustrates this. It was found that the cost and the ease of evasion is what affects the process of black income generation rather than the tax rate. (NIPFP, 1985).

The NIPFP Report discussed in detail not only the sugar industry but also the real estate sector. Both indicate that neither a higher tax rate necessarily leads to a higher quantum of generation of black incomes nor a cut in it reduces the generation of black incomes.

Real Estate Taxation
In the case of real estate, data from Delhi indicates that high value property facing high rates of taxes (but more specifically high rates of capital gains tax at the time of sale) was found to be under-valued by a far lower percentage than low value property facing lower rates of taxes (NIPFP Report, p. 236). For instance, it was found that at the time of sale, properties of declared value above Rs. 3 lakhs were under-valued between 15 and 50% in a majority of cases. On the other hand, an average property with a declared value of under Rs. 50,000 was under-valued by upwards of 200% and in many cases even above 400%.

The data contradicts the high tax rate hypothesis which would have required the high-value properties to be under-valued by far more than the low-value properties. It needs to be mentioned that the data mentioned above was supplied by the income-tax department and the percentage under-valuation was calculated by using the initial judgment value of the department and the declared purchase price (NIPFP Report, p. 232).

Further, the Finance Bill, 1977, announced that beginning 1 April 1978 (i.e., one year later), long-term capital gains would be exempt from tax if they were invested in certain specified securities (like bank deposits). Thus, for a high-value property which has often to pay the highest marginal tax rate, in the year 1978/79, the effective tax rate could have been brought down from 70% to 0%. This amounted to a substantial tax cut as opposed to the case of sugar industry where the excise duty rates changed only a few percentage points and may not be expected to have a substantial impact on compliance.

The income-tax department's data for real estate does not show an unambiguous reduction in the average percentage under-valuation for the year 1978/79 (p. 248). One possible explanation is that the other tax rates applicable to properties, like house tax, wealth tax and stamp duty, were not brought down so that the reduction in one tax rate is by itself not so effective. However, the sale of immovable properties could have been postponed from the year 1977/78 to 1978/79 to take advantage of the new provisions. This would have produced a dip in the number of sales for 1977/78 and a hump for 1978/79 (the provision was withdrawn from 1979) but this did not happen.

The assumption underlying the above argument is that property transactions can be postponed. The question arises whether this is at all plausible? The short answer is yes. The data for Delhi show that during the Emergency years the average number of sales of immovable property dropped dramatically to about 25% of the average for other years in the seventies (NIPFP Report, p. 249). The data from Bombay on the monthly sale and purchase of flats (NIPFP Report, p. 241) was even more revealing.

In July 1982, a provision was introduced in the Income-tax Act to acquire undervalued flats. The largest number of such transactions used to occur in Bombay. This number dropped to zero in July 1982 and only gradually recovered to a monthly average of 1,600 in 1984. From the stable trend in 1984, it could be projected that the average number of transactions before July 1982 may have been around 1,300 per month. Thus, in the period 1982 to 1984 people did modify their sales pattern.

Finally, it needs to be mentioned that capital gains tax on real estate is applicable largely to those investors who do not buy property for personal use but use it as a means of investment or speculation. This is so since capital gains on one residential property are exempt from tax if reinvested in a residential property within a specified period. Thus, if one is simply changing one's residence, one is unaffected by taxes. The real bite of taxation is meant for real estate speculators. These people can postpone their transactions.

From these arguments it is evident that even a massive reduction in the effective tax rate did not have an effect on black income generation in real estate. However, deterrence seems to have an immediate impact as indicated by the above mentioned experience during Emergency and the provision for acquisition of undervalued flats introduced in July 1982.

Examples from the NIPFP Report show that a high tax rate does not necessarily lead to a higher quantum of black income generation (in the case of sugar and real estate), contrary to the suggestion made in the chapter on causes (p. 283). It is surprising that after stating that 'studies which quantify the nature of the links between the level and structure of taxation and the extent of evasion are virtually non-existent in India' (p. 274), the relevant analysis in the Report itself is ignored. Unfortunately, prejudice is carried a bit too far.

Complex Laws and Administration

Theoretically, evasion possibilities increase with the difficulties of administration of the tax laws. For instance, in the case of cotton textiles, production involves output from handlooms, powerlooms and mills. Further, the processing for cloth may either be by hand or by power. In the early eighties, there was a separate tax rate for each category of output. To complicate matters, taxes were levied ad valorem (on the value of output) with the rate being determined by the count (roughly the fineness or coarseness of the cloth) and its value.

This meant that a very large number of tax rates were applicable and the mis-classification of cloth, was quite common. According to calculations, the loss of excise duty may have been an average of 20 per cent but possibly even 50 per cent of the duty collected. Sugar is a homogeneous commodity and had three excise duty rates applicable. Excise evasion in the case of this commodity was found to be lower, around ten per cent.

However, more detailed investigation suggests, the strength of the argument that black income generation is linked to the difficulty of administration does not appear to be overwhelming. If this was an important explanation for evasion, then one would not expect to see major year to year fluctuations in the extent of its evasion. The difficulty in administering tax laws has changed gradually and not in spurts.

It is possible that changes in the tax laws temporarily reduce black income generation by making the older methods of evasion redundant, requiring new mechanisms to be evolved and by introducing uncertainty in black economy operations.

The example (already presented) of acquisition of undervalued properties in Bombay illustrates this. All transactions came to a halt for months. Black income generation in this activity stopped and property prices declined by around 20 per cent. It was after more than a year and a half that the annual number of transactions reached the pre-1982 figures and the property values recovered. The builders and the real estate agents took this much time to evolve mechanisms to circumvent the new law.

The logic of the argument would suggest that constant changes in the law would keep tax evasion down. But this cannot be a policy since governance itself would be difficult. The role of the administration therefore becomes critical in any under-standing of the process of black income generation in India. The combination of complex law and an ineffective administration obviously facilitates flouting of rules. A professionally run administration, proud of its role, would be able to administer even a complex system of rules.

Even if the hypothesis of high tax rates is valid, it would be so for incomes which are derived from legal activities and which are reportable to the tax authorities. It is only on such incomes that the individual has a choice of how much income to report. She/he could do a cost benefit analysis on these incomes to make the decision.

These considerations cannot be applicable to incomes from illegal activities, like, drugs, prostitution, bribes and smuggling. These are considered social bads and are banned activities. Hence the non-reporting of these incomes is independent of tax rates.

But there are gray areas, like, undervaluation of properties, under- and over-invoicing and excise duty evasion. These are legal activities in which illegality is committed. If these illegalities were not committed then these incomes would have accrued as white incomes and would have been reported to tax authorities.

Once an illegal act is committed, the income is not reportable. The question then is what are the considerations which propel an economic agent to commit an illegality in legal activities? One aspect is the economic gain from the illegality. However, the most important consideration is one's commitment to society. If one feels that taxes are needed for society to function well, say, for one's old age or for one's children or for one's peace of mind, etc., one may pay taxes even if there is no compulsion or checking for tax evasion. Commitment is a social factor. Even how well the administration functions depends on the social commitment of the bureaucracy.

In brief, legality and illegality are relative terms and individual actions lie in a spectrum of legality or illegality; the exact point at which the activity will lie depends on the social situation. The tax rate may be one of the factors determining the extent of evasion but not a critical one. The tax rate hypothesis is hard to test since there are too many factors—social, political and economic—which enter into the considerations of a tax evader.

State, Controls and Black Economy

It is widely believed that controls and regulations are responsible for the generation of black incomes. It is popularized by the terms 'licence-quota-permit' raj or the 'inspector' raj. Kabra (1982) saw the issue as a part of the wider drive to 'remove-controls reduce-taxation'. He has stated that 'controls and taxation are necessary to curb certain activities in the economy. They themselves by no means create or help black economy. It is illogical to hold the laws governing economic activities themselves as constituting the reasons why people violate or evade the laws' (p. 162).

That controls have a history needs to be stressed. Uncontrolled speculation or price fixing by industry and trade has often resulted in public pressure on policy to institute controls. For instance, there have been demands for controls on the functioning of the share market or the prices of onions. With the growth of the black economy and opening up of the economy, the potential for unscrupulous manipulation of the markets has grown. Controls and regulation in many instances have been demanded even by industry and/or trade. George Soros, the high priest of international finance, has been demanding controls on international capital flows (Soros, 1997).

Since the mid-thirties, the world over, state intervention in the economy has grown. It began as a necessity to deal with the depression in the world economy. Subsequently, it was realized that there were various areas of economic activity where the markets do not function as they should. This is called 'market failure'. In such a situation, government is supposed to intervene to set the markets right. Markets fail in a large number of activities in the supply of public goods, merit wants, where there are increasing returns to scale and where there are externalities.

The government is also supposed to intervene to give the economy a direction, to enable optimum utilization of resources which may otherwise go waste. Finally, government is supposed to help achieve equity. For the reasons listed, the world over, governments have increased their intervention in the economy. As Table V.8 shows, in this decade, expenditure by government as a percentage of GDP has been in the range of 20% to 50%. Table V.9 shows that for different groups of countries, from the the sixties to the eighties, this figure has increased sharply. In the eighties, the increase was moderate for most groups of countries except in the South Asia. Over a longer time-span of a century, Table V.10 shows that for the OECD countries, the figure jumped between 1915 and 1935 and then again between 1960 and 1980.

For the developing countries, the spurt was in the early seventies and eighties.

The government was given a role in the faith that it can do what the market cannot. This faith has been shaken in the eighties since policies have been found to fail and the size of the government has stagnated or declined in many countries. Capital has extracted more concessions from society (Table V.11), one of which is the retreat of the state to enable the private sector to have a larger economic space for itself.

Public goods are those activities in which society consumes as a whole, like defence, law and order, municipal services, maintenance of forests, etc. Merit wants are activities like health and education. In these activities, the individual may not value the activity as highly as the society may. For instance, education of a girl child may not be valued much by families. A girl may not receive adequate medical attention since it is not a priority for the family. But this cannot be so for society since the health of children depends on the mother being literate and healthy. A poor family may prefer to send children to work rather than send them to school. But for society, the value of a literate population is great. In the case of an externality, the individual may simply derive a benefit from the activity and leave the costs to be borne by society. Like, a company may produce a good and make a profit but also pollute air and water leaving it to society to clean it. This creates too much pollution since nobody cleans up and the cost falls on society.

In cases of increasing returns to scale, monopolies emerge which fleece the consumer. Government has to step in to provide the services or goods from these industries or has to regulate the private sector or break-up monopolies. Finally, the market is not a democratic institution. Its functioning depends on the purchasing power of the individual and not on equity amongst them. If inequities grow in society, unbearable social tensions get generated so that the state has a role in mitigating inequity.

While theoretically the role of the government in the economy is clearly defined, with the growth of the black economy, as discussed in Chapter 4, policy fails and this has discredited state intervention in the economy. Policy failure and globalization are two reasons for the retreat of the state.

In India regulations and controls need to be understood in the wider perspective of the nature of the state. Policies designed to achieve wider national goals (like, equity) have not met with national consensus (more so amongst the ruling classes). Consequently, sectional interests have viewed policies either as so many impediments to be overcome or as tools of economic gain. The black economy emerges as the natural corollary of this process of subversion of national policies.

Such a hypothesis implies that the state is neither neutral between classes nor represents a stable set of sectional interests. Kabra (1982), while recognizing the intra-class conflict amongst the ruling elite, nonetheless suggested a political conspiracy to fool the masses as an explanation for non-implementation of policy and the emergence of the black economy. This need not be so, a non-conspiratorial hypothesis might also suggest that in an unmitigated pursuit of narrow sectional interests, the burden of adjustment would necessarily fall on the unorganized and the weak.

Further, it cannot be denied that vested interests have developed around controls and that they can be under-cut by removing controls. However, the critics of controls need to recognize that mere removal of controls not only does not eliminate the need of sectional interests to maximize their incomes but also helps them do so openly and legitimately. One cannot make a general case for or against controls. The concept of social accountability must not be thrown to the winds, specially when it is not even certain that doing away with controls would necessarily curb black incomes.

Subversion of Controls: Roots in the Political Process

The proliferation of controls and regulations results in complex laws and difficulty in administration. Flouting of controls and regulations in the economy to generate black incomes involves developing specific mechanisms.

The difficulty in establishing any link between the degree of controls and regulations in the economy and the size of the black economy lies in the inability to represent the former as a composite. It is far easier to see the link in the case of an individual activity which may be subject to 'controls and regulation'. In the case of the sugar industry, various degrees of controls have been imposed on its production and distribution for a long time. Yet, no link between the degree of control and the size of black incomes generated was evident. (See NIPFP Report.)

Real estate has also been subject to various controls, like the Urban Land Ceilings Act, 1976. It has been argued that this led to an acceleration of price rise in urban landed properties because of the freezing of excess land. It is well known that a rapid rise in land prices leads to an increase in black income generation. An analysis of data for Delhi shows that from the mid-1960s to mid-1970s, the average price of land increased from around Rs 15 to Rs 200 per square yard while the rise in the next decade took it to around Rs 3,000 per square yard and then to around Rs. 35,000 per square yard. The rate of price increase in land cannot be said to have accelerated after the imposition of the Urban Land Ceilings Act, 1976 or be the cause of black income generation.

Controls and regulations can be and are misused to extract a rent. For instance, anyone who has tried to construct a house in India knows how much harassment is to be faced. Delays are used to extract a bribe. Usually, flouting of a rule is associated with an economic gain and the advice for this is given by the concerned official. However, even when rules are not flouted, a bribe may be given simply to save time and trouble—'speed money'.

The concerned functioning extracts a rent by agreeing to ignore the violation of the law or for using its discretion. To extract a rent, a surplus must be generated in that cocerned activity. In other words, the bribe paid, is typically a fraction of the benefit accruing or likely to accrue from the twisting of the law. The experience of businessmen and the police 'hafta' bear this out. (See chapter 2).

The discussion, therefore, raises three questions. First, why have laws become complex? Secondly, why has administration become ineffective and demoralized? And finally, how can the flouting of rules persist over a period of time in spite of the checks and balances in a democracy?

Looking at the final issue. A legal structure may become complex because of rapid changes in society. New situations call for new solutions. Yet, the earlier social structures do not disappear all at once and the laws relating to them continue to be required. Sometimes, the old laws remain in the statute books long after they lose their relevance. In addition, poor administration of the law increases the complexity of the situation.

No law can cover all contingencies. A law has to be administered both in letter and spirit. A corrupt and inefficient administration either implements the law rigidly or not at all. The flexibility or the initiative required to deal with a dynamic situation does not exist. Thus, a large number of loopholes are evolved by people bent on taking advantage of the law. In response to this situation, legislatures go on modifying laws one after the other, in an ad hoc manner, to plug the loopholes and in the process make them more complex.

The other two questions will be taken up later since they relate to the prevailing political process.

1991: Reduction in Controls

The post-1991 era calls into question the hypothesis regarding reduction of controls. In fact, if there is a law, its violation results in illegality and incomes associated with this activity are generated as black incomes. Corruption is a part of this phenomenon. Illegality can end if the rule of law is either followed or abolished. But, the latter amounts to eliminating society itself and there is little left to discuss. Laws define the parameters of social functioning and need to be based on what is socially desirable.

When controls are removed an illegal activity may become legal. How does the tag legal or illegal matter? Take the case of gold imports. It is not so important that now gold can be brought in legally whereas it was earlier illegal to do so and was called smuggling. Gold import still creates BOP problems since it does not add to the official reserves. The economic impact of the activity continues, only illegality is reduced as compared to earlier. Today, social perceptions are changing so fast that legal or illegal hardly matters. Tomorrow, due to inability to curb theft, suppose it is legalized, would it generate security for the citizens because illegality has declined.

Suppose various laws are eliminated. By definition, certain incomes formerly called black would become white and illegality and corruption decline. What difference would it make? Gold imports were legalized in 1992 so that smuggling became legal importation. This did not change the nature of the economic activity. Inflow of gold has if anything increased so that loss of foreign exchange has gone up. Laundering of drug money and its use for criminal activities continues. Hence, what matters is the nature of economic activity and not the tag white or black.

Lower customs duties across the board may mean less smuggling but even greater importation of the same goods, loss of foreign exchange and setback to indigenous producers of those goods. Lower direct tax rates will mean continuing adverse movements in income and wealth inequalities and shrinkage of the market size in the medium run. Also, under the present regime it would mean lower rate of growth of public investment and social sector expenditures—redefining State's responsibility to society. Has this followed a change in society's priorities?

The real question that should be asked is *why has the Indian ruling elite resorted to flouting the rule of law on such a large scale*? This has little to do with the amount of government regulation or controls. It can occur even if there are few controls and may not occur when there are many of them. Controls are only the means of generating black incomes. They are the means and not the cause (which is illegality).

The stock market (regulated or unregulated) has been a major conduit of black incomes. Illegal construction is proliferating in metropolitan India even though it is unrelated to control of land. Zoning laws, essential for the efficient functioning of cities, are being flouted by the builders and the rulers leading to a breakdown of Indian cities. The crux of the matter is additional profits, over and above that which can be legally generated. This has not changed post-1991.

The causes discussed—the high tax rate, the degree of controls and regulations—are not the basic causes and only represent the necessary conditions for the generation of black incomes. In other words, if a tax or a law did not exist there would be no question of its evasion but it does not follow that if a law exists its violation is automatic. Hence having a tax or a high tax rate does not mean that evasion would occur. Similarly, it is not that controls result in black income generation; they are a source for making black incomes.

Other Causes of Black Income Generation

The various other explanations for black income generation listed are:

1. Inflation.
2. Low salaries of the public functionaries.
3. Scale of government spending.
4. General laws and regulations.
5. Political and bureaucratic corruption.
6. Political funding.
7. Standards of public morality.
8. Social structure.

These may be grouped into three. First, the purely economic, consisting of the first two in the above list. Secondly, related to government functioning, comprising the next three. Lastly, the general or the systemic, consisting of the remaining three.

Economic

It is argued that inflation results in greater incentive to evade taxes because those who gain from inflation do not declare a part of these gains since these are partly illegal. To the extent that some people make illegal gains in bouts of inflation, the cause cannot be said to be inflation but illegality. For instance, if due to scarcities, black premia rise then scarcity is the cause both of inflation and of tax evasion.

A combination of inflation and a progressive tax regime causes the average tax rate to rise since nominal incomes rise and fall in higher tax slabs. If one believes in the tax rate hypothesis then inflation becomes a cause of tax evasion. This argument does not hold for reasons over and above those already discussed. Income tax payers are a minuscule lot, about 1% of the population. These are mostly from businesses and the top echelons of the organized sector. Businesses usually gain from inflation since they raise prices faster than their costs rise. Their post-tax incomes rather than fall tend to rise, so this cannot be a cause for tax evasion. For the organized sector workers, tax is deducted at source so in their case tax evasion cannot go up unless they get income under the table. How much of their income they get under the table is determined by factors other than inflation, and if anything this would rise with inflation.

Low salaries in the public sector is given as a reason for public sector official's being prone to corruption. But then it must be asked what is a low salary and what would be an adequate level at which public functionaries would not take bribes or cuts? The answer has to contend with the fact that it is worthwhile for businessmen to give a cut or a bribe to get a work done by sharing a fraction of the profit with the functionary. What is given as a bribe bears no relation to the salary of the functionary; it depends on the benefit that the functionary allows to the businessman. Thus salary is hardly the consideration in a bribe. Following the logic further, can salaries be in crores if a minister or a secretary has to deal with contracts worth thousands of crores of rupees?

Public functionaries already get salaries which are a large multiple of the per capita income. They compare their salaries with those who they deal with, the private sector, which pays much higher salaries. But then with whom can they be compared, the employees of the private sector or the businessmen? The dealings of the senior functionaries are with the businessmen and there is no way that salaries can be comparable to the earnings of the businessmen or comparable to the inducements that businessmen can offer them.

It is not that relative incomes do not matter in society (their role is discussed later) but the factors underlying these differentials and their consequences are not directly related to corruption. There are several intervening layers of social actions which need to be analysed to understand the linkage. Public functionaries are supposed to work within the parameters of rules and if they do not, the reason is not just their salaries but something else.

Governmental Functioning

The three items under this rubric have a link with the black economy but the point is, are they the causes of generation of black incomes? Gupta (1992) identified the source of generation of black as the cause of black income generation. The same mistake is made in identifying political and bureaucratic corruption or governmental spending as the cause of generation of black incomes. Corruption accompanies black income generation. The question is why is there more or less of corruption? The cause lies elsewhere.

Higher governmental spending can potentially allow greater black income generation but this need not be the case. In OECD countries, governments spend a larger fraction of their higher per capita income than the developing countries do. But the size of the black economy is smaller in the former than in the latter. The real issue is to know why there a greater or lesser subversion of policy and generation of black incomes?

General laws and regulations are potential instruments for black income generation. What is it that makes this feasible? When can the power given to a bureaucrat be misused? That which enables the politician and the bureaucrat to misuse their powers is the cause of black income generation. And for that it is necessary to look at the systemic causes.

Systemic

Political funding relates to the political structure in the country and is a systemic problem. The form of political funding existing in a country depends on its institutional practices. In a corrupt system, political functioning would also get corrupted and take forms which subvert the system itself. What needs to be known are the reasons for the form of political funding prevailing in a society.

The standard of public morality will obviously be low where the black economy is larger. If illegality is widespread large numbers will be involved, and, therefore, moral standards can be expected to be low. This is a tautology.

If the cause of black income generation is systemic then it is futile to locate its cause in microeconomic issues.

But economists both from the Left and Right have ignored the black economy in their analysis. In spite of mounting evidence that it had become significant in the seventies itself and even though for the Left policy was critical and its failure evident, they could not see the link between policy failure and the growing share of the black economy since it was not a part of their framework.

Analysts from the Right used the fact of a growing black economy to discredit state intervention in the economy and used policy failure to attack the pro-poor orientation (at least on paper) of policies as populism. They turned the logic of the black economy around, and depicted state intervention as the cause of the black economy and economic failure. As already discussed this analysis based on a micro understanding is inadequate.

S. B. Gupta, distinguishing primary corruption (that in high places) from secondary correction (in intermediate and low places) characterizes India as a capitalist social formation in which there is a class alliance of the propertied with the middle classes.

This formulation raises many questions. Why is it that the capitalists cannot do what they wish to do without corruption? Why does it grow or when does it begin to decline? Is it true of all capitalist social formations? How do the political functionaries get away with increasing amounts of corruption in a democracy?

All this is linked to conflict in society and not the outcome of an alliance. A stable alliance would suggest a stable system which should be able to see its long run interest and act on it to make gains through the white economy and by reducing the size of the black economy which is the cause of much systemic inefficiency. On the contrary, if the black economy is the result of a deep and unstable (changing) conflict amongst the propertied in Indian society they would not be able to together define their long run interests or act on it.

Indian politics governed by conflict is playing havoc with institutions. It is conflict which has weakened commitment to society and made illegality acceptable to the propertied. The black economy as the means of making additional economic gains by cheating the system and the subversion of democracy is a natural corollary of this. Today, in India, many of those in power break any law they can. Whether it is a building bye-law, rent control regulation, industrial licensing, tax laws, child marriage, child labour and minimum wages laws, traffic rules, environmental and industrial safety regulations and so on. Courts are overflowing with pending cases and full of corruption. The sense of justice in society is missing. What needs explaining is why there this state of anarchy. Conflicts among the propertied, illegality, black economy, subversion of democracy and poverty are mutually interlinked and feed on each other.

Growth, Disparities and the State

The very concept of a poverty line defined in terms of the money value of the minimum food requirement of an average person is flawed for several reasons, two of which are: First, the minimum required by an individual in society is socially defined and changes with the context and the times. Second, expenses incurred to earn this minimum must also be taken into account in the definition. In today's world, transport cost has to be met to get to work. Health hazards are posed by the new work situations and expenditures on maintaining oneself and family are essential to life. Education for the children of the poor is necessary for them to break out of the poverty trap. It is the net income after meeting these socially necessary expenditures and not the gross income of the individual that is relevant for understanding poverty. It is akin to the case of a business, the income is not gross revenue, since the costs of doing business are to be subtracted from it.

Even if the poverty line is not redefined with respect to the changing social circumstances, a person crossing any given poverty line by a few rupees does not stop being poor. Besides, the subjective element of poverty which is socially determined needs to be considered. A person may feel dissatisfied with her/his relative poverty in a way they may not have done in a different social context.

With society in flux, relationships changing, traditional income relativities breaking down, conspicuous consumption abounding and ostentation the rule, relative deprivation is far more visible to the individual and becomes a cause for dissatisfaction. The number of people dissatisfied with their economic status is growing. It is not even that those in abject poverty are the cause of the growing social tensions in the country. Rather, it is the ones who have risen somewhat but less than what they aspire to who are responsible.

In other words, it is the growing economic disparities, rising aspirations and the lack of adequate opportunities to fulfill them that are a major reason for the growing social tensions in India. The black economy underlies each of these factors. However, with the growing role of government in the economy, the belief that government is responsible for the inadequate opportunities has taken hold. The demands on the state have increased.

Various economic interests realise that to influence government policy pressure needs to be applied through organization. Thus, hitherto unorganized sections of the population are being organized and politicized. Government subject to these pressures and operating within these constraints has lost the freedom of action. Its capacity to work for the welfare of the wider community has declined and policy failure due to the black economy has made matters worse.

An economy can reduce poverty by either redistributing the incomes (at a point of time) or by growing in size with a given distribution of incomes. However, it is also possible that growth may actually worsen the distribution of incomes and may not reduce poverty. This is called 'immiserising growth'.

Growth which leaves out of its ambit some sections of the population has this characteristic and as discussed in Chapter 4, the Indian economy with its growing black economy is an example of this. The role that each individual plays in an economy is determined by the prevailing social structure. It is conceivable that the role that some can play may become redundant or at least become less important as society changes.

Such sections tend to get marginalized in society and in the economy. The role of the poor unskilled labour in the face of advancing technology is one such example.

If growth is rapid, those getting marginalized have a chance of obtaining jobs but if the economy is growing slowly, then these people face unemployment. Thus, in the face of technological change, to prevent marginalizing growth, the growth rate has to be sufficiently high. As such, to reduce disparities it is not simply enough that economic growth be rapid but a) it must take into account the changing technology and its impact on employment and b) prevent worsening of disparities. The black economy comes in the way of both of these.

The Role of Income Relativities

That there is a link between economic disparities and the level of social tensions is generally accepted. While their link with the growing black economy has been pointed out, this relationship is not a simple one. Disparities have existed for a long time in most societies but have produced different levels of social tension.

A social structure with a given incomes ladder (which has prevailed historically) seems to be a source of social stability. Income relativities amongst different social groups seem to be important. A historical pattern of relativities (even when highly unequal) seems to carry with it a sense of economic justice and makes it acceptable to people.

In a rapidly changing society, as in post-independence India, where the income relativities have dramatically changed, social tensions aggravate. This happens with the creation of new possibilities for some groups and the elimination or the declining importance of (the work of) other groups. The ruling ideology in society reinforces such trends. In a capitalist society, the fixed income groups do not blame the business community for their declining standards (due to inflation) or act against it in spite of the latter's obviously rising standard of living. They accept the differentiation. Interestingly, they blame each other for trying to obtain a higher share of the national pie. These are the relativities they are directly concerned with in the social ladder even if these are not the cause of their economic decline. The pull of ideology is such that business practices have not only become acceptable to the middle classes but have been adopted them.

The obvious examples are of professionals (doctors, lawyers, teachers, etc.) giving up their own age-old ethics in favour of earning more by charging more, using the business principle 'what the market can bear'. The resulting contradictions are there to see. For instance, top civil rights lawyers can be seen presenting the case against the Bhopal Gas victims, the result of the worst ever industrial disaster. They defend the moneyed and other such people involved without seeing any contradictions. This is justified on the grounds of 'not guilty unless proven so'. Many a doctor make his patients run around from expert to expert to make money. Teachers create conditions so that tuition becomes essential. Chartered accountants sign on the dotted line and white-wash business wrongs.

In recent times, with consumerism gaining dominance, the income relativities have become even more important than earlier. Status is not dependent on the individual's work but on the show of consumption, so that income relativities become immediately apparent and the feeling of relative deprivation heightened. This hurts those who fall behind but till recently thought themselves to be equals or superior to those who march ahead. Most do not mind somebody they accepted as superior doing even better. The unorganized may resort to crime but the organized hold the rest of the society to ransom because of their capacity to manipulate the system.

Changes in income relativities are a major cause for corruption in the bureaucracy. Bureaucrats had a high status in society. Post-independence, their status has declined vis-à-vis the businessman. They cannot afford to entertain at home every day on their own salary. Their wives cannot have the saris and the jewellery to match what the businessman's wife has. Their children cannot afford the same school or the games that the businessman's child has. There is peer group pressure as well; each one tries to match the businessman's lifestyle.

It is easy to withstand the pressure from above—from the politicians or the boss or even the social circle—provided one has support from family and friends. However, when an honest officer becomes an object of ridicule, it becomes a different matter. One has to live with it all the time. The pressures from within the family to get extra income for ostentation are the hardest to withstand. The change in income relativities is important to understand corruption.

Conflict Between Capital and Labour

In the typical model of a capitalist economy, the basic conflict is taken to be that between capital and labour. This has been utilized by Kalecki (1971) and Rowthorn (1977) to analyze the phenomenon of inflation and stagflation in a capitalist economy. They treat these classes as undifferentiated. In Kumar (1983), it was suggested that in the case of the Indian economy, it is necessary to separately incorporate the unorganized sectors of the economy even though the basic conflict remains between capital and labour.

In Kumar (1986) it was argued that a conflict model of the Rowthorn kind would be inappropriate for analyzing inflation in the Indian economy since capital and labour cannot be treated as homogeneous due to the existence of the large unorganized section of labour which is unable even to bargain for maintaining a fixed real wage. The unorganized sector only gets the residual incomes left by the organized sector (Kumar, 1983 and 1986).

In other words, the existence of the unorganized sector, enables a conflict started by any shock to the economy to get resolved by a downward adjustment of the share of incomes of the unorganized sectors. This results in rising disparities and marginalizing growth in the economy. This is the basic conflict model which helps explain the generation of black incomes in India.

Today, the share in the national income accruing to a section of population depends not only on the wage bargaining and the price setting processes but also on government policies. Various economic interests in society have realized this. For example, a tax on wages reduces the share of the workers in the national pie by reducing their post-tax incomes. On the other hand, if the expenditures out of the taxes go to improve their welfare, they are no worse off. For the agriculturists the procurement price fixed determines their share, etc. Thus, conflict takes place over government policies which effects the shares in national income that different sections of society expect to receive.

However, the growing conflict over policies has become a major source of waste (and inefficiency) in the economy. It also limits the role the state can play since resources are preempted by conflict generated demand on public resources. For example, inadequate resources are left to be spent on primary education because the well-off sections get concessions on wealth tax, capital gains, property taxes, etc.

Resources are also preempted in managing social tensions resulting from the growing conflict and marginalization of the vast sections of the people. For instance, expenditures on law and order rise. In a situation of heightened conflict amongst themselves, the individual ruling groups seek other allies and organize and politicize groups which till then were peripheral. In the rural areas, the rich farmer is seeking to use the middle and the poor peasants as allies by mobilizing them against the more prosperous urban elite. Unviable regional development plans are drawn up to co-opt local elite. Most of the money allotted is simply eaten up. This happened in Kashmir and the North East.

Black economy adds to the conflict amongst the dominant economic interests. It is a way of increasing one's share beyond what is legally available. Since the fight is usually over the post tax incomes, two things happen. First, those who are successfully able to evade taxes shift the burden onto those who cannot shift it (say, the fixed income groups). This makes the latter feel that injustice is being done to them and they ask for greater concessions. Second, to obtain a given amount of revenue, tax rates have to be higher than they need be. This increases the sense of injustice amongst those forced to pay taxes.

In other words, the sharpening conflict amongst the ruling groups in India and their inability to resolve their differences without imposing greater and greater burdens on the state is both a manifestation of the growing crisis and also the cause. Such conflict limits the opportunities for the ruling groups and heightens the conflict amongst them.

There is another aspect of the growing conflict. Centre-State relations have deteriorated. The Centre has assumed more and more economic, political and social power in its hands. It has used this to play politics by flexing its financial muscle. This provides an opportunity to regional elite to lay the blame for relative deprivation on the Centre. Opposition governments in the states have mobilized opinion to fight the manipulations by the Centre. and where regional pride was hurt it led to a reinforcement of regionalism. Coming on top of the uneven regional growth, it has diverted attention from the economic dimensions of disparities to political and social factors.

Unrepresentative Politics: Truncation of Democracy

Indian democracy appears to be tottering. Corruption charges have been levelled against chief ministers and prime ministers. With no one owning responsibility, democracy is taking a beating. Some candidates seeking election have a criminal record. Many of them enter the legislature through manipulation and vote banks or due to blood relationship with well-known leaders (See Table V.10). Consequently, parliamentary performance or public opinion hardly counts.

The ruling groups have both weakened democracy and shown the way to emerging groups. They have manipulated every possible division in society to come to power. They have promised and not delivered. Punjab, Kashmir, Ayodhya, Mandal and so on have been used to garner votes. Garibi Hatao, Clean Government that works faster and Right to Work remained slogans that added to cynicism. In the recent past, each government that has come to power has had a hidden agenda which had no relationship to the campaign promises by that party. Kanshi Ram feels that it is not even important to have a programme. This is the source of widespread cynicism.

Take the elected governments of 1989, 1991, 1996 and 1998 as examples. SJP government in 1990 does not count—it did not promise anyone anything. Janta came to power in 1989 on the promise of a left of centre progressive and anti corruption plank. But they (and their allies) did little to educate the public on GATT even if they felt helpless in changing the course of negotiations. They started negotiations with the IMF on a loan and presumably on the conditionalities. They started the process of putting into place the New Economic Policies, including the present industrial policy. The Planning Commission was largely marginalized. There was no attempt to deliver on the poll promise of Right to Work. Hence, when cornered all they could do was to play the Mandal card, pending before the nation for over ten years.

The Congress in 1991 did not seek a mandate to implement the New Economic Policies but Mr. Rao initiated them within days of coming to power. In the 1991 elections, the real issues did not get debated—the economy, Kashmir and Punjab. The issues that came to the fore were Ayodhya and Rajiv Gandhi's assassination which swung 11% of the vote towards the Congress between the first and the second rounds of voting.

The government of 1996 with the Left as a component came to power with its constituents opposing NEP but implemented them with vigour. The BJP government in 1998 came on the plank of Swadeshi but further opened up the economy with a vigour not seen earlier. Corruption has been an issue time and again. This is surprising given that it has become a part of the existence of the ruling elite.

There is a gradual disenfranchisement of the poor. According to the Planning Commission, 37% of the people lie below the poverty line. The figure can be questioned but there is no disagreement that a vast majority of the people are poverty-stricken.

The manifesto of every party contains a commitment to eradicate poverty, etc. At one level, the task of any political party working to uplift these people is a straight forward one. Provide adequate productive employment to all. Yet, forty years after independence, the country is far from this target. One can only conclude that the poor, the bulk of the people in the country, do not find representation of their interests in the political spectrum.

The poor have no real choices from amongst the candidates who stand for elections since the various party platforms look similar and in terms of deeds, past experience has taught people that different parties behave in more or less similar ways. People are left to maximize their immediate and personal gain by voting for their own caste or community candidate, or for one who distributes some largesse at the time of elections.

Candidates for elections are seldom people from amongst the downtrodden. Increasingly, these are people whose qualification is their connections and/or money (Table V.10). They do not come through the democratic process and do not understand what it means to represent the interest of the poor. They are imposed from the top and are clear that they represent the interest only of their mentors: the monied and the political bosses. Such people without any roots in the masses are not only afraid of real democracy but are contemptuous of it.

Today, parties have practically become personal properties to be inherited by the sons and relatives. As a result, chief ministers are decided upon in Delhi and as a corollary, the list of election candidates are also finalized in Delhi. The question of representation or political standing in their respective constituencies are marginal.

In this situation, what matters for winning elections is whether the party has an adequate machinery in the constituency and money to feed it. (See appendix on elections). The party machinery is required not just at the time of elections but to maintain vote banks amongst the poor or the minorities. This is expensive business since local leaders have to be kept contented, power balance maintained among competing interests and patronage bought. Illegality is an essential part of these machinations. Administration has to be manipulated, strong men kept, etc.

A major interest of the monied classes is to make their wealth grow. In a land of grinding poverty, if true power rested with the people, this would be difficult in the best of times. It is then in the interest of the monied classes to see that power does not rest with the majority. In a system of parliamentary democracy, it then becomes imperative for the rich to have elected representatives who would pay only lip service to the cause of the poor while acting on behalf of the rich.

In the appendix on elections, a summary of interviews with fourteen political leaders is presented. By and large most admitted to having a nexus with big business, local industry and trade associations. They get money and help in kind from them not only for elections but also for day to day running of their politics. They admit to a quid-pro-quo for the help.

Following this logic, the political parties make a sham condemnation of the vast inequity in society. With private ownership of capital, some will earn high incomes so that as a populist measure, high taxes become necessary—to reduce incomes in the hands of the rich and to show a commitment to the principle of equity. However, loopholes are left in the laws and a blind eye is turned in implementation. This is the source of black income generation: the existing dichotomy between words and deeds of our policies (and politicians). This is the contradiction of our political system that those who apparently control it are not the real masters.

In a nutshell, the root of money power in Indian politics is essentially its non-representative nature and this is deliberate. *It is not that politics needs big money but money needs to control politics. Black money is a result of a basic contradiction in our system and the elite wish to control the political process for their continued charmed existence.* Elections are only the most concentrated form of politics and the tip of the iceberg.

From the experiences of political leaders in the 1998 election, it is clear that popular candidates with local support spent little while those without a base had to spend sums ranging in crores. Some of those interviewed stated that money spent was not the determining factor in their victory. However, everyone agreed that more and more money was being spent on elections because the voter is becoming cynical and easily attracted to divisive issues. This reflects, a loss of faith that the politicians would deliver on promises.

THE TRIAD

If it is true that it is not so much that politics needs money but that money power needs to control politics for its own ends then democracy would be subverted.

The connivance of the bureaucracy in the functioning of the black economy is a related issue. Its increasing corruption and demoralization need to be understood. The pressures from above (political) are obviously there with sectional interests all too inclined to subvert policy. There are pressures from below as well, as already discussed.

For an illegality to persist in the system, the bureaucracy and the politicians have to actively or passively be a party to it. Hence for the generation of black incomes, the businessman, the politician and the bureaucrat have to be involved. Even if one of the three is missing, there can be no black income generation. *This is the triad.*

The emergence of the Janta Dal in 1988 was seen as a positive development on the Indian political scene. It was termed as 'a turning point' for India. The origins of this event may be traced back to early 1987 when Mr V. P. Singh was abruptly eased out of the Finance Ministry and by mid-1987 out of the Congress Party itself.

Mr V.P. Singh's vigorous campaign against the industrialists, the businessmen and other white collar crimes had built up a strong lobby against him. In the early days of the Rajiv regime, the campaign against economic crimes did much for his image—'Mr Clean' and the 'government that works'.

Mr V. P. Singh without being able to check the growing black economy succeeded in posing a threat to those with large black incomes. He was seen to exceed the limits when Mr Kirloskar and Mr Thapar were arrested. This let loose powerful forces amongst the Big Business lobby which worked for his ouster. Later these interests worked to dislodge him when he became the Prime Minster.

Mr Singh tried the carrot of lower tax rates and liberalisation of the economic regime while using the stick of the tax raids and arrests. The national dailies howled in protest arguing that the prestige and the image of industrial leaders built over decades ought not to be sullied in this fashion. It was also said that when the private sector is trying to raise massive resources, its image ought not to be tarnished. In other words, the illegality of the rich ought to be tolerated.

Once Mr Rajiv Gandhi's images tarnished by late 1986, Mr V.P.Singh stood out as an alternative. Consequently, Rajiv and the lobbies had a common enemy which needed to be neutralized. Apparently, a rift was created between Mr Rajiv Gandhi and Mr V. P. Singh by creating a suspicion in the former's mind that the latter was seeking to expose his close friend, Mr Bachchan.

The HDW submarine deal and the Bofors issue burst upon the Indian political scene in quick succession and shook the government. Various other issues of corruption in high places came to light.

Diversions were sought to be created through trying to involve Mr V.P. Singh in the Fairfax and St. Kitts cases. This seems to happen all the time when vested interests are sought to be curbed. As a result, 'honest' politicians and bureaucrats have learnt to compromise and honesty has become limited to not taking money personally but not interfering with vested interests and turning a blind eye to illegality.

The bureaucracy and the judiciary play different roles in a democracy. If the bureaucracy refuses to carry out illegal acts or the judiciary acts firmly when cases are brought before it, illegality cannot become systemic—it would remain sporadic. It is in this sense that the judiciary and the bureaucracy are clubbed together in the triad. The pressures on the judiciary to subvert it are similar to those on the bureaucracy, as discussed earlier.

The public does not know its rights because of a lack of transparency. Continuation of archaic rules on the statue books long after their usefulness is over, enables the bureaucracy to retain power. For instance, registration of bicycles and radio and TV continued far longer than needed causing enormous harassment to the public.

In the judiciary the need for notarization of documents can be cited. These mean little, since anything can be notarized even with a back date for a fees. The signatures of a lawyer can also be had by paying a fee. The public is harassed and loses money.

The lack of transparency, corruption (specially at the lower levels) and delays involved in getting justice have brought the entire process into disrepute. Justice is above all needed by the weak but they are the worst sufferers of the convoluted process; the rich are the beneficiaries. They can always obtain fresh dates for hearing to slow down or speed up proceedings.

Delay in tax matters in the courts means huge savings for businesses. Undertrials are known to have spent far more time in jails than justified by the crime they may have committed. In contrast, Mr L. M. Thapar could get the SC to give him bail at midnight. Accident insurance is known not to be paid for a decade or more. The suffering of families of victims does not count.

Take for example the case of a trade union leader who was fired from his job for calling another colleague a 'chuha' (rat). The Supreme Court could not believe this and refused to protect him. The High Court said that all the procedures were followed so there was no remedy. The leader went to the labour court and the case has dragged on for 18 years and he had no money left because after a dismissal he could not get a proper job. It has become an example to others not to take on powerful employers and an example to employers as to how to manipulate matters. (See Chapter 2).

As one lawyer put it, justice is a matter of favouring one over another. There is a certain degree of subjectivity in any judgment but when this becomes systemic, the judiciary is affected. A sense of social injustice spreads and commitment to society weakens. One kind of lawlessness breeds another. Those who suffer are willing to adopt other means to settle matters and bypass society. Illegality is justified and criminalization spreads.

One aspect of the weakening of the bureaucracy is what one keen observer has referred to as 'Over 55 syndrome' Lal (1995). He suggests that the post-retirement work is an important aspect of the behaviour of these people. Lucrative jobs await these people if they have been subservient during their service. One can build links with the private sector by obliging them while in service. This yields directorships or arbitration work. It may yield employment in senior positions or as liaison officers. Many from the army have retired to become middle men of arms dealers. Those who keep the political bosses happy have been rewarded with governorships, chairpersonships of committees, and so on.

The influencing of the bureaucracy begins early, even before these people get into decision-making levels. Offers of postings or of fellowships abroad are other inducements. However, the offers from multilateral institutions and UN agencies are the most prized ones and compromises are made voluntarily to get such postings. Many wait for a cue from these agencies to take the 'correct' line. Data not made available to Indian researchers is easily handed over to officials from these agencies.

It is not that honest officers do not get posted abroad, like, Mr. Arun Bhatia. But they get the worst postings. The purpose is to remove them from the scene so that they may not be able to do further damage to the functioning of the triad.

In brief, the independence of the judiciary and the bureaucracy is under great pressure, given that there is prevalence of some amount of corruption in them in direct and indirect ways. The system puts a gloss over the illegality of the vested interests. The sense of social justice is dented so that the public become cynical and accepts the triad as inevitable.

The Media

Indian media is vibrant and active. Many an expose of scams and corruption appear from time to time. However, few are followed to their logical conclusion. The public has a short memory and exposes have come with such rapidity that few remember what was important a month back. Romesh Sharma and his possible links with Dawood Ibrahim were hot news for a couple of months in late 1998 and then relegated to the background. It was quickly overtaken in early 1999 by the sacking of the Navy Chief, the Bihar massacres and the imposition of the President's rule there, the killings of Christians and so.

The media has the capacity to expose the illegality of the triad. But this potential has remained without adequate follow-up. The public suffering from fatigue, feels helpless and has given up.

The effectiveness of the media has been circumscribed. In spite of the exposes and scams the decline of institutions has continued a pace.

The media has substantially got coopted in the triad. It is supposed to act 'responsibly' and not rock the system. The rewards for good behaviour have taken the shape of facilities like travel, housing, import of computers, jaunts and guest house facilities.

Many an editor is closely linked with the properties of the paper. The owners have commercial interests which require favourable policy-decisions. Exclusive stories depend on journalists maintaining links with those in power. This often requires keeping close links with select groups of politicians and bureaucrats. When powerful groups begin to fight, exposés about the opponents come out. Inspired leaks and plants are resorted to. Since there is little commitment to get to the bottom of frauds, stories start with a bang to end in a whimper—as equilibrium amongst the groups is restored.

The media persons are happy with their sense of power. They get work done for relatives, friends and others—railway reservations, passes for the Republic Day parade, school admissions, telephone connections, etc. This is only possible as a part of the system and not by pushing the system hard by taking things to their logical conclusion.

The perspective of the media is short-sighted. To gain the label of exclusive, stories are done in a rush. There is inadequate research to prove things conclusively. With exceptions, professionalism is missing.

The social set the media people move around with is that of the powerful. They at times even represent the interests of this set. Hence they take a cynical view of society. They often analyse events by asking who gains from it and attribute motives accordingly—right or wrong. Since most belong to some group, naturally they adopt the point of view which suits their group. Wider social concerns are characterized as soft areas and a narrow time frame for analysis is all that is feasible. In brief, the vested interests have co-opted the media into the triad thus neutralising the threat it may pose. The role of the proprietors in the co-option is critical.

Eroding Will of the Elite: The Criminal in the Triad

With the rise of illegality, breakdown of institutions of democracy and criminalization in society, it is little wonder that criminals are today a part of the triad. The politician, the businessman and the bureaucrat may receive certain favours from the criminal and even act at her/his behest.

Today, the Indian state is multilayered with several sources of authority competing with each other. The legal state headed by the prime minister is only one of the layers. The prime minister is often a prisoner of some of the other layers and groups, and, therefore, not a free agent to act in the wider public interest. These other layers operate through their influence on the politics of the land. They create problems for the legal state if they are touched.

At times, these other layers are more effective in getting their work done than even the prime minister may be. They use all methods, inducements and physical threats, to get their work done. Since the writ of the prime minister is based on legitimacy and in recent times it has been severely dented, its effectiveness has been eroded. The porous administration and the non-compliance by the citizens makes the legal system ineffective.

Into this vacuum have stepped in these extra-legal power centres who wield either local or all-India influence. Some of these groups are said to be controlled by foreign powers, mafia groups operating from other countries and business groups headed by powerful individuals. They have established links at various levels of administration and where links do not exist directly, they use money power to purchase influence, to get policies suitable to their requirements and subvert those not suited to their needs. In other words, make policies fail.

This has created a vicious circle of contempt for non-functional policies leading to individuals resorting to illegality. Many find it advantageous to become a member of a group and thereby legitimize a typical masala Hindi film. The demoralized citizen is forced to accept non-legal functioning, either by collusion or through silence. The feeling of social injustice and alienation gets entrenched. Faith in institutions is sapped and citizens become apolitical.

CONCLUSION

The cause of the black economy is illegality or functioning beyond the pale of social norms. The elite finds it comfortable since capital is able to expand its share of national income and politically and socially maintain itself in power. The cause does not lie in some esoteric economic law. So the solution cannot be a simple and mechanical one. (See Chapter 7).

The size of the black economy represents the extent of extra-legal functioning of society. This illegality cannot be affected by either reducing regulations and controls or lowering taxes. *Controls and taxes are mere sources of black income generation but not the cause. Abolishing taxes and rules and regulations is like abolishing society.*

Frameworks which try to understand the black economy as the actions of individuals making optimum gains are fundamentally flawed and limited. They provide an ex-post justification for that which is happening but do not have anything to say why individuals are acting in certain ways and at their own long-term cost? The social aspect is missing and basic improvements are not feasible in this framework.

Trust in others and in society is based on a sense of social justice amongst individuals. It is an essential ingredient of social functioning. It also simplifies social functioning and thereby reducing costs and waste and makes actions efficient. No set of rules can be foolproof or complete. Much has to be left to the judgment of people and if they feel a sense of belonging they would do that which is in the long-term interest of society.

Social functioning must depend on a minimum of punishment and rewards. There has to be voluntarism in society. The attitude today is 'what I can get away with I will try and if caught I will see what to do'. This attitude represents a narrowing of the citizens horizons. Partly this is a result of rapid change in society and confusion about social values. The definition of right and wrong has undergone a shift in unpredictable directions. With the decline of institutions, the few moorings that existed have also got demolished. Principles have been eroded as they are always seen in relative terms—in relation to self. Rapid change has led to the selection of those who think in the short run and ignore the long term social interest. There is a process of marginalization of good.

The rule of property in India is weak. Property rights are not adequately defined and there is a constant conflict over what they are. Capital has tried to interpret it in the form most suited to it but that has been contested. To advance its interests it has tried to use means which are pre-capitalist, often feudal in character, so not suited to a modern capitalist society. This has led to growing conflict.

State functionaries, politicians, bureaucrats, judiciary, police and others have become party to defining and maintenance of property rights by whatever means. The challenge of democratization and equity has been subverted through the black economy. The conflict that underlies it is like class struggle by other means.

The New Economic Policies attempt to define the property rights more clearly and independent of the rights of the non-propertied. Will they then help curb the growth of the black economy? The issue is not just whether corruption will decline. Formally it might, but if the non-propertied react through greater conflict, illegality would not decline unless there is authoritarian rule and democracy is truncated.

The problem of black economy is not just an economic one. It is one of whether the nature of economic activities will take on socially more desirable forms? The New Economic Policies are not based on such considerations. Since these policies have sharpened conflict, different forms of making black incomes are being devised. Illegality has grown in a more permissive environment for capital and others are responding to this in whatever manner they can.

Today, the need is to analyse the causes of growing illegality and devising ways of checking it. Unfortunately, the causation is being reversed and corruption (and efficiency) is being used as an excuse for making the state abdicate its responsibility to people.

What emerged from the present analysis is that behind the growing illegality lies the triad. The businessmen interested in making additional profits shares a part of it with the politician and the bureaucrat for allowing her/him to do so. Over time, the criminal has become a part of the triad or controls it.

In the appendix, the experiences of politicians fighting an election is presented and and it is found that they have close links with business and bureaucrats. Politicians get funds for elections and promote each others' interests. The choice of the candidates depends often on the support from the triad and not on local popularity. In many cases, the candidate may not be a local person; someone who may have done work in the constituency. The local triad manages the election. Being representative of the people is hardly a criterion for selection and candidates remain beholden to vested interests. In the process, democracy is subverted.

The solution to the problem of growing illegality (and corruption) lies in raising public consciousness and making the system responsive to people. That will be true reform: the present reforms have only enabled the triad to tighten its grip over the system.

6

Consequences of the Black Economy

The principal consequences of the existence of a significant black economy are found to be the loss of control over policy and its failure, the unplanned internationalization of the economy and growing illegality. Some of their consequences for the quality of life of the citizen are spelt out here.

It is argued by some that the black economy generates employment, so, a) its existence should not be a cause for concern, b) it is not all bad and c) the inability to accurately estimate its size is a mere statistical problem. In brief, there is no need to be alarmed by it. This issue can be addressed at two planes, the narrow economic or the more general social one.

As traffic becomes more chaotic, more policemen are required to regulate it. As more accidents occur, more mechanics, doctors and medical staff get employment. Does this imply that accidents are good for society? Not only society loses due to accidents but chaos increases travel time for everyone resulting in individual and social loss. If most drive at night using high beam, an individual cannot be an exception since her/his chance of having an accident goes up. Everyone is equally blinded and the probability of accidents rises. Poorly lit roads and lack of social concern lead to this habit which then continues even on well lit ones. One problem leads to another and loss to society.

A car flashing a red light and demanding right of way is no more taken to be indicative of an emergency but of someone trying to pull rank and the public resents it. Police drivers are often seen breaking rules—driving on the wrong side, parking incorrectly or at a turning, switching lanes without signalling, etc, setting a bad example for the public. When the upholders of the law become the law breakers, criminalization spreads and even the offenders suffer. Policy loses its meaning and goals cannot be achieved. Even the most powerful suffer—Giani Zail Singh's car was hit by a truck in spite of all the protection.

When the fence encroaches the field, can anything be safe? If driving licenses are issued without tests (for a consideration) drivers are likely to have little idea of the rules and there would be chaos on the roads. Someone breaking a law usually feels guilty but not the Indian drivers because they often do not know they have broken a rule. Instead, they become indignant accusing the other person for coming in their way. Some have even run over traffic policemen who were trying to wave them down for an offense.

The existence of the black economy signifies illegality and if the phenomenon is as widespread as the numbers imply there is much to worry about. The black economy has had a strong demonstration effect in society. Those with large black incomes live ostentatiously and not only get away with it but also because of their position in society enjoy a prestige so that they have become examples for others (specially, the young and those aspiring to rise) to emulate, glorifying the use of illegal means to success.

Today there is almost no area of public life where work is done as a matter of routine; it is done as a favour. Either one needs contacts or money or both to avoid facing harassment. Those in power derive strength from it. It also suits the rich since they have the money to jump any queue or to buy influence. This is done with sophistication. Liaison or middle men have sprung up every where in the corridors of power. They can get work done, legal or illegal.

The economic consequences are serious. Poverty has hardly declined and has taken a harsher form and resulted in increased social tensions and crime. Even if it is accepted at face value that the percentage of the population below the poverty line has declined, a rise in consumption by say Rs 10 or Rs 100 per person per month would hardly categorize that family as non-poor.

By all appearances disparities are growing. Luxury living is evident all around what with the proliferation of private vehicles, CTVs, VCRs, ice cream and video parlours and the like. In contrast, the poor still appear as under-nourished, ill-clad, illiterate, and on the streets as they ever were, even if on the average instead of 1 now they have 1.4 square meals a day, fifty years after independence. The last survey giving income distribution is the one by NCAER conducted in 1975-76. It suggested that the average income in the highest income category (Rs 60,000 and above) was Rs 80,000 while in the lowest income category (Rs 1,200 and less) it was Rs 800, i.e., a ratio of 1:100. The NIPFP study on the black economy despite its several errors, is indicative that inclusive of the black incomes, this ratio becomes 1:1200. The black economy worsens the income distribution in the country.

SECTORAL CONSEQUENCES

The role of state intervention in promoting rapid ecomonic growth is accepted today. At independence the private sector was weak and needed state support to create infrastructure and to grow. But overtime policies became less and less effective with the growth of the black economy, and failed to deliver what was expected of them.

Policy Failure

Social Infrastructure
The black economy affects social infrastructure directly and indirectly. Indirectly it has an impact due to the shortage of budgetary resources, consequent to tax evasion. The allocations for these sectors have not been raised commensurate with the needs. These sectors are considered to be soft so that they face the first cuts when there is a short fall. Finally, since these subjects fall in the jurisdiction of the States and they are short of resources (because of the black economy) due to inadequate tax collections and transfers from the Centre, allocations have been inadequate.

More directly, the money spent is siphoned out in a variety of ways so that the expenditures are ineffective. In brief, policy failure has two aspects—inadequate allocations and ineffective expenditures. Education, health, drinking water, sanitation, housing, etc., comprize social infrastructure. On paper, the numbers look impressive but quality is woeful. In comparison to progress achieved in many other developing countries, the achievements are unimpressive.

Education: Formally, the target of 6% of GDP for education has not been achieved but even more needs to be spent to catch up with the advanced nations. Whatever resources do exist, the black economy leads to their sub-optimal utilization. (See appendix).

Those with resources, the rich, have found an individualized solution to the problem of declining standards. They are increasingly sending their children abroad at massive resource cost to society. The create a problem both by not paying taxes resulting in resource shortage and then deploying them outside the country so that the education system here is deprived of these funds.

Private resources are poured into tuition, coaching, training colleges, studies abroad, etc. If these are added up, they would be enough to pay the best salaries to teachers so that the best talent could be attracted to this profession. Today, children waste their time first trying to learn in the class and then at home from parents or tutors. The resources are spent but wastefully and society as a whole loses.

Good institutions, teachers and students are the exception. Some self-motivated students do well in spite of the systemic problems but this is accidental and inadequate to the national needs. Most 'good' institutions are mediocre by international standards and unequal to the task of producing highly skilled workers or high quality researchers.

As discussed in the appendix on education, for many academics making money and manipulating to gain power has become primary. This has led to loss of dynamism all around and imposed a huge cost on society through brain drain not only to West but also through diversion of talent to less essential social functions. Many academics simply recycle theories originating in the West and this is often considered 'good' work. This label gives credibility but social reality begins to be viewed through western prisms. This creates a vicious circle in which society bypasses institutions of learning preferring to go to the original sources of knowledge in the West. It is tragic that when ideas are given, the first question asked is where else in the world (read the West) has it been tried? Good students prefer to go to the original sources for research but then research here languishes.

The feeling that resources are scarce has spawned conservativism. Learning is taken to be a burden on society. Many use education as a parking place till they get a job. Administrators try to move students into the job market at the earliest opportunity. Learning for its own sake is discouraged. Why cannot there be a plumber with a Ph.D. in philosophy?

In brief, education should be about the finer things in life and building a better society. This requires idealism but if educational institutions and educationists are involved in corruption, they become cynical and cannot perform this essential task. It is the quality of education which determines the quality of doctors, managers, plumbers and drivers. Without commitment, standards fall and there is loss of dynamism—another name for poverty.

Health. Primary, secondary and tertiary health centres are now seats of widespread corruption. The primary concern seems to have shifted from cure to making money. Without the necessary commitment, cure has become difficult even if there is the slightest complication. Due to corruption, these centres often have unhygienic conditions and poorly maintained facilities. At times, test reports of patients are mixed up or samples lost. Many lives are lost due to negligence. Doctors working under tremendous pressure often miss complications. By and large, patients have to be cared for by their attendants. This imposes additional pressure on the limited facilities of the hospital. Conditions outside the big hospitals are insanitary in the extreme with patient's relatives camping there. In this vicious circle, often attendants fall sick. The citizen is trapped between the greed of the private sector and the apathy of the public health system.

A well-functioning public health (and education) system is a check on profiteering in private institutions. However, since the former are woefully inadequate, the latter are able to charge monopoly prices and fleece the public (when they are vulnerable).

For instance, if AIIMS in Delhi charges for a heart surgery say, a lakh of rupees, it would be difficult for the private sector to charge say, five lakhs. But if good doctors were to leave AIIMS en mass (for whatever reasons) and the quality of service was to deteriorate, soon the private sector would begin charging at least that much.

Doctors and health systems are supposed to cure irrespective of other considerations but the black economy and the penetration of the market has diluted these considerations. The well off and the powerful have switched to the private sector or they go abroad at enormous resource cost to the nation. Resources are wasted without the health system improving—a sub-optimal use of resources.

Housing and Civic Infrastructure. The black economy affects most aspects of housing. Most urban dwellings fall in one of three categories. They are either built on encroached public land (even if later regularised) or purchased by partly paying in black or receive a rent which is partly in black. As a consequence of these illegalities, further illegalities are committed. Bribes have to be paid to avoid harassment.

Encroachment is not feasible without the connivance of the local muscleman, the policeman and the local authority. The encroacher has an uncertain tenure and has to constantly keep the muscleman happy. This overseer is a small time leader with links in the police, municipality and the local representative. She/he keeps all these layers happy to enable encroachment to continue. (See Chapter 2).

Due to the illegal nature of these settlements, civic infrastructure like roads, parks, sewage, electricity and water is often lacking. Surrounding open areas are converted into latrines and garbage dumps. Scavenging is left to the pigs and animals. Electricity and water are stolen from adjoining electricity poles and the water pipes.

Civic amenities come under severe strain. Shortages of water and electricity are aggravated. Water from damaged pipes gets contaminated and loss of electrical energy rises due to sparking which often results in tripping or damaged transformers. Health standards are poor resulting in repeated illnesses. Putting a strain on the limited public health services and the family budget.

Residents in formal, legal housing, undervalue their property to escape taxes—income tax, capital gains tax, property tax and possibly wealth tax. They bribe the municipal assessors to accept a low valuation for their property. They bribe for deviating from their sanctioned building plans and for encroachment on public land. In many cases, extra floors are built or built area exceeds the sanctioned area and balconies extend over the roads (sometimes close to the electricity wires). Such encroachment is profitable (in spite of the bribes) since it yields extra rental income or provides valuable space for the family.

The consequence is that the local body gets much less tax than it should and has to meet the additional costs of providing services to those who are encroachers. Due to corruption, to provide a given level of service, budgetary allocation has to be higher. Say, sweepers exist on paper to enable the supervisor to draw their salary. This results in higher budgetary deficit and poor quality of service. Finally, even if corruption was not to degrade roads, sewerage, police services, etc., due to tax evasion, the municipalities lack the resources to give the requisite level of infrastructure.

Systemic Inefficiency and Rising Costs. Apart from the fact that the citizens, whether the well off in select pockets or those in slums, have a poor standard of living, they also have to bear the costs of collective inefficiency.

Few officials do their work in the routine way either so as to extract a bribe or because they are demoralized. If the banker takes time to cash someone's cheque, he faces the music when he goes to pay the electricity bill and alongwith the electricity man he faces delays at the railway station while buying a ticket.

Citizens bear unnecessary costs whether in the form of time spent or as bribe or when the quality of work is poor and expenditures on maintenance are high. Rectifying non-functioning telephones requires repeated reminders and possibly a bribe. Electricity of the incorrect and fluctuating voltage increases breakdown of appliances, requiring expenditure of time and money.

Even if each individual gains something through earning a black income, there is a loss to each through collective inefficiency of the system. To meet the contingency, individuals who can afford it have gone for individual solutions even though these are expensive.

To overcome water shortage, individual water purification plants, tubewells and pumps are used. The unit cost of water from such facilities is many times the cost of municipal water supply. Similarly, the provision of generators and inverters for electricity is an expensive solution to power shortage. Electricity from an inverter costs ten times the charge by the Delhi Electric Supply. To counter voltage fluctuation, stabilizers are required for many appliances, raising costs.

The private expenditure on tubewells, pumps, purification units, etc., would be enough to double the capacity of municipal water supply and there would be no shortage of water even for the slums. When water is available only for a few hours, it is stored and later thrown away. This waste may also decline. If slums have provision of water, damage to pipes would be reduced and its contamination prevented. Savings on health costs would be enormous. Parents would breath easier since they need not worry that their children may drink tap water in the school or elsewhere.

Assuming that five lakh inverters and generators operate in Delhi and their average price is Rs 25,000/-, this would imply an investment of Rs 1,250 crore, enough to set up 400 MW of electricity generation capacity which would suffice to overcome the current shortage. Electricity availability would rise and reduce the use of batteries and the need to charge them. Voltage and frequency would be more stable and of the correct value reducing breakdown of equipment. Use of stabilizers would decline. Noise pollution and fumes from diesel and kerosene generators would come down improving the environment.

If the estimate of Rs 1,000 crore of annual loss of revenue for the Delhi Electricity Board due to theft of power is accepted, Delhi could install 300 MW of additional generation capacity annually. Not only would there be ample amount of power for all but the Board would be making profits (not losses) at current charges.

In the above examples, the kind of privatization currently practiced is not the solution to shortages since its costs are high while the benefits are few. If public provision of these service becomes efficient, it would not only be cheaper but there would be benefits which are not available through privatization. But this requires curbing the black economy. Choosing the privitization route means accepting a less optimal use of resources and reduced welfare for even those who can afford it; the welfare of the poor who are excluded from these markets is certainly reduced.

There is privatization of another kind. Namely, handing over the public sector to the private sector. Profits which were accruing to the triad through the black economy accrue to the companies buying the public sector assets. In most cases of such privatization of municipal services, like, garbage collection and sewerage, a sub-optimality operates. This is a choice forced on society by the black economy.

Criminalization

Deteriorating law and order is a consequence of the growing black economy and an example of waste and sub-optimality. One senior officer suggested that every additional police station means more crime. Contacts developed by policemen for non-criminal activities like allowing encroachments, have spread to other activities like leakage of question papers, black marketing of goods in short supply and so on. The next step is to develop links with criminals, pickpockets and the mafia.

Citizens have also increasingly got involved in illegality. The insecure housing tenure in the slums opens the way to illegality for many slum dwellers. The local dada has to be kept happy. He draws unemployed youth into activities like crime, drug trafficking and prostitution. The upper classes have come to accept illegality because of their own involvement in it. For instance, those in the public or the private sector who give or accept bribes or take cuts from suppliers, among others, stand compromised. Tax evasion amongst the middle class or resort to misuse of office facilities has played an important role in acceptance of illegality as a way of life.

Criminalization has its most serious impact on the weak in society—children, the old, women and the poor. The socially weak need the protection of society the most. When illegality grows, laws are systematically flouted and might becomes right, the weak suffer due to misuse of power. The strong subvert democracy and its institutions to gain undue advantage at the expense of the weak.

Extortion and kidnapping have grown. Individual remedies are not available for this. Protective walls, gadgets and guards are no match for determined criminals. Further, intelligence gathering cannot be organized by individuals since that is prohibitively expensive. Preventive steps against potential threats are therefore not feasible. The intelligence provided by a corrupt police force is not only undependable but may be false or likely to be available to the criminals from whom the rich may be seeking protection.

In short, the beneficiaries of the black economy are themselves victims of the rising crime wave. Individuals keeping black money, gold, jewellery and other undeclared assets at home are in no position to register the theft of these assets with the police. Those paying off criminals abroad cannot complain about extortion and kidnapping since their funds are illegal. Such individuals are easy targets for criminals. Information about the black wealth of individuals is available to criminals through those who may have helped generate this wealth.

In brief, criminalization in society is the result not only of the rising graph of illegality but also the decline of resistance to it amongst the populace and both these are the result of the proliferation of the black economy in legal activities. The beneficiaries of the black economy are also the victims of criminalization but the worst sufferers are the weak in society. Expenditure on law and order machinery has grown but since it has developed a vested interest in crime, it has aggravated the problem. Society is caught in a vicious circle—the police is needed but as more police is deployed, crime has increased. Another example of waste and sub-optimality.

Impact on the Environment

Environmental degradation in India is linked to the violation of the laws and the growth of the black economy. Even though in 1995 the per capita income in India was around $ 340 and that in the advanced countries about $ 25,000 (75 times that of India), the levels of pollution are comparable. The major metropolitan centres, underground water sources and the rivers in India are now some of the worst polluted in the world.

The Bhopal gas tragedy symbolizes the short cuts taken by industry to make extra profits. Polluted air and water are released without treatment to make extra profits. Waste products are improperly disposed of. Inspectors are bribed to look the other way.

Industry indirectly also adds to pollution through producing poor quality or adulterated products. These products either breakdown and need replacement or repairs at additional environmental costs or lead to wastage during use. For instance, adulterated petrol results in reduced life of engines, increased breakdown, more of air pollution and greater consumption of energy for the same work.

Similarly, when electrical gadgets are not made to specifications, their use leads to sparking or leakage of current, greater breakdown of equipment, and to a shorter life-span. For instance, bulbs have to be more frequently changed, plugs and sockets melt and need replacement more often, and toasters and heaters need frequent repairs. Poorly designed houses, require more heating, cooling, and cleaning up, and, therefore, more of energy. Due to this kind of waste in every activity, consumption of inputs per unit of output is high and this adds to pollution without adding to welfare.

No doubt, poverty is a cause of pollution since the poor cannot afford the expenses required for cleaning up or for producing good quality products. They buy cheap products to improve their living standard. Producers of such products cut corners and violate various laws. They use child labour, produce without safety precautions, dispose off untreated waste and so on. These illegalities make them a part of the black economy.

Poverty is a cause of inadequate civic infrastructure and, therefore, of pollution. On the one hand, the poor receive low salaries and cannot afford to pay the full costs of these services (therefore, they get few). On the other hand, the black economy raises the cost of the services due to corruption and the high cost of land. The gap created between affordability and provision is high. This is a systemic problem. Cities need labour services to function but since employers pay the labour poorly they are unable to spend on the basic services. The employers are also not willing to pay taxes which could enable municipalities to subsidize these services.

The point is that services are inadequate not because of resource shortage but because they are not mobilized and go waste. The employers neither pay labour adequately nor pay the taxes correctly. For instance, provision of clean drinking water does not require any foreign technology or water from outside. The problem is tax evasion and diversion of resources allotted to drinking water.

Finally, even while the poor pollute due to their situation in the system, their consumption is so minuscule that the total amount of pollution produced by them is likely to be a small fraction of the total. Taking black incomes into account the differential in incomes between those below the poverty line and those in the top 3% of the incomes ladder is at least of the order of 1:60 (see chapter 3). If consumption constitutes 20% of the income for the well off, twelve of the poor equal one of the well off. The poor produce little waste and recycle most of it, the well off waste without recycling so that the differential in resource use is likely to be much worse than 1:12. The pollution created by the top 3% is greater than by all those below the poverty line.

Recycling must be put in proper perspective lest it give the license to the well off to increase consumption. They could argue that they pollute less than the average citizen in the advanced nations. Recycling adds to pollution though less than if the same goods were produced from raw materials. Recycling wastes from nuclear establishments, batteries, paper, plastics and other chemicals causes serious pollution and at times this makes dangerous than producing the good.

The problem becomes worse when wastes are received for recycling from the rich countries. Examples of this are battery and plastic wastes or ships for breaking. The international division of labour is pushing production from polluting processes to the the developing countries. Capital sees profits in this and some argue for this in the name of development. Low paid labour in the developing countries suffers the consequences. This also explains why pollution in India is greater than implied by its consumption level.

In brief, widespread illegality and the black economy are a major cause of pollution and deterioration in the living conditions of the citizen. The poor contribute directly to pollution due to their poverty and indirectly because of the illegality surrounding their existence. They are the victims of the black economy and of the development path. The well off, the major contributors to pollution, are also unable to escape its consequences. The situation is sub-optimal—even for the beneficiaries of the black economy.

Waste

Social waste is like digging holes and filling them. Pollution is an example of this. So are the failure of law and order and the scarcity of power and drinking. In each of these cases, a problem is created and then attempted to be resolved. The net benefit is far less than possible so that the social welfare is not enhanced as much as the level of activity indicates. There is activity but social welfare does not improve directly (only to the extent of employment generated and enhanced consumption).

Waste leads to activity and transactions which are not essential; they add to the costs. Individuals try to load these costs on to society to generate a profit for themselves but social welfare is not enhanced by this amount since someone else has to bear the cost. For instance, a leather unit may dump waste water into the Ganga to increase profit. But society has to bear the cost of cleaning up so its welfare does not rise as much as would be indicated by the profit of the industry.

The existence of the black economy results in increased transactions without the social welfare rising. For instance, as criminalization rises, more locks and security devices are needed, none of which enhance individual or social welfare. To evade taxes, separate accounts are required to be kept, lengthy procedures are adopted to hoodwink authorities, extra accountants are employed, more tax lawyers are needed to prepare cases and finally, tax officials have to be kept happy in a variety of ways including bribes.

When work is delayed to extract a bribe, time is wasted, quality may be poor, deadlines are not met so that costs rise due to inventories or cancellation of orders. All this leads to higher cost of production and lack of competitiveness in international markets.

Another example of waste is the transport pattern in urban agglomerates. People criss-cross the city to go to work. Land speculation, aggravated by the black economy, forces most workers to live far from their place of work and commute. Urban transport is both energy-and capital-intensive and India is short of both so that the resource cost is heavy. This problem would exist even if there was no black economy but it gets compounded manifold due to illegality.

While there are any number of examples, a final one given here concerns packaging. This industry has grown phenomenally in India in the last twenty years and specially in the consumer goods sectors. Earlier goods were available in loose or bulk quantities so that the price paid was mostly the cost of manufacture of the good purchased. Now the cost of advertising, transport and packaging in many cases is comparable to that of the useful good packaged. Take for instance, water in bottles, milk and edible oils in tetra packs and lubricants in pouches. A bottle of water costing Rs. 10 may not have water worth Rs. 0.1 in it.

To make extra profits, adulteration in edible goods and production of inferior quality products has proliferated. Packaging and brand names have emerged in response to breakdown of the consumer's trust in open and loose purchase of goods. With the proliferation of the black economy, even packaged products are adulterated or of inferior quality. For instance, the introduction of dropsy in mustard oil and urea and chalk powder in milk. Branded medicines may be spurious or syringes recycled. Many branded products carry a warning against counterfeits. In brief, branding and packaging have grown because of the black economy but at tremendous cost to society and the black economy is in the process of undoing its effects also. To conclude, the black economy leads to enormous waste and rise in costs and at times production occurs without an increase in social welfare.

Missing Pride in Professional Commitment

There is a lack of professionalism/commitment to work not only amongst those in the media but also amongst teachers, doctors, lawyers and chartered accountants. For this there structural reasons.

It is not simply a matter of punishment and reward. Who is to police those who are to punish? If the prime ministers themselves are perceived to be corrupt, how can the system punish? If individuals get away with corruption, no monetary reward can be greater. If policy makers can make crores in cuts, a salary can not match that. Obviously, doctors feel that the money they can make on recommending unnecessary expensive tests is more than they can legitimately charge as fees. Punishment and reward cannot substitute for professional commitment to one's work.

It is often argued, especially in the context of sports that Indians lack the killer instinct and that is the reason for their lack of excellence in the world arena. The failure of Indian professionals to excel has to do with the lack of attention to detail. Many are happy to do slipshod work which would not be acceptable in many other countries. If a doctor is interested in prolonging illness, there is no need to diagnose accurately since diseases are self-limiting and often will get cured anyway. If a teacher is not interested in communicating knowledge in the class, slipshod work would be tolerated all around.

The growing black economy and the associated non-performance of work by various sections of the population is then a major reason for the non-professional attitude of these highly educated sections. Over a period of time, this attitude becomes a part of the milieu, 'everything goes' (*Sab chalta hai*).

In sports too, this attitude prevails since it is a part of the training right from school. Finer points of training are usually ignored if one has gone a certain distance. However, in the international arena this simply will not do. Our cricketers are no doubt talented but lack the attention to detail and are erratic. Talent comes up accidentally and not because the system picks it up and grooms it into a world beater.

Some of those reaching the top in their fields of endeavour are doing so not on merit (with exceptions) but due to other considerations—connections, sychophancy, etc. Even the talented people at the top have had to resort to these devices to become successful. Consequently, the mental make-up of those who reach the top is not based on confidence in their skills and they reproduce the system through which they came up.

Take the example of police officials who may be appointed because they are pliable. Often the vice-chancellors of universities are beholden to their political masters and not to their university peer group. They in turn appoint their favourite teachers in key positions so when required they can be manipulated. Creative people are 'difficult' since they do not do the bidding of others. They need to be kept away from key positions. Honest police officers can be posted to 'dry' postings except when difficulties arise. They may be sent to Nagaland or Punjab to fight terrorists. In the private sector, key managers should connive in the generation of black incomes for the owners. Boards of directors should constitute 'yes men'. Editors in the Press should say 'yes boss' to the proprietors.

In brief, amongst professionals, commitment to work is missing (with isolated exceptions). The system is based on reproducing mediocrity at all levels. If this is not changed the system will remain rundown.

THE FALSE DEBATES

The exclusion of the black economy in the analysis of current problems has led to many false debates. Solutions based on incomplete analysis become meaningless and they simply reinforce prejudices resulting in the aggravation of social conflict. A few examples of such debates are:

a) Efficiency of labour versus that of capital.
b) Unorganized labour versus organized labour.
c) Monopoly versus competition.
d) Open versus closed economy.
e) Public sector versus private sector.

Organized vs Unorganized Labour

The Right in India lays the blame for the ills of the Indian economy on labour and that too organized labour. For them, trade unions are like a red rag and need to be neutralized if not abolished. The Left has pinned the blame on capital but it no more demands nationalization since a) the public sector in particular, and policies in general have failed, b) the Soviet Union has collapsed and c) China has gone the capitalist way. Globalization has forced the Left to modify its position.

In the competition of capital and labor, it is true that capital gets a smaller share of the national cake, labour will get a larger one and vice-versa. The two shares have to add up to one. This is the basic conflict in a capitalist economy. The growth of the black economy implies that the share of capital in the true economy goes up and at the expense of share of wages.

Labour is depicted as indisciplined and the cause of overstaffing, corruption, low commitment and much else. Unionized labour which demands inflation indexing of wages is blamed for inflation and for low wages in the unorganized sector. This is incorrect. Inflation indexing only keeps the real wage unchanged. If productivity is rising, then keeping real wages unchanged results in a rise in the share of capital. The Central Government employees who are the best organized section of labour in the country constantly lose with inflation so that a pay commission is set up every ten years to revise their salaries.

In fact, organized labour in the private and the public sectors adds up to 28 million out of a total work force of about 350 million, that is, about 8% of the total. They are therefore too weak to push through their interests. The share of the organized sector is rising in the economy but employment in it is hardly changing and the share of labour in the income generated by the organized sector has been falling (See Table III.1).

Indian labour is among the cheapest the world so that labour costs per unit of output in spite of over-staffing and inefficiency are small. As per RBI data, in the cost of production of the organized sector, the share of labour is hardly 10%. So even if half the labour force is sacked, the saving in costs would be 5%. This is nothing compared to the additional costs due to the black economy (See appendix 6.1) which add up to 115%. Organized labour is falsely attacked for being responsible for the plight of the unorganized workers since its share has fallen, not risen. The falling share of wages in the organized sector has been accompanied by a static share of wages in the unorganized sector (See Table III.1). If the black economy is included in the analysis then the share of wages has fallen dramatically.

The crux of the problem of costs and who gets what share of the national cake is the black economy. Labour has been reacting to its declining share through the only means it knows, by acting sullenly and holding society to ransom as and when it can. This is true not only of organized labour but also of highly-paid professional white collar workers like pilots and engineers. Capital's actions of increasing its share through the black economy has caused a reaction on the part of all workers; conflict has grown without resolution.

Competition and Efficiency

Indian industry is supposed to be inefficient because of a) lack of competition b) the economy being closed, allowing monopolies to emerge and c) lack of economies of scale.

In major segments of Indian industry there have been far too many firms so that world scale plants have not come up, in spite of the large size of the market. For instance, in items of mass consumption. In these sectors, competition should have been fierce but this did not materialize since oligopolies emerged. In some sectors, like automobiles, where the size of the market was small, oligopolies emerged naturally.

If world scale plants are to be set up, then in most cases, very few firms would be required and oligopolistic behaviour would be reinforced. One cannot have both. Indian industry could have been competitive even with a two- to three-generation-old technology and in spite of not having scale economies because of cheap labour. However, this has been thwarted by the black economy which raises costs and generates waste. The business practices and not the number of firms or scale economies is the issue.

Ignoring reality, it has been suggested that opening the economy to global competition would discipline Indian capital. However, this opening up has no relation to the black economy signifying illegality, and Indian industry is unlikely to reform itself. Foreign industry which may come will seriously affect Indian industry because of its technology, advertising skills, and financial muscle. Further because its capital intensity is much higher, it would provide little employment aggravating the unemployment problem. Rather than solving the problem it would create a bigger one; a bit like chopping off the nose to cure a cold.

Some argue that opening up has benefitted the consumer by giving her/him more choice and better goods. That is true but at what price? Who is the consumer? The businessmen and the workers. How can that which reduces their incomes be good for them? One has to earn before one can consume. If Indian capital and labour suffer, can the consumer be better off? Only those employed or connected with MNCs can benefit and they are but a tiny minority of the population.

Has India been a closed economy? The degree of openness is measured by the ratio of imports to GDP. This has been of the order of 8-10% for India which is about the same for Japan and the USA. Then why is that not good enough for India? The problem of Indian industry clearly lies less with the degree of openness but elsewhere; the size of the black economy.

Public Versus Private Sectors

It is often argued that the public sector is inefficient while the private sector is efficient. The former is supposed to be characterized by overstaffing and low profitability while the latter is imagined to be well run and profitable. The public sector management and workers are assumed to provide poor service while the private sector, driven by the profit motive, is presumed to have service orientation. Public sector is supposed to be slow to react while the private sector is taken to be dynamic.

These notions are caricatures of the reality. There have been many profit-making public sector enterprises (140 out of 250 at the Centre). But there are loss-making private sector ones. The number of private sick units in March 1995 was 2.71 lakh. The private sector has not anticipated changes in technology and turned sick in a big way. With few exceptions, it has shunned R&D and what it has called R&D has largely been market research. The little R&D that has taken place has been in the public sector. The private sector has resorted to repeated import of technology absorbing little of it, the public sector has absorbed some of the technology it has imported.

Corruption plagues both the sectors. The private sector suffers other inefficiencies too—it siphons out profits, reinvesting only some of it and slowing down growth. India could not have lagged so far behind other countries if the private sector had been dynamic. It got cheap infrastructure from the public sector and a lot of state patronage. Capital siphoned out profits from the public sector for short-term gains and thereby reduced its own effectiveness.

The rate of profit in the public sector has been low. This is a result of the siphoning out of profits. If these were added back to the declared profits of the public sector, its rate of profit would rise several-fold. If one were to consider the white economy alone, the public sector is a drain on the household sector's savings but the reality is more complex. The picture is not so stark when the black economy is taken into account. The public sector was set up to command the economic heights (to hasten development) but the black economy has thwarted this.

The point about the public sector is not just profitability. It was not set up for this purpose even though one aspect of the public sector was that it would mobilize resources for further investment. The real function of the public sector was that it can do that which the private sector is not willing to do (in India). It could take risks which the private sector would refuse to take—in R&D, in long gestation projects, where large amount of capital is needed, in strategic industries and in continuing to invest even when profitability in the economy is down (say, in an economic down turn).

Growing illegality in the private sector has meant siphoning out of profit by the promoters and to loss of dynamism of the company. Funds are shifted to other units leaving the older units in a financial crisis. Additional profits are made without technological advances. This has created a mindset in which attention to detail, quality, technology, etc., have been secondary to manipulation. In other words, capital has tended to become parasitical, losing dynamism.

Finally, the private sector cannot cater to the basic needs of the poor since there is little profit to be generated from them. The black economy makes the economy high cost, keeps the real wages of the poor low and hinders the generation of adequate employment. It is in the context of poverty that subsidies play an important role. The public sector has to help alleviate poverty if social tensions are to be kept down.

Curtailing the role of the public sector or making it like the private sector misses the point about why it is needed and is a sub-optimal solution. The problem is not one of choice between public and private but how to curb the black economy which affects both the sectors. If this is done, both the sectors will become viable and complement each other.

THE MACRO CONSEQUENCES OF THE BLACK ECONOMY

Far more attention needs to be paid to the macro aspects of the black economy, like investment, the split between productive and unproductive investments, unemployment. The impact of the black economy on the monetary sector should have been obvious but has not been adequately dealt with. One needs to know the institutional practices to decide whether the velocity of circulation of money is a) different between the black and the white economies, b) whether the mechanism of circulation differ and c) the ease with which the black and white liquidity can convert from one to the other and the channels available for it. If, indeed the velocities of circulation are different, the impact of monetary policies on the black economy may not be predictable and may have unintended consequences, other than those suggested in the literature.

Consider speculative activity. Government may tighten monetary policies in order to curb liquidity to control speculation in commodities in short supply. However, liquidity from the black economy can quickly thwart this so that there may be little impact on speculation and prices. The velocity of circulation would rise sharply. In other times, funds may wait for opportunities so that the velocity of circulation may drop and economic activity slow down.

As argued in Chapter 3, the black economy is concentrated in the hands of the top 3% in the incomes ladder. Since the black economy is growing faster than the white economy, the implication is that this group has gained proportionately more than others in incomes and wealth. This is important, to understand what is happening to the savings propensity in the economy.

It has been argued by some that the existence of a significant black economy does not lead to a significant underestimation of gross savings. The question arises why has a large concentration of incomes and wealth in the hands of the high savers (the top 3% or even the top 5%) not resulted in a large increase in the observed average savings propensity specially in the eighties? Either the savings propensity is underestimated, or these people have a different savings behaviour out of black and white incomes, or the growing black economy does not lead to concentration of income and wealth. These questions were discussed earlier but many others need to be addressed; only a few are dealt with below.

In Chapter 4, it was pointed out that the growing shares of the black economy, the property incomes and the tertiary sector in the total economy are interlinked. Many economic consequences follow from these relationships which are otherwise inexplicable.

Crisis and Fiscal Policy

As the share of these three variables in GDP increases, there would be a time when the economy would be producing only services in the black economy and all incomes would be property incomes. As mentioned earlier, this is unrealistic and long before an economy reaches such a situation, there would be a breakdown. In other words, if the black economy grows unchecked, the total economy would head for a crisis.

Can fiscal policy play a role in preventing such a crisis from building up? Say by taxing the surplus in private hands so as to reduce its quantum. This would slow down the opening of newer channels of generation of black incomes and reduce the coupling between the two and thereby help decelerate the growth of the black economy. But this does not eliminate the black economy as long as a positive coupling remains. The tax can only be on declared property incomes but with the growth in the black economy, its share would continue to fall, so that, over time, the tax base would narrow and a *fiscal crisis* would ensue. The black economy share would continue to grow even if more slowly, in spite of the couplings being weakened by policy.

The phenomenon of a rising proportion of the services sector in GDP is now common to all the countries of the world, irrespective of the rate of growth of the black economy. So what is different in India's case? That the black economy has become a special reason for the rapid growth of the services sector. The link works through the growth of the surplus.

Relative Stagnation

The implication of a rising share of the black economy is that the share of surplus expands and the private sector's capacity to invest goes up. Simultaneously, the government finding it difficult to raise tax revenue is forced to resort to borrowing to finance its expenditures. The growing surplus in private hands is the obvious source for such borrowing but this comes at a price. The private sector extracts concessions to lend to the government (as discussed earlier), further aggravating income distribution.

The growing trinity of the black economy, property incomes and tertiary section is consistent with stagnation or low growth in the economy as a whole. Since it causes the share of wages to fall, it leads to a tendency for deficiency of demand for mass consumption goods and persistence of excess capacity in these sectors. A low over-all growth in the materials producing sectors is also likely due to the shift of demand in favour of the services sector.

Demand for luxury goods rises due to the growing share of the surplus and of the services sectors. However, this saturates quickly so that in the net, consumption demand stagnates and results in a low overall growth in the economy. This is not to argue that in the Indian economy there may not be other reasons for deficiency of demand like inadequate public investments. However, such explanations are unable to account for the persistence of relatively slow growth and deficiency of demand in spite of the stepped up expenditures and budget deficit by the government, even as a per cent of the GDP. As pointed out earlier, it is the black economy which has blunted the role of deficits in pumping demand into the economy.

A number of analysts have suggested that deficiency of demand is the cause of the relatively slow growth in the Indian economy. They have based their argument on a worsening income distribution. However, critics have countered that evidence for a more skewed income distribution in India has not been clear-cut. The debate has remained inconclusive since the arguments were based only on the revealed picture of the economy. If the black economy was taken into account, concentration of incomes and growing disparity in the factor income shares follows. This is the missing link in the debate on why the rate of growth in the Indian economy has been slow.

Prices and Terms of Trade

The rising level of services required to distribute material goods, as suggested earlier would imply that the difference in the price that the producer receives and the consumer has to pay increases. This ought to show itself in a consistently faster rise in the Consumer Price Index as compared to the Wholesale Price Index. However, the collection of the Consumer Price Index data in India is unreliable and the black premia on goods are not reflected in it. In spite of this shortcoming, this phenomenon is now visible.

The trinity has implications for the terms of trade between industry and agriculture. In the case of agriculture a regional concentration of production of the marketed surplus has taken place. This has meant an increase in trade, transport and other services required for final sale leading to an increase in the gap between the price paid by the consumer and that received by the producer. The agitation by the rural farm lobbies reflects this concern. The middlemen are accused of earning large margins and of preventing the farmers from getting the full gains from their produce.

As a result of stagnant demand for mass consumption items and specially for foodgrains, if output per head remains unchanged, prices would decline. Alternatively, if prices are maintained, unsold stocks would grow. Thus, for foodgrains, with average purchase per head unchanged (with fluctuation) but output per head rising (with fluctuation) stocks have mounted and prices have shown relative stability in the seventies and eighties. In the nineties, the growth in output per head has slowed down and prices allowed to rise so that stocks have continued to be a problem.

In the seventies and the eighties, the government had to intervene in the foodgrain markets and this meant rising costs of procurement, setting up public distribution, storage and transport. Due to inefficiency and corruption, the costs went up. Thus, not only did the gap in prices increase due to the operation of the private markets but public intervention was unable to counter this trend. In sum, the margins included in the final price of agricultural produce have risen and led to a reduction in the price received by the producers.

For industry, concentration in production has proceeded faster than in agriculture. The relative weight of the organized sector in the total has increased. In the case of the stagnant industries and the growing consumer durable industries, the fight over market shares has taken the form not of price-cutting but of increased expenditures to protect and enlarge the market shares through advertising and other such services.

Prices of manufactures have mostly risen even under recessionary conditions in the economy. This is a result of the rise in services costs per unit of output and a rise in the unit cost of the declared production because the cost of the undeclared part is also added to it.

To conclude, the growing black economy would lead to a faster rise in final prices in industry than in agriculture. Other relevant factors in this context are the differences in the rise in the degree of concentration and specialization and the pricing mechanisms in the two sectors. All these factors cause the terms of trade at the level of the final sales to turn against agriculture even if they turn in its favour at the wholesale level.

Consequences of Unthinking Globalization

The globalization that has been imposed on the economy not only due to the pressures from the West and its multilateral institutions but, as pointed out earlier, is a result of the operation of the growing black economy and the associated loss of dynamism in society. It has several negative consequences for India.

Products with international brand names are now available— from Coke and Pepsi to CTVs, cars and primary gold. Indian companies are raising money abroad and foreign investors are buying shares in the national stock markets. Television has been invaded by foreign channels while Doordarshan has to face the competition is copying them through film-based entertainment. Fashion and pop shows have brought the Indian TV viewer on par with the rest of the world. There is a telecom revolution sweeping in the country. That India is opening up in the widest sense is without doubt. But, what does all this add up to?

For the Indian elite, it is a chance to join the international elite. One can now legitimately buy a Mercedez or a BMW or Pierre Cardin label in India without having to look over the shoulder. It is possible to holiday abroad and maintain an account there to meet expenses—no obligation to anyone.

For the middle classes, the range of goods available has expanded and the chance to get a child employed in an MNC has improved (even if marginally). Entertainment at home throughout the day (on TV) is possible. It is another matter that there is less time to read or that children have less time for studies or that the violence and sex being beamed down to them is affecting them psychologically. Criminalization amongst the middle class youth and default on credit cards and consumer loans are symptomatic of rising aspirations without the means of fulfilling them.

The appetite of the youth for going abroad to earn a fortune has been fed by the images of a good life in the West or the Middle East. Indian dreams have changed. Earlier many migrants to cities dreamt of saving to buy land in their village and returning there. Today, their dream is to get a visa to go to the US, UK or the Middle East for employment and to settle down there. As the joke goes, if a referendum is held, middle class Indians may vote to become the 52nd State of the USA.

There was a joke in 1992 that the West may be asked to appoint the Indian prime minister since Indians are proving to be incompetent. Human rights and labour standards are likely to be discussed at the next round of negotiations under WTO. The US has proposed to the IMF that good governance and delivery of justice should be placed as items for discussion on its agenda. These may be part of conditionalities for giving loans in the future and these will most likely be supervised by personnel from the advanced nations.

The widespread illegality in the country has so adverdely affecting the ruling class that they cannot even think of good governance on their own or of improved labour laws. The elite should have taken pride in building a civilized society, instead they see a threat to their lifestyle if the West imposes some of these conditions.

What of the rest, the poor? Globalization is scarring them deeply. They are at the receiving end of this bewildering change. The goodies are there but not for them. They are becoming even more marginal in their own country since international capital is the determinant of national priorities. The signal is loud and clear. Money may be made by any means and better still as a non-resident—no guilt is attached to it. All this is the result of India globalizing to someone else's scheme; not its own.

Worse, today the world is changing rapidly, unlike in the earlier era. Information travelled in months and years. Attitudes and expectations used to change over decades and centuries. There was time to correct mistakes. Now, by the time a mistake is discovered, it may be too late to correct it. Globalizers argue that the economy will improve. But, if they are wrong, by the time they concede the mistake, it may be too late. It almost happened on the issue of convertibility in 1997.

Globalization is not just an economic phenomenon but has social, political and cultural aspects. Yoga, meditation, ayurvedic medicines and handicrafts have acquired a new meaning only when they have been accepted in the West and recycled to India, packaged in a modernizing framework.

Globalization of media would mean flow of information through the western filters. Reading *Time*, *Economist* or the *Wall Street Journal*, one may get the impression that India is not news worthy or at best a quaint country. These agencies determine the agenda of current issues and debates. Even the proponents of swadeshi pick up these issues and quote these sources.

The crowning of Sushmita Sen and Aishwarya Rai as beauty queens in 1994-95 tells another tale of the globalizing Indian culture. Indian beauty measured in Western terms can stand up to the best in the world. The standards are Western. At the Miss India contest where the two ladies were selected, the judges were briefed to select a package which could win the Miss Universe title. The aim was not to select an Indian beauty in the classical Indian terms. The consequence has been that with full media glare, the standards of beauty to be emulated by Indian middle class girls have become western. Perhaps there is nothing wrong with this but this is globalization as a fashion but without a design.

The forces shaping India's globalization are powerful and in command. They have taken advantage of the weaknesses of the Indian ruling elite and is slowly marginalizing them. They are inevitably killing whatever dynamism had survived the growing black economy. Today, they cannot even be challenged without a concerted national attempt based on an Indian design and a will. Unfortunately, the black economy has left little that can be called a national will.

BLACK ECONOMY: THE SYSTEMIC CONSEQUENCES

The discussion till now suggests that every aspect of the citizens' life is affected and society as a whole is in crisis. The crisis in the system is not just an aggregation of the problems in each of the sectors but is more than that. Further, it is the systemic crisis which reacts back on the crisis in individual sectors. So that while there are differences between the sectors depending on their specificities the similarities in the mechanism are overwhelming. In this sense, it is the crisis of the system which determines the problems in each of the sectors.

Black Hurts Interest of National Capital Most

Capital appears to gain unambiguously from the growing black economy since it yields extra profits which are not declared to tax authorities, and, therefore, result in higher disposable incomes in their hands. Businessmen are bound to believe this.

Analyzed carefully, it turns out that the black economy hurts the interest of capital the most. As discussed in Chapter 4, the growth of the black economy slows down increase in demand, and, therefore, growth of output and profits. Thus, the size of capital does not grow as much as it could have. This is important in international competition.

Next, if it is accepted that government is not neutral and acts in the interest of capital (no matter what the rhetoric is), budgetary expenditures can be taken to favour the propertied. This is the so called 'non-populist' part of the budget. Hence if policy fails, its largest impact would be on the interest of capital. Inadequacy of law and order, education, health, rural infrastructure, power, transportation and communications hurt the interest of capital more than that of the poor.

Due to the rising share of the black economy, the policy-maker loses control over the flows of capital within the economy and its leakage outside. Not only does the share of capital in national income rise, it becomes a channel for its further expansion through obtaining more concessions from government and society, but to what effect is this gain, since it only deepens the economic crisis.

While all this is attractive for capital, it results in a high cost of production in the economy (See appendix 6.1). This could have been avoided if resources had been mobilized through direct taxes. They are not a prime cost in production and do not enter the pricing formula of firms. If revenues had been raised through direct taxes, the production structures would have been insulated from the inefficiency of the system created by the growing black economy.

Finally, the leakage of black profits from the economy and their investment abroad is like having capital account convertibility. Indian capital has become internationalized through this route. Mobility has thwarted policy and become another mechanism for extracting concessions. Internationally also, greater mobility of capital has strengthened it against labour. This is apart from the fact that trade union strength has fallen in most countries of the world. Capital mobility has forced nations to make competitive concessions and raised the share of capital in output world-wide.

Globalizers favour removal of protection for indigenous capital. They suggest free access to the Indian market for foreign capital. WTO under TRIMS requires national treatment to foreign capital. Given the disparity between the consumer in India and in the advanced world and between foreign and Indian capital taking all the factors into account, this policy favours foreign capital.

Neither the consumer nor Indian capital will benefit in the long run unless the basic problems of the economy are tackled first.

Those opposed to unthinking globalization recognize the inequity in the international markets and want to give Indian economy a chance to catch up. They argue for globalization on equal basis and not under dictate from the advanced nations.

In brief, for national capital the use of the black economy to raise its share in income is inefficient since it reduces the growth impulses in the economy, raises costs of production, creates BOP difficulties and leads to policy failure and reduced effectiveness of the state. In brief, it lowers its own capacity to work in its own interest and surrenders the initiative to outside forces.

Strategic Retreat of the State

A serious consequence of policy failure has been the discrediting of state intervention. Markets even though they fail in a wide variety of situations have become the favourites. Neo-classical theory suggests that in real life, free markets neither exist nor do they work efficiently and that when they fail, then for efficiency all markets must be taken over by the state. Yet, the tide of ideology so sharply favours the markets that this literature is ignored.

In most advanced nations almost half the GDP is spent by the state. (See Tables V.7 to V.9) India's record is poor in comparison even though the need for efficient intervention by the state is greater here than in the West. Markets cannot cater to the basic need for health, housing, education, for the bottom 70% in the incomes ladder in India since there is little profit to be made in this market. These people have no option but to depend on state intervention. In a drought, only the state can give succor. The market, on the contrary, aggravates the situation through speculation. Similar is the case for other basic needs, like, housing.

State intervention for the poor is supposed to be the least efficient so that it is considered optimum for the state to retreat from these areas. This argument is being clothed in the garb of properly targeting intervention and excluding the undeserving. In a situation where there is a non-functional and corrupt bureaucracy which can neither identify nor deliver specifically to the poor, the programmes will simplify fold up, leaving the poor in a lurch.

In contrast, where capital needs state intervention, it is considered justified in the name of promoting growth. The structure of the economy is being modified (Structural Adjustment, called SAP) to make it conducive to capital (international more than national). Infrastructure is being given concessions so that private sector can obtain it cheaply. Speculation is encouraged in the stock markets. Import of luxury goods at a big resource cost to the nation is allowed. Even if the poor go hungry or children go without education, resources are to be allowed to flow into speculation and import of cars and other luxury goods. This is not termed populism but essential for 'efficiency'.

The argument is not for autarky. This requires a strategy based on total involvement of the nation but the black economy comes in the way of such a scheme. As already argued, the black economy is a reflection of irreconcilable conflict amongst the ruling groups. The strategic retreat of the state and globalization which marginalize a large section of the society from economic gains can only lead to further strife and collapse of the national will.

Marginalization of Issues in Elections

The collapse of the national will is reflected in the electoral process where issues have ceased to matter. A quick look at the party manifestoes is illustrative.

The issues facing the nation are well known—poverty, unemployment, inflation, Kashmir, and so on. The manifesto drafting committees don't need to discover them but simply clothe them in a readable form. Issues are framed with sufficient ambiguity to provide enough escape routes during elections and later, if the party does come to power.

It is not that the issues contained in the manifestoes are unimportant but election after election there is a history of broken promises (by the party which comes to power). On the plea of pragmatism, anything can be justified—inclusion of a maximum set of policies in the manifesto and their non-implementation while in power.

In 1991, Congress(I) did not deliver on rollback of prices to the 1989 level within 100 days of coming to power. Actually, no one expected it to happen. The Janta Dal hardly attempted to deliver the Right to Work or to Housing contained in its manifesto in 1989. Reservations for the backward castes happened accidentally due to internal party conflict.

The mere incorporation of an issue in a manifesto is no guarantee of action by the party. A well-drafted manifesto containing 10 or 100 points can be produced in a short span of time. Leaders are not involved in the drafting till the last stage and appear to be unconcerned with the logic of the exercise in its totality. Coherence of views is unimportant since implementation is not expected.

In the absence of a perspective, individual issues in the manifesto are not worth the paper they are written on. Both because they may contradict something else in the document and because they are unlikely to be acted upon.

Of course, if there is a groundswell in favour of an issue, it cannot be ignored by the parties. That was the case with the acceptance of the Mandal Report. Every party ended up supporting the implementation even though none of them really wanted it (they paid lip service to it). Given the rising dalit consciousness, no party today is able to ignore granting of concessions to dalits. Without any programmatic understanding, to score a point, the BJP backed the BSP government in UP.

Even when movements have come up, cooption by vested interests have blunted their edge. For instance, in the case of Mandal, reservations are being introduced at a time when they have become meaningless with public sector cutting back employment and total employment generation on the decline. At times, demands have been partly conceded prematurely so that the movement gets confused and peters out. For instance, in the case of Panchayati Raj, Rajiv Gandhi by prematurely creating these institutions preempted the issue of decentralization.

As issues have ceased to matter, national politics has become dependent on personalities and their whims. Elections are not being won on positive issues but on the basis of public disenchantment with the ruling party. Candidates are fielded not for their commitment to the party programme but for their affiliation to a) the party leaders and b) the winning caste and community combination. These factors matter because the manifestoes do not.

This may change if the public gets a memory—it remembers how it got fooled by its representatives. The record of voting by parties on the various issues of interest to the people should be brought to public notice. The danger however is that all the parties may have a similar dismal record, and, therefore, the public may not have any choice. But it is worth a try.

Intellectuals who labour time and again to produce manifestoes seem to have accepted the devaluation of their documents. Most actually believe that this is justified to achieve power for their group and perhaps hope for a share in power. This is convenient to the politicians.

In brief, today, parties are governed less by issues than by individualities so that the issuing of manifestoes makes everyone other than those seeking power look silly.

Subversion of Institutions of Democracy

The black economy represents illegality and it operates by subverting the various institutions of democracy. There is a two way relationship so that the weaker the democracy gets the more the black economy flourishes. As more and more sections of the population get drawn into the net of the black economy, public opinion gets diluted. It is like in the police either a person is a part of the hafta system or feels helpless to stop it. As Buddha said, let the one who has done no wrong cast the first stone and no one could. Today, no section of society is able to provide leadership. Intellectuals are not generating ideas and are by and large demoralized. The visible ones from the academic community are pliable, swayed by offers of committees, foreign trips and other inducements thrown at them by those in power who wish to coopt them. This is one aspect of loss of dynamism.

It may be too much to expect politicians, bureaucrats, policemen, lawyers, doctors, businessmen, and the like to provide moral leadership. This is not to argue that there are no honest people amongst these groups but that is not enough to change things around. In many of these groups, like, in the bureaucracy or the police, honest people are an exception. The honest ones are unable to even lead their own group, and, therefore, it is that much more difficult for them to lead others. As a nation, the level of distrust is so high that no one accepts anyone else's leadership. This adds to the disarray.

In this atmosphere of distrust, lack of social concern and cohesion, accountability has become a victim. Accountability is defined in feudal terms to one's own group or mentor. Right or wrong is defined in terms of the interest of the group. My group's corruption is acceptable since it may benefit me in some way. Principles are adjusted to suit the group.

Those who believe in honesty in the wider sense of accountability to society at large, are being marginalized. Actions of the principled are predictable. They neither help in bending rules nor create problems when rules are followed. Socializing with them does not yield returns (favours) when rules have to be bent so that association with them is not useful. It is those who are willing to bend principles and are likely to help when the need arises who are useful and need to be kept happy. Thus, those who are honest are marginalized within their peer group as well as in the wider society. How does one build society under the circumstances? At best, groups which work for their members' interest emerge. By definition, they would be antagonistic to other groups.

The politicians and political parties are the prime example of such behaviour. They are not interested in delivering on promises so they resort to untruths to maintain themselves in power. Cynicism in the public and individual's alienation from society are useful for them to maintain their hold on power. If people cannot act together, they cannot replace them.

Those in power behave like a mafia. They maintain silence about each other's wrong doings. Anyone who breaks rank is marginalized in a variety of ways. Each institution has its own mafia which links up to form the bigger one. Change of power means changing the faces in the mafia. Teachers keep silent about each others wrong doing and that prevailing in their institutions. When the head of an institution changes she/he brings own trusted people around her/him. Institutional functioning is discouraged since it is hard to control and manipulate. Malleable people are needed to head various positions. Other professions do the same. In this milieu, accountability is to the group and not to society.

Accountability can only have a long term context and cannot be to individuals. In its absence, society faces sub-optimality on many fronts. Take for instance education. Educationists who are incharge of framing policies have bureaucratic ambitions and what they mean by management is maintining control. The creative ones are sidelined since they do not conform and are 'unmanageable'. Their ideas create the possibility of matters going beyond the management's controls. This attitude is reflected all down the line. For instance, the basis of relationship between the teacher and the taught should be trust. But this missing. Teachers are often only interested in keeping control in the class and discourage questioning. Students sensing the teacher's dishonesty lose respect for her/him. The relationship between the school and the parents is also based on distrust. There is much manipulation that goes on, on both sides. The result is a sub-optimality for all concerned.

Today there is lack of accountability in the most important institution of democracy, the parliament. A party when in power proposes something but later, if it loses power, opposes it. From this to switching parties for power is a short step. In effect, the defection of the politician begins in the mind much before she/he switches party. Today, what counts for a politician is power and not priniciples. In this sense, there is no defection at all and no democracy is truncated. In brief, the propertied who resort to the black economy to increase their share in national income end up subverting accountability and the various institutions of democracy.

CONCLUSION

The black economy results in policy failure both because of inadequate allocations and due to ineffectiveness of expenditures. Primary schools intended to be set up do not materialize. Roads either do not get built or are of sub-standard quality needing frequent repairs. Badly laid water-pipes burst leading to both shortage and contamination of drinking water. Investment gets diverted to unproductive sectors leading to shortage of savings for real investment. Scarcity of foreign exchange prevents import of essentials and technology. Society is unable to achieve its goals.

The black economy has many economic ill-effects. While some argue that there are a few beneficial effects, in the net, the social impact is negative. A change in name, *illegal to legal,* does not eliminate the economic ill-effects of an activity—this is window-dressing. Consequently, modern day India does not present the image of a civilized society.

The black economy and the erosion of institutions of democracy are interlinked. The institutions of democracy, legislatures, learning centres, judiciary, bureaucracy, police, media, etc., are all compromised due to the functioning of the black economy. They are not doing what they should be doing and people's faith in democracy has been eroded. Issues in elections have ceased to matter, devaluing the electoral process. As people's pressure has declined, illegality has grown. The involvement of the country's elite in illegality has eroded their commitment to work and this pervades society. Criminalization, waste and sub-optimality have penetrated deep into the Indian society.

Since resources are wasted, there is greater conflict over what is remaining. This along with the subterranean character of the black economy has fuelled a number of false debates on current problems. Rather than look at the common cause of the failures, blame is sought to be shifted to others and debating points scored.

The nation is not short of resources but because of the existence of the black economy a large chunk of them are not only wasted but are either lying idle or are siphoned out of the nation. *Paradoxically, the interest of those who have benefitted most from the black economy has also been hurt the most since growth has been stunted and dynamism has been eroded.* Much of the activity in the black economy is like digging holes and filling them. Many are employed but society makes little progress and remains poor. As policy fails, individual solutions are sought, which results in making the resource shortage look worse and weakening the commitment to national goals. Social action is discredited and demand for the state to retreat gains legitimacy. Important social functions are going unattended. In turn, this causes further policy failure so that a vicious circle gets created. This *has produced a mindset in which the citizen expects that 'the usual is the unusual and the unusual the usual'.*

Another paradox is that even though while resources exist, the citizen has been led to believe that the nation is short of resources—it is poor. This has led to the voluntary acceptance of an unequal globalization on the terms laid down by the outsiders. Indian capital has accepted a junior position because of this and its weaknesses brought about by its flirtation with the black economy in the last thirty years. The result is a deep impact on the social and cultural milieu in the country, making it even less dynamic. Indian politics, believing there is no alternative (TINA), has even less space to represent the interest of the weak in society; weakening its democratic fabric.

Checking growth of the black economy has become the single biggest task for the nation.

7

Remedies for Curbing Black Economy

In Chapter 4 it was argued that the major macroeconomic problems since the seventies have been integrally linked to the growing black economy. In Chapter 6, it was shown that the black economy has systemic consequences and affects all aspects of the citizen's life. Hence it should have been a significant factor of analysis in the Indian economy. Its non-inclusion in analysis resulted in a partial understanding of the Indian economy and often to incorrect policy pronouncements. The need to incorporate the black economy was not simply an empirical matter but a theoretical necessity. The circular flow of incomes changes with the black economy. The theoretical analysis yields counter-intuitive results with regard to tax evasion, investment and savings, subsidies, BOP and so on.

Capital is able to raise its share in national income using the black economy but paradoxically hurts its own interest. It reduces its own capacity to grow rapidly (by narrowing its markets). While this makes it more dependent on the state to generate demand in the economy, it also reduces the effectiveness of the state to do so because of policy failure. It blunts the instruments available to it for its own rapid growth for the sake of short term gains.

Prior to 1991, it was widely argued that to curb the growing black economy, controls needed to be reduced and tax rates lowered. Since 1991, many of the controls are gone and direct tax rates have been drastically reduced but from available indicators the black economy has continued to grow. For instance, the buoyancy in direct taxes when calculated over the relevant tax base (business incomes) has remained unchanged (See appendix 7.1). Another indication is the growing number and size of scams in the nineties (See appendix 1.0). Other pointers are the continued rapid growth in the tertiary sector and increase in speculative activity.

The design of New Economic Policies (NEP) ignores the implications of the activities carried out in the black economy. As argued in Chapter 5, legalizing the formerly illegal activities, like in the case of gold smuggling, does not solve the problem since neither the growth impulses improve nor the leakages from the national economy decline. What is required is to change the nature of the activities associated with the black economy (now or earlier).

In a nutshell, that which is the corrective to the policies pursued before 1991 is also the corrective to the ills of the New Economic Policies. The black economy needs to be tackled head on and its more pernicious elements eliminated from the economy. Concessions to the propertied under NEP will not achieve this goal. They will have to change the basic nature of their economic activities. In this, the fiscal monetary policy governing the functioning of the marketized economy can and will have to play a major role. The policy regime itself will have to undergo change from that which has existed in India. That is the real alternative before the nation—an indigenous one based on the nation's own resources.

Available literature is full of suggestions for dealing with the black economy. There are a large number of government reports with hundreds of suggestions to check the growth of the black economy. The government has tried out a range of schemes like, amnesty, tax cuts, demonetisation and acquisition of undervalued properties. Some of these are discussed later along with the reasons for their failure. Some proposed solutions are absurd since they suggest elimination of direct taxes (See appendix 7.2) or an end to rules, etc. These amount to abolishing society itself.

Eradication of rules or of roads or of traffic police is no solution to chaotic traffic since that would be like obliteration of traffic. The point is that traffic should be orderly—rules have to be obeyed voluntarily. This requires everyone to have faith in them.

In traffic, the conflict over right of way takes extra-legal forms. It gets resolved only when everyone follows the rules.

Traffic rules are designed to be democratic. They do not give the right of way to say, a truck over a bicyclist. The solution does not lie in having more traffic policemen who in the absence of consensus over the rules and public confusion have simply used the abuse of rules to extract money.

Giving a higher salary to the police is no solution. Salaries have to be commensurate with the work performed and should be seen to be fair. They should never be based on the coercive power of how corrupt one can become since there would be no end to this and it would never acquire legitimacy in the eyes of others.

When rules are violated, black incomes are generated. As discussed in Chapter 5, the rule or the control are not the cause of black income generation but they are the source of black income generation.

A remedy lies in removing the cause of black income generation and not the source of black income generation. Often it is argued that removal of controls or elimination of income-tax will curtail the growth of black income generation. In fact, if income-tax is eliminated, there will be no black income since there can be no income-tax evasion. But this is what in mathematics is called a 'trivial solution' and amounts to saying eliminate society itself.

If society is not able to check crime since the police may have a nexus with the criminals and gets a share of the booty (hafta), and therefore has a vested interest, does it follow that theft and pick-pocketing be legally permitted? This would certainly improve the figures for crime but would it have any meaning? As legal crime increases, the citizen would become more insecure and take law into her/his own hands resulting in a free for all and new the rule would become 'might is right'.

Following the logic of legalizing the illegal can one argue that one stops charging for electricity or telephones or maybe eliminates them all together so that this kind of corruption ends? Clearly, this would be retrograde. If society is not functioning properly, rather than eliminate it or reduce activities, would it not be better to reform it?

The need is to control activities which are not in the interest of society. By eliminating such controls or laws, society does not become better off. One needs to curb the non-reporting of factor incomes to tax authorities rather than eliminate the tax. The undesirability of illegal factor income generation is the point; it is the activities which are undesirable for society. From the micro-point of view these are not undesirable since they lead to efficiency but from the macro-point of view they need to be checked to help the economy to grow or to enable society to function better.

LESSONS FROM KEY SCHEMES TRIED

Voluntary Disclosure Schemes

Voluntary disclosure schemes have been announced from time to time. These schemes give amnesty to those who have generated black incomes in the past. The last of these was the highly publicized voluntary disclosure scheme (VDIS) of 1997. Rs 10,000 crores of taxes were collected through it.

Whether VDIS was a success or not can only be gauged in the context of its implications for the economy. On this the confusion prevails. The confusion begins with the name itself. The scheme should have been called Voluntary Disclosure of Wealth instead of Income. What has been declared is the past accumulation of assets in the form of bullion, real estate, bank balances, etc. Since the financial year does not come to an end till March 31, incomes generated in any year can be declared upto the time of filing the return for that year and there can be no question of declaring them under VDIS.

Incomes in earlier years which were not declared in the tax returns for those years can only be declared by filing revised tax returns for those years. This would require revealing the source of those incomes. Since under VDIS this was not asked for, it cannot be said that past black incomes have been revealed. Consider this; X reveals the earlier purchase of an undervalued real estate when she paid some black to the seller, say, Y. X had transferred his black savings to Y who holds it till she/he deploys the funds. The income-tax department should prosecute Y for having undeclared income but this is not feasible under the rules of VDIS. It is no good taxing X alone, the declarant under VDIS.

The tax is paid by X on the undeclared value of the transaction in the year the transaction supposedly took place. In subsequent years, the value of the property has not only appreciated but also it has probably yielded undeclared returns. None of these are taxed under VDIS, as they should have been under an income-declaration scheme. Thus, the effective tax rate under VDIS worked out to a fraction of 30%. In some cases, it may have been only a few per cent (effectively zero). Apparently, the scheme's success had much to do with this low (intended?) tax rate.

The 'success' of VDIS 1997 apparently made no difference to the Indian economy. It should have, if the black economy is the evil it is and if the success of VDIS made a dent on the black economy in India. Many analysts have argued that since the latter part of the statement is not correct, no effect was likely. However, others may argue that the black economy is not bad for the economy so no effect should have been expected, except budgetary. Either way no impact on the economy was expected. Is this correct?

To sort this out, the distinction between income and wealth needs to be appreciated. Income flows from current production in the economy. Out of this income, a part is saved and the rest consumed. What is saved results in the accumulation of wealth. The relationship between income and wealth is complicated.

The declarants under VDIS revealed a part (or in some cases even the whole) of the accumulation of their wealth and paid a tax on the declared value of the concealed assets. Many of these assets are unproductive in nature whose declaration does not alter the production process in the economy and does not effect income generation. Hence no direct impact may be expected. Indirectly, the payment of tax on these assets requires funds, so liquidity was squeezed. Those declaring their black assets had to generate funds from current activities, black or white, to pay the tax.

Further, VDIS increased uncertainty for the investors, most of whom hold black assets. They had to make up their minds about the fraction of their black assets to reveal. As was evident from the rush in the last weeks of the scheme, they waited till the very end to make up their minds. In the meanwhile, they had to keep liquid to pay the tax. Perhaps, they delayed investment decisions till they were clear. Uncertainty also resulted from the raids and the pressure from the income-tax authorities on those transacting, say, real estate, during this period.

Uncertainty has been a major cause of the economic slow down since 1996. The end of VDIS did not mean that the situation reversed. The 'whitened' assets were not converted into productive investments or used to increase consumption. Consequently, demand did not rise and recession continued. If the declining prices of gold and real estate were to divert investment into the productive sectors some impact may have been observed later but this has not happened. Demand for gold has been growing year after year. Real estate has been facing a slump since the middle of 1995 and demand is unlikely to decline further.

Will VDIS plug further black income generation and result in more investment in productive sectors? Under the scheme black income sources were not required to be revealed and the information provided under VDIS cannot be used in the future. Worse, such schemes trigger further black income generation due to the expectation that more of them will be initiated later. After all, another government facing budgetary crisis could initiate a similar scheme. Finally, disclosure schemes discriminate against honest tax-payers and weaken their resolve to stay honest. In effect black income generation is not affected by such schemes.

VDIS is actually a VDWS. Rs 33,000 crore worth of assets were declared under the scheme but the present value of these assets may have been many times this amount. Since detailed data will never be revealed, the exact amount will not be known. The implication is that the State which went down on bended knees was again cheated.

Be that as it may, what seems to have been revealed is a tiny fraction of the vast hoard of black wealth accumulated by the Indian elite in the last forty years. This fortune is held partly in India and partly abroad. An estimate is difficult at the best of times. If it is assumed to be ten times the annual black income generation, then it could be Rs 56 lakh crore in 1997. In brief, one per cent of the black wealth may have been revealed. This is corroborated by the case of gold which was declared in large quantities. At least 10,000 tons of gold have been smuggled into India in the last forty years which at 1998 prices would be worth Rs 5 lakh crore. The amount declared constitutes a few per cent of this hoard. The same situation is likely to hold with respect to other black assets.

Since taxes (Rs 10,000 crore) on declarations under VDIS had to be paid out of current white incomes, black incomes (about Rs 6 lakh crore in1997) do not enter the picture. The additional taxes collected during 1997-98 turned out to be at the expense of regular tax collections. In essence, the scheme did not strike at the root of the process of black income generation, and, therefore, apart from the budgetary implications, the ill-effects (which are many) of the black economy on the national economy continued. Whatever be the name, VDIS or VDWS, there was little cause for celebration.

Measures adopted from time to time, like, bearer bonds and voluntary disclosure schemes actually aggravate the problem. They allow easy convertibility of accumulated black funds to white. Thus they further reduce the already low cost of evasion and thereby encourage the expansion of the black economy. They build up the expectation that these schemes would be repeated sooner or later so the reason for paying taxes now and complying with the law of the land is eroded. These schemes may have been considered attractive if they had at least mopped up a major portion of the black funds and had made an impact on the generation of black incomes in the future.

Disclosure schemes send the wrong signals to the tax evader and to the honest citizen. The former is encouraged to indulge in more of illegality (not just tax evasion) while the latter who loses faith in the system feels it is unfair and tries to gain through other means. Either way, the system loses and the black economy is encouraged.

Gold Mobilization

Gold has been one of the important assets with which the black economy has had a link. The idea of mobilizing its available stocks, in private hands, for shoring up the foreign exchange reserves of the country is a good one. However, this has to be done carefully. Since, as argued above, any concessions to black income generation end up being counter-productive.

The liberalization of the import of gold since 1992 has actually increased the demand for gold. This was expected because even white savings may be held in the form of primary gold given the preference for it. Three is an increased leakage of savings from the economy which can destabilize the rupee viz-a-viz the foreign currencies. Holding gold is like holding foreign currency and its importation amounts to capital movements, like, with convertibility on the capital account.

If gold is mobilized through a gold bond scheme floated by the banks, there are serious implications for the budget. If the gold so mobilized is held idle, there is a loss to the banks who have to pay an interest and this would have to be covered by the government. If the gold is sold as a means of shoring up foreign exchange reserves, it will entail a loss since the international price is at least 25% lower. If gold is advanced to the exporters of jewellery, it will also be like export of gold and will be at international prices. A loss will then accrue. In each of these cases, the budget would have to make up the losses.

Further, the sale/mortgage of gold outside the country will mean lower stocks in the country. This may set up expectation that gold price will rise and increase the demand for gold. In fact, the amnesty implied in the bond scheme would give a fillip to demand for gold from the black economy. It is possible that gold becomes the preferred route to convert black to white and vice versa. If the demand for gold rises from both the black and the white economy, loss of foreign exchange due to greater inflow of gold into the country into private hands maybe much greater than any gains from the gold bond scheme.

In fact, it could be argued that since the import of gold has become legal, the government could simply buy gold in the free market to build foreign exchange reserves. This would drive up the gold price in the domestic market and promote further inflow of gold. For the gold scheme to succeed, some people holding primary gold should want to off-load their gold holdings for a small return so that no increase in the inflow of gold into private hands takes place. This does not seem plausible since at present more and more gold is being held even when the average rate of return is far lower than in alternate uses, like shares.

In fact, gold is held even though it is not associated with production so that its quantity remains unchanged, only its money value appreciates. People prefer it because of liquidity, risk and other considerations. To overcome these factors, so that people part with their gold holding, a high rate of return may have to be offered. This would be specially true if banks are involved in the collection. Banks lack credibility due the high levels of corruption and people may fear fraud. When they go to deposit their gold, they might be told it is of lower purity than it really is, among other reasons.

The gold scheme would amount to borrowing by the government. If it is entirely or even partly kept as a reserve, the size of the fiscal deficit would rise. If gold is simply held in the country, it would not be able to earn any interest and the government would have to pay this out of its other receipts.

If a real 2% rate of return is to be allowed then at the current rate of inflation, the interest rate would have to be about 10%. Clearly, the fiscal deficit would shoot up. Even if a part of the gold is sold outside, there would be capital loss and the interest earned on the sale proceeds held outside would be inadequate to pay the interest in India. The fiscal deficit would rise. If the rate of return offered on the gold bonds is high the budgetary position would become worse.

The only advantage of the scheme would be that it makes available foreign exchange which is otherwise scarce. The rupee cost may be well worth the expense in a crisis only. The foreign currency reserves of the RBI also earn a return but the net cost (opportunity cost) is in foreign currency. The gold bond scheme will convert this into rupee costs.

To know whether gold would be deposited by people, one needs to know the gold-holding pattern. Gold holding by the different asset-holding groups and the preferences of these groups are not known. As pointed out, the average annual purchase of gold by households in India is small (4 grams). Even if it is believed that only the top 2% of the families in the country hold gold in primary form, to hold their black savings, the average annual purchase would be about 200 grams per such family. This is not big money and may not become available for the gold bond scheme.

There is a need to distinguish between those who generate black money and hold gold as a form of black savings and others who hold it for family reasons. It is the former who maybe expected to use the gold bank and the bond schemes. These are powerful people with political clout. They would clamour that these deposits should be allowed liquidity, i.e., loans should be allowed against these deposits. If this is done then the possibility opens up that there may be an expansion in money supply, speculation, price rise and devaluation.

In a nutshell, the gold bond scheme needs to be thought through cautiously lest it gets little but ends up destabilizing the rupee and encouraging the black economy. Steps to control the black economy and to change the asset preferences of the top 3% in India are needed prior to floating the gold bond scheme. A proper sequencing is a must.

Lessons from the Financial Sector Scam

The share market has become the mechanism for a few people in the know to make money at the expense of the gullible middle class. Some suggested that a lack of computerization was the reason for the scam. This argument does not hold water. In the advanced nations where extensive computerisation exists, various kinds of manipulation takes place including fraud. Computerisation does not prevent frauds, in fact, it aids international speculators to make their business into a fine art. This was more than evident in the failure of the Baring Bank or the South-east Asian Financial Meltdown.

Only public pressure and transparent functioning can prevent the financial scam that took place in 1991-92. Business secrecy has to be curtailed and business practices have to be made more transparent. Raising greed to a high pedestal through policy, that is, encouraging speculation, has to stop. Finally, responsibility for policy failure needs to be fixed. In other words, accountability needs to be built into the entire system. Today, hardly anyone in the top echelons of the bureaucracy or the political leadership gets prosecuted since the chain of command is always fudged.

Top policy-makers bear clear moral responsibility for creating the environment in which the scam could occur. The scam became an occasion for playing politics and to push through favourite policies. The Narasimham Committee Report and its recommendations needed to be reassessed. Pushing through reckless liberalization without adequate safeguards only opened the doors to many more scams. The need is for appropriate regulatory mechanisms and curbs on private greed. The absence of the former and too much of the latter have created problems for the Indian economy.

Speculation in the secondary share markets has continued in the post-scam period and along with that the generation of black incomes. This is based on manipulation by those holding enormous financial power. The chairman of Tata Tea in his 1997 report to the General Body meeting bemoaned this trend with regard to the shares of his company. He pointed out how tens of thousands of shares of his company were being traded in the stock exchanges but a tiny fraction were lodged with the company for transfer. These trends need to be checked to control the growth of black incomes in the share markets (See appendix 2.8).

The Land Market: the Corrective

Speculative activities in the land markets also illustrate this point. It is essential to control them for social reasons and for stopping the circulation of black incomes. While on the one hand, this speculation dampens the investment climate and slows down the rate of growth in the economy, on the other hand, it makes the access to land for the genuinely needy more difficult (at least in the urban areas). The problem is serious on both the fronts. The bigger question it raises is can the undesirable trend of funds shifting from productive into unproductive activities be controlled?

As discussed in Chapter 2, speculation in real estate has been rampant and has enabled the circulation of black incomes. It has also led to the diversion of investment from productive to unproductive channels. This activity then needs to be curbed. The rate of return on certain kinds of landed property can be shown to be a multiple of the rate of inflation. The high capital gains lead both to creation of black incomes and to attractiveness of investing black incomes. A self-perpetuating boom then follows.

Clearly, if the expectation of capital gain is broken, the vacant and under-utilized properties would be sold by their owners. Then prices would decline. To achieve this through policy would require a complete package and it has to be asuumed that the political will and an effective administration exist. Without these two elements, there can be no policy. The two key policies would a) discourage sale and purchase of real estate purely for profit; b) to stop the transactions in real estate between individuals must be stopped. It must be only through the state. The power-of-attorney sales for government-allotted properties as well as for cooperative societies must be discouraged. The hundred fiftieth report of the Public Accounts Committee had held (in 1983) that sales under a general power of attorney are not legal.

Since such sales are illegal, government can take back possession of properties where this has happened. It must signal to any prospective purchaser that they are taking a risk in making a power of attorney purchase. Without first tackling such transactions, sale and purchase through the government would be unenforceable.

In addition, social amenities in a premises like telephone, electricity and water may be provided either in the name of the allottee of the property or of the legal tenant. The general power of attorney ought to have a restricted period of validity. These measures would increase the risk and the inconvenience of such transactions.

Large parcels of land must be released so as to soak up liquidity of the speculators and to make land available to those who genuinely need land for their need. The availability of social infrastructure should be evenly spread out rather than being concentrated at a few locations.

The idea of routing transactions through the government before they become legal is not tantamount to nationalization. People can build for themselves but cannot transact. This would curtail speculation since government would transact at given prices. A rapid rise in the value of the property would not be assured and the major reason for speculative investment in land would disappear.

Simultaneous with this, the sale and purchase of real estate should be made simple and new properties or those being sold to the government may be allotted on the basis of first come first served. This would encourage people to relocate according to proximity to their places of work.

Property taxes must also be based on the government (local authority) fixed current market prices determined for the various zones of any city. This would make the holding of vacant property or excess property expensive. It would not only boost municipal taxes but also bring into the market (to the government and then to the public) the surplus property in the hands of a few who would find it expensive to hold. They would no more be interested in cornering real estate as they do at present.

Property tax can be viewed as a charge for the privilege of having urban social services. Municipalities will then have adequate funds to provide the requisite level of infrastructure. The decline of the cities would be checked. There *may* also be a relocation of employment to smaller towns with cheaper land. Decentralized urban growth may get encouraged. Today, in spite of all talk, there is unabated growth of the metropolitan centres.

Preventing speculation in real estate would increase the profitability of economic activities by keeping rents low. Also, by keeping returns on real estate low it would prevent funds from being diverted from productive activities. Finally, construction for rental would become less desirable since people would prefer to construct for themselves on land which would become available.

If speculation is curbed, the problem of rapid rise in rents would end and Rent Control Acts made redundant. The problem of rent control is due to the rapid rise of rents and the inability of individuals to provide themselves the housing they need at the prevailing land prices driven by speculation. Landlords who do not maintain their properties because they yield a low rent would start maintaining them if they get market rent. In fact, the tenants could be allowed to buy out the property from the government at the pre-determined prices. They would then maintain the properties rather then let them decay.

Concessions to industry cannot by themselves raise demand or profitability if demand itself is low and profits are not to be had. But by making unproductive channels of investment less profitable, funds may be forced into productive areas. Simultaneously, if the lower middle classes and the poor pay lower rents, demand for industrial goods would increase. Finally, with easier access to land, construction activity would rise and generate further demand for manufactured goods both directly and indirectly (through creating more employment).

Curbing speculation in land would be beneficial from the point of view of economic activity in the country and would curb the circulation of black incomes. The suggestions made here would result in decentralised urbanisation and prevent the decay of metropolises. Above all, citizens would be better able to fulfill their need for shelter and improve their living conditions. (See Kumar, 1994).

Demonetization

Black money (unaccounted cash) is recognized by Prof Kabra as only one of the components of black wealth. However, on the premise that 'there are sizeable quantities of money floating in the black economy', the author suggests 'the importance of demonetisation of high denomination currency as a means for unearthing as well as cancelling out a good part of black incomes' (Kabra, 1982, p. 111).

This raises many questions which must be settled for demonetization to be viable policy. For instance, given the interpenetrating nature of the black and the white economies, how can one distinguish between the white and the black money hoards? Further, consequent to demonetization, would the black component of prices collapse? Would near-money forms emerge? A clear answer to these questions is an important pre-requisite to suggesting demonetisation as a viable policy.

Demonetization of large denomination currency notes has been suggested from time to time as a restrictive measure. In 1978, the high denomination notes (Rs. 1,000 and Rs. 5,000) were demonetized even though they could not have accounted for any major chunk of the black hoards, There were only Rs. 165 crores worth of them in circulation. The bearer bonds experience is also worth mention. At least temporarily (until government spending increased to put currency back into circulation), black currency hoards tendered for exchange were demobilized.

Demonetization imposes heavy costs on the economy, causes inconvenience to the citizens and yet its outcome is both unknown and uncertain. In any case, demonetization does not eliminate the root cause of the creation of the black economy. Hence, if at all, it would have a minor one-time impact.

Finally, the discussions with income-tax department officials in charge of raids is revealing, how come during raids on builders they did not catch large hoards of cash? When asked the officials replied that even when they did catch large sums of cash the builders were able to explain the cash flow within a matter of days. As already discussed earlier, cash is a means of transactions and is not immobilized. Demonetization of high denomination currency notes would only demobilize, very little of black hoards of cash. In fact, those in the villages who may not be able to convert their money are likely to be the losers not the businessmen or the corrupt politicians and bureaucrats who may actually have some hoards, but can quickly get them converted.

Lower Tax Rates: No Remedy

The major issues in the context of the hypothesis of high tax rates leading to black income generation, namely, what constitutes a high tax rate and whether, tax rates are high in India have been left unanswered in the NIPFP study. It quotes data from EARC to show that the combined incidence of income and wealth taxes has been high (NIPFP, 1985, p. 280). However, the norm for defining a high tax rate has not been discussed. It is tautological to argue that tax rates must be felt to be high because there is a large black economy.

In a poor country like India, with a per capita income of Rs. 14,000 per annum, the current tax exemption limit, including standard deduction (but not other deductions) is, Rs. 75,000. It may be asked that in a country where the minimum wages in most areas around Rs 50 per day (and mostly unenforcable), what ought to be the allowed level of disparity? This can be the only criterion to decide on taxation. But on this, the Report is silent. The Report does not even show that a reduction in tax rates would lead to a decrease in black income generation and, yet argues for a reduction in tax rates.

The recommendation for reducing the income-taxes rates ignores the available data which showed that hardly 1.5 lakh individuals paid an average income-tax rate of above 30% (Kumar, 1985b). As discussed in Chapter 5, the picture has not changed since then. Actually, the number of tax-evaders is much larger and not directly linked to those paying high taxes.

J.R.D. Tata addressing a press conference on 4 March 1985 is reported to have said, 'the punitive incidence of taxation, both personal and corporate, has only provoked contempt for taxation laws. ... these restraining factors should be eliminated without further delay.' This was a forceful plea for cuts in direct tax rates. Contrast this with the report of another dialogue. L. M. Thapar, chairing the Indo-Candian JBC on 23 April 1985, was asked by a Canadian delegate whether tax-rates were high in India. He is reported to have said that given the existence of enough loopholes, we hardly need to pay taxes. This was not contradicted by other businessmen present. The implication is that even legally, tax rates have not been high and the contempt for tax laws that Mr Tata spoke about arises for other reasons than that 'tax rates are high'.

The alternative to this hypothesis is that a large number of black income generators probably completely escape the tax net and remain unaffected by tax rate changes. These people may respond to how strictly the law is implemented and to deterrence. The example from real estate, given in Chapter 5, showed that deterrence does seem to work.

Apart from the general recommendation to reduce taxes, the Report suggests a reduction in stamp duties. Unfortunately, this suggestion would further encourage black income generation. The reason is that if implemented this provision would lower the cost of transaction and raise the rate of return from real estate and lead to a new infusion of funds into this sector. This would aggravate price rise and speculation in real estate and cause large capital gains to be generated. Not only would this be socially undesirable but it would also cause the undervaluation of immovable property to increase. Speculators would be further encouraged to shorten the period of holding their investments. Something like this has already happened earlier when the definition of long-term capital gains was changed from properties held for three years to those held for one year.

Post-1991, income-tax rates have declined and income-tax collection has risen sharply (See Table VII.3). It has increased as a share of both the GDP (See Table VII.4) and the total taxes collected. Does this imply that as tax rates have been cut, there is better compliance so that black income generation has declined as tax rates have become reasonable? At first glance, this seems to be correct. However, this is not the correct interpretation. This result is also possible if income distribution gets highly skewed in favour of the tax-payers. Under NEP, this has happened since business incomes and the incomes of managerial class had risen sharply. The rate of growth of the non-agricultural organized sector has been high (See Table VII.3). Within this sector, the managerial salaries have increased by over 400% since the upper limit to salaries has been almost eliminated. In most years since 1991, corporate incomes have spurted by 10 to 30% (See Table VII.5) for a sample of companies. This is well above the rate of growth of GDP.

Between 1997 and 1999 there has been a spurt in income-tax collection due to the award of the Fifth Pay Commission and the arrears paid for the period 1996 to 1999 and VDIS. If all these special factors are taken into account, direct tax collection should have risen even faster than what has been observed if compliance had improved.

However, there was one reason why tax collection from the corporate sector improved in the period 1994 to 1996 but this had nothing to do with the tax rates. It had to do with the threat of takeover hanging over Indian companies. In the post-1991 period, takeovers have become easy since now the government (through the financial institutions) *d*oes not automatically support an existing management.

To counter this, managements of Indian companies have increased their holding in their own companies (the Tatas have done so openly) so that someone threatening takeover has to have a larger share of the equity. This also reduces the floating stock of equity and increases the price of that share and makes the takeover that much more costly.

The managements have tried to further increase the price of the equity of their companies by improving balance-sheet profitability. This makes takeover even more costly. For this purpose, the companies have converted some of their black incomes into white incomes by reducing the share of undeclared output and increasing that of the declared output.

The conclusion is that in the period 1994 to 1996, increased corporate tax collections had nothing to do with reductions in tax rates and its observed high growth rate was a result of a looming threat of takeover. The rate of growth of the black economy in the corporate sector certainly came down and possibly became negative. However, it continued to grow in the other sectors of the economy like, the tertiary sector and the unorganized sector, so that overall it had a positive rate of growth in the economy.

In discussions with small businessmen it became clear that their decision to declare profits is based on how much white incomes they need for their business and this had nothing to do with the tax rates. MNCs generally are less involved in evading output but as the ITC case showed, they have been transferring money out of the Indian economy. Further, using transfer-pricing, profits have been siphoned out of the Indian economy. It has now come to light that foreign employees have been paid large dollar salaries abroad and for this profits were siphoned out. The income-tax department has been investigating this.

It is a reflection of the contradictions of our system that we are not thinking of doing the obvious and simple things but attempting complex exercises of dubious merit instead like reducing tax rates. What is really needed is simplification of the tax structure and the removal of redundant laws, controls and regulations. The point is that the merit of each action must be established independently and without resorting to the false arguments that they generally result in the generation of black incomes.

Review of Some Technical Suggestions

Kabra (1982) suggested various administrative measures which the bureaucracy could implement. For instance, nationalized auditing, formation of a 'real estate corporation', or introduction of a 'Central Taxes Pass Book'. He feels that these and other measures are likely 'to improve the anti tax-evasion potential of tax administration . . . weaken the channels for interference by the politicians . . . contribute to building up of the morale of the actual, man-on-the-spot to go ahead with his bounded duties . . . .' (p. 138). What seems unclear here is how by adding a few more powers can an administration, demoralized and collapsing, be made to turn the corner. This is not to suggest that nothing can or should be done.

The attempt clearly is to restructure the market itself, a prerequisite for the success of the above policy. Clearly, most practising liberal economists of the 'remove-controls, reduce-taxation' brand cannot be expected to view with favour the above set of suggestions.

Acquisition of real estate which is being under-valued when sold has been a part of the income-tax laws. This is to deter the circulation of black savings through real estate transactions and to collect the correct amount of tax on capital gains. It also enables the property tax to be correctly estimated and collected. However, this scheme has failed since valuation of a property is difficult and most transactions are managed through bribes.

Another suggestion has been to make cash transactions difficult. This has been attempted by forcing businesses to make payments in cheque. Transactions above a certain amount, say Rs 10,000 have to be in cheque. Banks are supposed to report large deposits and drafts are to be issued from bank accounts, etc. However, none of this has come in the way of black income generation. It has only made the laws more complicated.

In this age of computerization, many have suggested that computers can help curb the growth of the black economy. This eliminates the human element which is supposed to be corrupt and uses discretion to make money. This has also been suggested with respect to taxation—customs, excise and income-tax. In the case of income-taxation, Permanent Account Numbers (PAN) have been allotted and cards issued. The idea is to keep track of transactions in which black incomes may be used.

A computer may automatically match the reporting of transactions so that under-invoicing and over-invoicing may be detected and payments which are not reported may be kept track of. However, for the last twenty years, the scheme has been tried in different phases without success.

In the eighties, PAN were not allotted for years. It was perhaps feared that people may obtain false PAN numbers and split up their incomes and legitimately evade taxes. With the kind of computerization available it was difficult to keep track of the data and coordinate it for checking evasion. A simple change in spelling of name or of the address is enough to fool the computer into believing that these are separate accounts while post will get through since the postman corrects for these errors while delivering the mail.

In the case of banking, there can be no hard and fast rule for giving credit. The human element is critical in judging credit worthiness. It is in allotment of working capital limits and loans that bribes are received for exercising discretion. Certainly, there is no problem in computerizing, savings and current accounts, time deposits, cheque clearance and posting of cheques, and so on.

In another instance, in Delhi, telephone and electricity billing have been computerized. This has not prevented fraud from continuing. Electricity meters can be fixed by the meter reader or lines tapped from the poles and overhead wires by paying off the staff, so that theft of power continues. In fact, in feeding of data, additional problems are created for honest citizens. To get a correction made is far more difficult now. The same is true in the case of telephone department. If the line is tapped from the box and given to someone else, the computer cannot detect it. If the line is not repaired till a bribe is given, there is no remedy. If the new connection is not given till money exchanges hands, it is difficult for the computer to do anything. At best now it is easy to tell that so many complaints were registered or that there was a delay in repairing or installing the phone.

As technology advances more and more computerization is feasible. Like the setting up of automatic teller machines to dispense cash. But here there is no element of discretion. Similarly, it is conceivable that one day the amount of electricity consumed by a consumer is automatically monitored from a central exchange. It may be possible that soon robots will read the meters and repair telephone lines eliminating the need for human intervention.

But the question arises, can society run automatically, say like a colony of ants or bees? Can there be no discretion or trust? Today even the cabinet has not been taken into confidence in some important matters. The recent example of Pokhran blast comes to mind. It was done in such secrecy that even the Defence, the Finance and the Home Ministers knew little about it in advance to enable the country to take a strategic view of the situation. Will the cabinet also be automated? Should not society reassess itself and recreate itself on the basis of trust rather than think of abolishing itself?

Human ingenuity is such that in the absence of consensus over policies and erosion of sense of justice, each law is being circumvented in newer ways. In response, newer laws have been promulgated making them ever more complex, making circumventing them even easier. *The system is based on a lack of trust of the citizen while the individuals running the system themselves cannot be trusted and are collaborating with those they are supposed to keep in check.* This systemic contradiction needs to be resolved to check the growth of the black economy.

In the examples considered in this section, various technical solutions have been considered and each one of them appears to be reasonable on the face of it. Each one of them assumes that there is a functioning bureaucracy. If the instrument which is to implement the laws is itself eroded then where is the possibility of checking illegality?

In this sense, checking the growth of the black economy is not a technical problem but a systemic one. Why is the fence eating the field instead of protecting it? For this, the system has to be reformed. One needs to consider that in the last forty years there have been dozens of committees which have looked at the various aspects of the problem and made hundreds of suggestions for tackling it. Some, like the acquisition of under-valued property, bearer bonds and reduction in controls have been implemented but without producing a dent on the generation of black incomes. The examples considered in this section suggest that black income generation is not linked to either the tax rates or the controls in these activities. Violation of rules is often for reasons other than these two. *In brief, it is not that the black economy has not been checked for lack of technical solutions.*

TOWARDS A REMEDY

It is now evident that the black economy has to be tackled at a different level, than a purely technical one. The growing illegality at the heart of which is the triad of the politician, bureaucrat and businessman, has led to a system being created in which an honest individual belonging to any one of these groups is marginalized. The problem is systemic and its resolution also to be likewise.

The linkages in the triad need to be broken. Since the activity of the politicians and the bureaucracy (including judiciary and the police) is in the public realm, policy can have a stronger effect on them. Once their link is weakened, the businessman or the criminal who controls the triad (or is its members) would find it difficult to sustain illegally.

The function of the politician is to represent the people and carry out their will. The bureaucrat is to work under the direction of the politician to carry out policy and both have to function within the framework of the constitution—the law of the land. The judiciary is to oversee that the law of the land is not violated by anyone; including those in power. There are different requirements to tackle each of these.

Given that the politician and the bureaucrat operate in the public domain, the public is perhaps in the best position to check wrong doing. But why are they not already performing this task? The reason is that democracy in India has been truncated and weakened. Often, the citizens are handicapped by secrecy because they do not know a) what is going on and b) what should happen. The Right to Information would empower them.

Right to Information, Judicial, Bureaucracy and Media Reform

The entire system functions non-transparently so that the citizen has little idea of what is going on whether in the government or in the private sector. Companies manipulate their balance-sheets to hoodwink the investing public and the financial institutions. Many in the government, secure in the knowledge that their wrong doing will not be exposed, commit all manner of wrong. They have created a system in which participants have a vested interest in its continuity. A Mr Khairnar was marginalized since he could not produce documentary evidence to support his charges. Similarly, in the Bofors case, even though several opposition politicians who claimed that they had evidence have been in and out of power, conclusive proof has not come out.

This explains why in spite of growing corruption, no politician or bureaucrat has been prosecuted unlike in some of the advanced nations. The public has become so cynical that it has repeatedly elected leaders who have been known to be involved in corruption or crime but have not yet been prosecuted. Everyone who should know, knows of the police hafta system but no one has been able to stop it so that crime continues to increase. Accountability of those in office is missing. They either hide information on the plea that the system should not be rocked or destroy it.

In the Bofors case, Madhav Singh Solanki, the then Foreign Minister could pass on a note to the Swiss Minister to delay the Bofors case but no one knows till date on whose behest he did it.

Often, the public is denied information so that it is unable to fight for its rights. Budgetary allocations are made for schemes about which the public does not know and, therefore, unable to ask for their implementation so the money either lapses or is diverted to other schemes. This defeats the purpose of having policies or budgets approved by the legislatures.

Public must be given information as a right and not just on the basis of need to know. There are few things that involve national security and these may be kept a secret but this may not constitute more than a tiny fraction of the total number of documents involved. Even most of the papers related to defence need not be kept secret. It is absolute secrecy that has been responsible for the increase in corruption in the armed forces, like in procurement and canteen.

Non-transparency in functioning has permeated into every aspect of governmental functioning. Even in the universities secrecy is practiced when no matter relating to defence is remotely involved. While examination-related activities may be required to be kept a secret for a limited period of time nothing else need be hidden from the public. Non-transparency has become a mindset, emboldening functionaries to believe they will not get exposed.

Bureaucracy in India is a relic of the British rule which needed an instrument of control over the local population and to facilitate the expansion of its industry into India. Service to the people or development were not on its agenda. Its functioning was based on non-transparency and accumulation of powers in its own hands. Accountability was only to the British rulers.

In the post independence period, while the rest of the structure of the bureaucracy has remained unchanged, accountability has got eroded. The bureaucracy does not have one master—though the people should be its masters, in reality, as a partner in the triad, it has become the master.

Decision-making in the public sector is different in the public sector as compared to the private sector. It requires commitment and understanding. Often a decision may seem alright in the macro context but may seem to be bad viewed in a limited context. For instance, if to develop a backward area, an industry has to be set up at a great infrastructural expense, the decision at the micro level is irrational since it could be more profitable near a metropolitan centre with its fully developed infrastructure. What may appear to be rational to upper echelons of the decision-maker may seem to be irrational at the lower levels, and, therefore, may not be properly implemented. Private sector decision-making suffers from no such dilemma since its goal is to maximize profits and not develop infrastructure.

Public sector managers and bureaucrats tend not to take clear decisions since if proved wrong, they would face flak. They try to spread the risk around by not taking decisions and by ensuring that blame cannot be pinpointed. Accountability is the victim.

The elite character of the bureaucracy, a residual from the colonial times, and its incorporation in the triad are responsible for its non-responsiveness to the common man. To change this, its perks and privileges must be reduced substantially. In a national perspective, its status must be brought down to that of the common man and certainly in relation to other more important tasks facing the nation, like, R&D.

Today the world has become so complex that it is not easy for a generalist to understand the technicalities and decide on the correct course of action. To deal with this complexity, the practice of appointing generalists for important jobs must end. Policy-making powers must be with committees consisting of specialists. Further, there is a need to promote institutional functioning with wide delegation of responsibilities.

Rules should be simple and clear so that decisions can be taken at the lowest level of interface of the bureaucracy and the public. The practice of files going up and down should end since it is both time-consuming and wastes resources. Simultaneously, since responsibility can be more easily fixed in a decentralized system, there must be swift action against those indulging in corruption or harassment. This will restore the credibility of the bureaucracy and eliminate middlemen.

The Right to Information will impact the bureaucracy immediately since they would not commit themselves on paper to a wrong action or allow others to make them the fall guy. The triad would have a chance of getting snapped.

The judicial system needs urgent reform. Judicial delays have to be tackled urgently. Incidents, like Mr L M Thapar getting bail at midnight from the residence of a Supreme Court judge while undertrials languish far longer than any punishment they could get should end.

With the growth of litigation in courts the judges are really hard pressed since they are required to go through a number of cases in a limited time.

The judicial process needs to be simplified and the number of stages through which a case goes should be reduced. The timetable for the hearing of the case should be set up in advance and given to the parties involved when the case is admitted to a court. Adjournment in cases should be allowed in the rarest of instances and not as a matter of routine. Litigants need to know the judicial process better. Today, they may not even know that it takes time for an order to be implemented so that getting a favourable order is not enough.

For certain small cases, there should be summary trial with no more than one sitting and the litigants allowed to argue their own case. Courts should produce booklets giving the details of how to fight different kinds of cases. Trust should be promoted. For instance, documents may be self-authenticated. Deception in court should be heavily penalized. For instance, if a cheque issued to court or on instruction of the court bounces, there should be swift action.

Lawyers also need to introspect. They may delay matters to benefit their clients and themselves. The court should penalize such lawyers. Some keep the client in the dark about various things. An agreement should be required to be signed between the lawyer and the client and it should be presented to the judge hearing the case at the start of the case. The record about a lawyer should be available with the bar council and made available to the clients. This should give the number of cases dealt with, their outcome and the number of cases pending. Lawyers' charges for cases should be made known in the public domain and certain norms for charges should be fixed by the Bar Council.

The judges need to keep a distance from vested interests like the corporate world, lawyers and politicians. This is easier said than done but must be a part of the self-discipline of judiciary. There has to be some form of social recognition for those judges who observe such a code of conduct. Judges should be appointed to places other than where they practiced as lawyers.

The police needs drastic reform. But who is to police the police. Their link with criminals will get weakened if the political authority and the public get activated. Since the political system itself is weak, it is public pressure that has to be brought to bear on them.

The public should have the right to have its complaint registered. Any complaint of non-registration of a case should be sufficient ground for punishment of the officer involved. Recording of false cases should also be severely dealt with. The record of each thana—cases registered and solved—should be put up in each thana and performance should be rewarded (increments and facilities for the personnel of that thana). Action against the corrupt should be well-publicized.

To tackle the 'Over 55 syndrome' retiring personnel should be prohibited from taking up any employment for at least five years after retirement. Simultaneously, the retirement age of government personnel may be raised to 62 years so as to utilize the services of senior employees a little longer.

The role of the judiciary should be strictly in the implementation of the law of the land, as it exists—good or bad. The role of the bureaucracy is implementation of policies as formulated by the legislature. It is necessary to maintain these boundaries, however blurred they get at times. Maintaining such distinction in functioning provides a system of checks and balances. It should be classified that in this section a mere outline of reform is presented and it is not a complete package. No one aspect of the outline will achieve success and the entire package consisting of adequate checks and balances will be required to be implemented. In other words, a systemic change is needed.

Media is important both for the Right to Information and the checks and balances on those in power. It can play a significant role in building public opinion. However, media has increasingly been coopted by the vested interests. It either represents the interest of the top 3% in the incomes ladder or has resorted to yellow journalism.

The complaint from the politicians that they are paying media by the column centimetre during elections and giving individual journalists money suggests the extent of spread of yellow journalism and blackmail. The number of national newspapers in which the business owner has directly interfered with the newspaper and in which editors are marginalized has gone up. One newspaper started a 'Human Rights' column after a member of its owner's family got implicated in a serious offence.

The association of media persons with those in power is a major factor in their cooption. They become a part of the day to day politics with stories being fed to create a climate. Competitive journalism with its dependence on scoops requires journalists to have working relationship with those in power. Trust between the journalists and those in power is the basis of a nexus between them and soon this turns into cooption.

For individual journalists, cooption enables them to get work done for family and friends. Telephones, railway reservations, appointments at government hospitals, gas, work with the police, and the like, become possible due to the contacts developed. The network expands as time passes since those helped become a part of the network. In some cases, this process may begin by helping genuine cases of those in distress but it soon develops into some thing else.

In brief, media needs autonomy both from the government and the commercial interest of the promoters. Autonomy must be built into every stage of the media—of the newspaper and the TV channel from their owners and the government. For this, the role of the editor is critical but unfortunately, this is a dying institution. Journalists too must be able to exercise independence from their editors. Accountability to society can come only from autonomy of the individuals and the institutions. The Press Council and Prasar Bharti should be statutory bodies with powers to prosecute those in the media and those outside who infringe the autonomy. Since this depends on public awareness and pressure, ultimately the problem again is one of raising public consciousness.

There is a lack of professionalism in the media (as also in other professions). This is a result of a culture of scoops and quick responses as well as dependence on some favoured sources for these scoops and shortage of resources with the media. A journalist may cover a political story one day and the next day write on an economic aspect and a third day cover a civil rights violation. There may be inadequate preparation for what is written and this results in shoddy work in an increasingly complex world. All this brings into question the professionalism in the media.

Reform for Business Incomes: Problems from the Alternative Budget

As already discussed, today the tax laws are far too complex to be implemented meaningfully. No income-tax officer can have the time to properly scrutinize the return submitted by even a small businessman or a professional. Taking advantage of this, those who wish to evade income-tax submit incorrect returns and then bribe the officer to have them accepted.

The remedy for this lies in a simplification of the tax laws to the point that it is easy to catch those who are fudging accounts. For this, three steps are required. First, all manner of deductions that are today available have to be removed from the statute books. Secondly, all income should be treated on par rather than allow special treatment to some incomes. Tax must be levied on income from agriculture, from holding shares, etc. Thirdly, there should not be special treatment to capital gains or savings like provident funds.

The argument is often made that this third suggestion would be a disincentive to save. This is not true. The tax concessions are found only to change the form in which savings are held. People save for the future for a wide variety of reasons, like for a house, for old age, children's education, for expanding businesses, for illness and other contingencies. Only the form in which they hold their savings changes with tax concessions. Government is also forced to give tax concessions to attract funds for its own use (called 'small savings') but this would not be required if the black economy is checked and taxes collected.

Simplification would also allow a meaningful computerization of the tax payees data. Today, there are a vast number of parameters that need to be checked even for a small businessman or a professional and this becomes impossible with the resources available. Not that computerization solves the problem but it can be a useful tool if the system changes.

Today, businessmen pay tax on their net business income. As already argued, they inflate costs to generate black incomes. Since costs are manipulated, tax should be on gross rather than net profits. Of course, the rate of tax could be adjusted to allow for some normal level of costs. The only costs which may be allowed to be netted to define gross profits should be wage and salary income (excluding managerial salaries which are like a profit sharing arrangement), purchase of inputs (like, raw material and energy), depreciation and interest payments. Since taxes are deducted at source (TDS) out of wage and salary incomes, this would be known; there would be a counter-check on this component. Inputs are purchased in bulk so that there would be a small number of such transactions which could be effectively computerized. Depreciation is well defined in tax laws so it cannot be fudged beyond a point and interest payment would be someone else's income so it would be easy to check.

All other expenses of business should be incurred out of incomes on which taxes are paid. It would be the prerogative of the management how the income would be spent—on travel, entertainment, and so on. Today, the incentive to save on costs is low since a part of it is paid out of taxes not paid. Paradoxically though companies would be free to spend, they would save on these costs to raise their profitability and become more competitive than those companies which do not save on costs. So, apart from simplification and possibilities of computerization, there would be greater competition amongst companies and reduction of waste would also follow.

As far as the public sector is concerned, they should have day-to-day autonomy in functioning. Interference from the bureaucracy and the politician should be eliminated. Accountability should be to the parliament. At the time they are set up, there should be a well-stated purpose which should be mandated by the legislature and the PSUs should be judged by those criteria. The top management team and the board of directors should be given a clear mandate and tenure and not be subjected to threats of dismissed and transfers.

The PSUs should have normal accounting practices where all costs are shown clearly and if subsidies are required to be given they should be reflected in the balance-sheet and be compensated for by the government. For instance, if PSUs are asked to supply goods cheap, the budget should compensate them for it. If some expensive technology or equipment from specific sources is to be purchased because of strategic reasons, the budget should reflect this as a grant. These steps would enable the profitability of the public sector to be correctly reflected. The performance of the management should be judged using this as a yardstick.

Accounts of companies, public or private, should be transparent. The board of directors of companies should include independent directors representing the public interest, not only of the fragmented public holding but also of society at large. The board of directors should not be merely ceremonial positions but should be accountable to the public and be held liable if fraud is detected in a company. The board of directors should be a check on the owners and the managers of the companies. A public limited company is not only built on the capital of individuals but represents the stake of society.

Society's interest needs to be safeguarded by checking malpractice and black income generation. The financial institutions which grant companies loans and working capital should have their nominees on the board of directors. They should be independent people—unrelated to the business group, government or politicians. Further, no one should be nominated to more than one board. Auditors of companies found to be indulging in malpractices should be made liable to the share holders.

To check the black investments in real estate, apart from the steps discussed earlier, wealth and property taxes should be levied on all property. A simplification should be achieved by eliminating deductions. Valuation of wealth should be based on the current market value. Say, in the case of real estate, valuation for property tax could be based on the location of the property and the amount of built-up area allowed on it (FSI). An average cost of construction could be used and the current market value of the land in a zone could be applied to arrive at a figure of the value. This mechanical formula would fix the value of all property in a zone and leave little to discretion.

This valuation would be independent of the amount of construction on a piece of land and the kind of materials used in it. It would also not be based on the historical value of the land so that neighbouring properties would be charged the same tax and not depend on when the construction took place. This would reflect the true value of the services provided to a plot of land. It would also reduce speculation in real estate and bring down the prices of land to realistic levels.

As all property gets taxed (whether through wealth or property tax or both) benami property would come into the tax net. To pay the tax, an income would have to be shown so that black incomes whose savings flow into real estate would be revealed to tax authorities. *This can be called interlocking of taxes.* Since property cannot be hidden, a tax would have to be paid. This would force individuals to reveal their black incomes and also force more property to come on to the market.

Interlocking of direct taxes, their simplification and computerization would make their collection grow rapidly. Through this package the number of those paying these taxes could be raised from the present 14 million to about 50 million. Twenty-eight million would be organized sector employees and the balance would be businesses and the self-employed. The additional direct taxes collected from these people would help lower the rates of indirect taxes or to completely eliminate them on essential goods so that the inflationary potential of the economy would decline. The details of such a package and the benefits from it are provided in the Alternative Budget (See Kumar, 1994). This package would not only curb the growth of the black economy but rectify the macroeconomic problems of the Indian economy. However, this requires political will.

Economic offenses should be treated on par with criminal ones like dacoity and robbery. They represent a different kind of breaking in and when detected also lead to physical attacks. For instance, witnesses are threatened or eliminated. Owners/ managers committing fraud should be held personally liable and should not be allowed use of company's resources to defend themselves in courts. Their personal wealth should be attached to clear their obligation to the company.

In brief, to tackle black income generation by businessmen, laws should be simplified and discretion be minimized to make implementation feasible even by an incompetent administration. Direct taxes need reform in this direction and they should be interlocked so that a cross-check is possible. Companies should be under public scrutiny, their accounts more transparent and their board of directors accountable. There should be at least one independent-minded person on the board of directors of each company. Auditors should be held liable to the shareholders if fraud is detected. Laws should be strictly enforced. If businessmen find laws cannot be subverted, they would not be able to generate extra profits; they would have nothing to share with others and the triad would tend to fade away.

Reform of the Political System

The third arm of the triad propelling the black economy is the politician. In some ways this segment is the most critical one since politicians are assigned the task of controlling the entire system. In a democracy, the system is supposed to be what people want and the politician as the representative of the people is supposed to implement their will. When the politician joins the triad and works for the vested interests, she/he subverts the will of the people.

The NEP are changing the politics of the country. The coalition of the ruling groups in India unable to resolve its internal contradictions has been forced to undergo a change with the inclusion of international capital as the dominant partner. Certain sections of the former ruling elite—the rural elite, small business and the middle class have been marginalized. Politics has turned even more undemocratic than it was and poses a deeper challenge to the system than before—conflict can only grow.

Can it be said that democracy is on the wane in India? It needs to be remembered that democracy is built gradually through a process in which sometimes it is strengthened and at other times weakened. Currently, two contradictory trends are visible. One of growing democratic consciousness amongst the citizens. Whereas earlier they believed they had no choice who their leader should be and voted for whosoever the village leaders decided in favour of, today that has changed. Those in power are repeatedly being defeated in National and Assembly elections due to their non-performance. Citizens feel empowered to change them because they are not satisfied.

However, simultaneously, there is the other trend of decline of institutions and of growing cynicism amongst the people because they do not have a *real* choice. The leaders they have thrown up have been coopted into the power structure by the vested interests, weakening democracy and leading to a growing black economy. Strengthening democracy is then essential for the political process and for curbing the black economy.

The link between the politician and money power needs to be broken. As discussed in the appendix on election expenses of politicians, elections involve all manner of malpractice and the' building of links between those in politics and the vested interests. Often there is no distinction between the two with vested interests putting up their own candidates. It is suggested that election funding needs to be changed so that those not linked to money power can also win elections.

State Funding of Elections: No Solution

The influence of black money in public life has received attention from time to time. To reduce the influence of money on politics, two things are suggested. First, state funding of elections, and secondly, openly allowing the private sector to contribute to party coffers. It has been argued that these steps have made a difference in other countries.

The logic of the proposal is that a) large sums of money are needed to fight elections, b) by not allowing parties to legally get these funds, they are forced to get them illegally and c) this forces them to compromise with vested interests.

To break these links, it is argued that the present illegality be legalized. Election expenditure limits be raised and those desirous of giving money, especially the private corporate sector, be allowed to do so. It is argued that bringing these links into the open would reduce the influence of money in politics. State funding of elections would reduce the dependence on vested interests for money and enable parties to represent the interest of the people, thereby strengthening democracy.

There are a number of questionable links in the above argument. First, the present set of political parties are keen to represent the people but are prevented from doing so by lack of enough money. Secondly, these parties are interested in eliminating the influence of money (and more specifically of black money) on politics. Thirdly, money is needed by political parties only for fighting elections. Each of these arguments need to be assessed.

State funding of elections will not eliminate the need for money, black or white, to run Indian politics in its present form. In the interviews with politicians it became clear that they need funds every day and not just when elections come. For this they depend on the vested interests and will continue to do so even if elections are funded. During elections, since state funding cannot match the needs of the political parties, extra funds would continue to come from the vested interests.

Today, the official limits on election expenditures are so low that even if state funding is up to the full limit, it would hardly meet 20% of the expenditures of a major candidate. Even if the limits are raised, it is unlikely that in a poor country, they would be raised to the level of the present actual spending. Political parties will continue to supplement funds through other means. How will expenses on booth-capturing, employing muscle men, setting up alternative candidates, maintaining vote banks, bribing the voters, etc., be shown legitimately? (See Table V.11, V.12 on election expenditures.)

Having said that, it is true that some genuinely popular candidates who have a base in their constituencies will benefit from state funding of elections. They may be able to shake off their tenuous links with vested interests. But even among these as shown by the interviews with MPs large sums of money are spent to match the opposition and accepted illegal funds. One of the MPs in the sample who had been winning from his constituency and held important ministerial berths lost in spite of the base since the politics of the constituency changed. To retain his base he would have had to make compromises with the vested interests. This system will not change with state funding even if a few benefit.

Some of the politicians interviewed did state that money alone was not the determining factor in their victory. A wave, a tie- up, propping up of weak candidates, dividing votes by putting up candidates are critical for victory. Some of these need money. The vested interests use these tactics to prevent honest people (and opponents) from winning elections because they would be a threat to their activities. They do not want the politicians to represent the interest of the people since they perceive that to be against their own interest

One may ask, how do discredited people or criminals or those with criminal records get elected? This represents the public's disenchantment with the false promises of the non-criminal politician. The unscrupulous element is like a Robin Hood and makes a show of delivery. She/he can promise what an honest politician will not. While the latter will talk of the national issues the former will talk of the local issues and even of bending the discredited law. She/he would enable encroachment of land. Would get a road made even if it gets washed away, would get a health centre sanctioned even if the money is misappropriated, etc. The public consciousness about all this has to change and given the cynicism, this will take time.

As far as the question of company donations are concerned, which political party in India would like to be seen to be legally taking large sums of money from the private corporate sector? They know that the walls will be plastered with slogans that they are the agents of the vested interests and this matters in a country where 70% of the population is poor. Political parties want to hide this fact under all circumstances and that is why they do not openly take such money. Clearly, a change in the law will make little difference.

It is also suggested that party accounts must be audited, to prevent the use of illegitimate money. This is a good idea but when annual audits do not deter even small businesses from making black incomes, how would it stop political parties in their illegality.

Would some genuinely representative parties come up because of state funding? They could get a core funding for their election needs. In other words, could this be the thin edge of the wedge which could change the nature of Indian politics? The experience of the left vitiates against any optimism on this account. Using far less black money than other parties and having cadres to campaign they have not managed to grow or alter the nature of Indian politics dramatically as portrayed by proponents of state funding. Clearly, the power of the monied and their ideology are far stronger.

Further, state funding is likely to be limited to the main parties and this would preclude the new or the small parties which may be more representative. These parties would have to grow on their own steam to reach a minimum critical size. If they are genuinely democratic, they could continue growing with limited resources by adopting the pattern of financing that helped them reach the critical size and would not need state financing.

The former Chief Election Commissioner attempted some reform of elections but as one of the politicians interviewed said, he succeeded in driving expenses underground. Election meetings and posters are visible but constitute a small part of the total expense on elections.

The critical reform required is to make politics more democratic. Parties and the people's representatives have to be under public scrutiny. It is the public which alone can act as a check on money power. State funding can then help maintain such a system. It cannot by itself bring forth democratic functioning to loosen the hold of the vested interests who have a stake in perpetuating the present system.

What needs to be understood is that *it is not genuine politics which needs huge illegal (black) funds but it is that the vested interests want to control politics* so that they can form the triad to make extra-economic gains. *The causation is from black economy to unrepresentative politics.* What is needed is electoral reform which makes Indian politics more democratic and representative.

Electoral Reform: Make the Voter King

There is a cynical view that a government should do its own thing, independent of electoral promises—people are supposed to be illiterate and manipulable. Many argue that all the tough economic decisions called 'non-populist' (read, pro-rich) can only be taken in the first two years after a national election since after that the party in power has to look after the electoral politics and indulge in 'populism'.

This elitist view ascribes wisdom to a select few and legitimizes cynical manipulation. This clearly undemocratic view does not take into account that it a) weakens democracy in the long run and even undercuts their interest and b) opens the doors for manipulation by those who may care little for the country like foreign powers or criminals.

For a vast and heterogeneous country, survival requires a vibrant democracy where the will of the people rules—'populism' or not. This is the only way people's faith in the country and its system can be kept up. The task of the political parties and *genuine* leaders is to educate the public about the real issues and get them to accept even tough decisions which require sacrifice. While most citizens are used to sacrificing, it is the elite who would not agree since it expects the system to deliver to them a higher and higher standard of living by whatever means.

Today's ruling ideology of 'efficiency and optimality' is based on the principle of consumer sovereignty. That is, the individual knows best. 'Efficiency' is supposed to follow by enabling that to happen which the 'king' consumer wants (and not by fooling him). In the market, if individuals want Coca-cola, Wrangler jeans and Macdonald hamburger, that is what they must get for the sake of 'efficiency'.

Those in favour of consumer sovereignty and allowing the consumer a free choice are the ones arguing for denying her/him this right on the most important issue of all—the choice of the system she/he wants. On the issue of democracy, those suggesting sovereignty of the individual in the market place argue that it is not such a good idea because the citizen is illiterate. Some of them even suggest that voting rights be limited to the elite.

It is clear that by making campaign promises to obtain votes and then not delivering on them when in power, consumer sovereignty is violated and efficiency sacrificed. According to the theory of 'efficiency' the rulers or the government are not supposed to have their own preference and even if they do, these should not be superimposed on the desires of the people as expressed in the outcome of the vote. They should only represent the electoral outcome for achieving efficiency, otherwise, the market for policy fails and inefficiency follows. The elite in control of the system contradict themselves when they argue for choice in the market for goods but deny a choice in the market for votes. Since the latter is far more important than the former, there is inefficiency overall.

The failure in the market for votes needs to be rectified. The rulers must be made accountable to the voters. This requires two things. First, the representatives must be made to deliver on their promises. This is possible if the gap between the elections is reduced so that there is no time to play with the promises to the citizens. With a smaller gap between elections, the rulers would face the scrutiny of the voters more often. Secondly, citizens should have a genuine choice and not between Tweedle-dee and Tweedle-dum.

The voter's choice can be enlarged by enabling her/him to either vote 'none of the above', that is, no one in a panel deserves her/his vote, or to give a 'negative vote', implying a strong negative preference for someone. One may have a strong preference against a criminal getting elected no matter who else gets elected. Or, one may wish to penalize someone who promised but did not deliver. The first choice, 'none of the above', would signal to the parties that they need to be more responsive to the public.

These options, by enlarging the voter's choices are likely to increase the voting percentage. Today, because of a lack of a choice, many have stopped voting altogether and in spite of booth capturing and such malpractices the voting percentage has dipped. Parties would be forced to a) put up candidates with a clean image and b) deliver on electoral promises. Perhaps sensitivity to the negative image associated with electoral malpractice like booth capturing, will also reduce these activities.

Elections could be held every two and a half years. If the increased cost is a consideration, half the legistalture can come up for reelection every two and a half years with the new legislative party electing a leader (new or old) every two and half years. Many modifications on this theme are possible.

An extra two thousand crores of rupees every other year on elections is only 0.07% of the GDP while the gains of a genuine democracy based on accountability built into the system will be immeasurable. Indians may actually begin to lead a civilized life. This will repay the cost many times over. The need of the hour is to restore sovereignty to the voters.

Other Suggestions for Electoral Reform

Democracy is linked to representation and to empowering people. Since representation is based on electing candidates belonging to parties, two things are necessary. First, representatives should have primary responsibility to the people electing them and not necessarily to the party leadership as it has become today. Secondly, parties must reflect what people want and not some hidden agenda of the leaders (who may be in league with the vested interests). No doubt, this is easier said than done.

The first step should be to promote inner party democracy. Leadership at every level should be elected. Today, it is often imposed from the above and manipulated by the vested interests. Many of the present and former leaders had no grassroots experience and came to positions of power simply due to their family connections. It is a structural feature of our politics which can be rectified. If the parties are not democratically structured, they cannot suddenly become democratic when in power. Even if a party has a highly elitist agenda there is nothing wrong with it. But to get to power let it convince the people of its programme and get to power.

The objection cannot be to someone representing people, whether from a well-established family or not (like, Pandit Nehru) but it is to someone who has little idea of what the people want and has no touch with them. Leadership in the parties should be elected from one tier to the next. From the village panchayat or the municipal ward to the district level to the State level and then to the national level. They should simultaneously be members of these bodies and participate in their activities and not be absentee leaders as happens today.

Similar to the party structure, there should be three tier and interlinked representation in the legislatures. One should not be allowed to fight a higher level election unless one has represented the lower level for at least one full term of that body.

For instance, there may be a local legislature, a state legislature and a national legislature. If there is one local representative for every 200 people, there would be a total of 5 million local representatives. From amongst these and those who have completed a term in the past, 5000 should be elected by the people to the state legislatures. Similarly, 500 out of the above pool should be elected to the National Parliament. Thus, each person getting elected would have had exposure to the problems of the people and unless in touch with them in a continuous way would not get elected.

There can never be a guarantee that manipulation will not occur. Yet, putting in place information that the voter can use to exercise choice is useful in a democracy. The voter should have information on the candidates and the parties they belong to. The parties themselves put out information about themselves and the candidates but that is partisan. There is a need for an independent agency to monitor the voting in the legislature and compare the performance of the parties and the representatives with the promises made in the preceding election. Such information should be made available to the citizens.

The independent agency which can perform this task may be the election commission or the legislature itself. Such a step may force parties and representatives to act more responsibly and not make wild promises to the electorate. The parties would be forced to do more homework on what they promise. The election commission should get a detailed profile of each of the candidates and circulate its salient features to all the voters so that they can make an informed choice.

Each representative and recognized party should have a secretariat for analysis of the issues on which it would take positions and make promises. Today, all this is rather ad hoc. The state should fund these secretariats upto a well defined limit. To make democracy function, it is necessary that our parties and representatives be well informed; the extra cost incurred would be worth it. It is conceivable that some parties and representatives would misuse the funds so provided. However, such entities would suffer in the long run and lose out to those who are better organized about the issues and deliver on promises. The steps suggested here would enable better representation of the people, a prerequisite to checking the growing black economy.

REMEDY: GENERAL CONSIDERATIONS

The preceding sections have argued that the system needs to be reformed so as to release it from the stranglehold of vested interests and to make it responsive to the public. To achieve order out of a situation where disorder has been growing is always difficult. One may consider the example of entropy in thermodynamics. Increase in entropy represents growing disorder and as work is done, disorder increases. When it is done most efficiently, disorder increases the least (it increases nonetheless).

When one digs holes to fill them, as with the black economy, entropy increases without any useful work being done, even leasing does not take place.

Further, when gas is allowed to expand from a small space where it was confined to a larger volume in which a vacuum was maintained, there is an increase in disorder. Each gas molecule will criss-cross the vessel and go back to the original small space from where it started but will the entire gas go back to its original corner from where it started? There is a probability that this may occur but this chance is so small that it will not happen in any foreseeable future. In effect, *while there may be micro-reversibility, there is seldom macro-reversibility.*

In brief, going from order to disorder is often easy but the converse is not true. The same is true of society. Building institutions is not easy but destroying them is. Once institutions decline, there is a history that gets embedded in them and makes a reversal difficult. The black economy which has led to the decline of institutions, erosion of the work-ethic, build-up of cynicism amongst the people, has caused disorder and entropy to increase and reversing it is going to be difficult.

In modern day societies, governments have created many institutions but in India many of them are hardly performing their designated tasks. Some in these institutions and in society continue to do their own work irrespective of what happens to the government so that society continues to function. However, good governance enhances the impact and effectiveness of what these people do. Their work carries a greater meaning when situated in a societal framework.

Individual scientists or sportsmen may be very good but they are not able to achieve their potential since the system is run down. Indian scientists are supposed to perform well abroad but on their return to India they get normalized to what exists here. Due to the system, in sports, India has always remained an also ran in the Olympics while countries smaller than Delhi have been able to win gold medals. Systems are critical for nurturing talent but with a rampant black economy and that which should happen not happening performance hardly counted.

To change the situation citizens need to be convinced that there is social justice; that things will happen as they should and the elite will not act lawlessly. The black economy has to be wound up so that the rule of law can prevail not only in letter but also in spirit.

No set of rules and laws can ever be complete or foolproof. With the growth of the black economy and the associated illegality, laws have become more and more complex and thereby problematic. For instance, to prevent cynical defection by legislators for narrow gains, an anti-defection Bill was promulgated but it has made little impact on defections and the decline in Indian politics.

If anything, as shown by the JMM case, buying and selling of representatives has scaled new heights. Worse, parties themselves have lost meaning since they now have no ideology. They are breaking up and realigning with each other purely for the sake of power and without any considerations of ideology. In this sense, everyone has become a defector. In effect, rules and laws can work only in an environment of trust with the unwritten rule that the spirit of the law will be followed.

In India with the gradual breakdown of trust due to the lawlessness and the growing black economy, on occasions leading to widespread policy failure, India is seen to be a Banana Republic by foreign powers.

India is not seen to be a state implementing its national will. The legally elected government has become one aspect of the Indian state since it coexists along with several other powerful entities—the mafia consisting of smugglers and drug lords, some big industrialists and foreign powers—which are able to carry out their designs. They use money or threat to have their orders implemented—a consequence of the black economy and the growth of criminalization in society.

This is not to argue that the legally elected government is distinct from these other structures and acting purely in the national interest. As already argued, the politicians and the bureaucrats are a part of the triad which is often controlled by criminals or other vested interests. Thus, even the legally constituted part of the state may function as a mafia carrying out its own agenda. Further, it enables the other entities to get a grip over the Indian state and carry on their agenda. The consequence is that the gap between what is declared and what is achieved is wide.

The attitude of the Indian elite is clearly illustrated by its attitude towards the Foreign Exchange Management Act (FEMA) and the proposed Money Laundering Bill. FEMA is to replace the FERA in the changed circumstances when the country is moving towards easing of controls on the flow of foreign exchange. Businesses have objected to stringent provisions against the usual manipulations they indulge in.

As the economy opens up, businessmen's illegality becomes harder to catch. International transactions are hard to trace as the Bofors case proves. There are people in the international arena who specialize in laundering money. They have hundreds of companies in tax havens and they transfer money from one to the other and then close them so that they cannot be traced and the money disappears. Thus, if the Money Laundering Bill has to have any meaning, it has to be stringent.

It is well-known that criminals are laundering their money to capture legitimate businesses and control/enter politics. Yet, all the business associations have opposed the stringent provisions of the Bill. Clearly, they are worried about what the impact on them could be. What is remarkable is that they are not willing to forego their little illegality so that the larger threat to the economy may be dealt with stringently. To ask for leniency in dealing with such a major threat once again illustrates that national capital thinks in the short run and takes a sectarian view of the situation—a national perspective is missing.

The absence of a national perspective amongst the elite, the existence of several layers of structures in the Indian state and the denting of trust within the cabinet has affected governance. Because of various factors delegation of responsibilty has ceased, resulting in centralization of power in the Prime Minister's Office.

The black economy which has undermined trust in society and eroded institutions has created a no-win situation for the citizens. Trust is an essential ingredient of social functioning since not everything can be spelt out in advance. With trust, even when things begin to go wrong, they get rectified. In its absence, they go further wrong since everyone takes advantage of the mistakes. No one is committed to rectification. In effect, *with trust, systems are self-correcting while in its absence, they become unstable.* One may say, for social actions to be simple and efficient, trust is necessary.

When trust prevails, laws can be simple and greater transparency is feasible which in turn enables laws to remain simple. If laws remain unimplemented they lose meaning. While complex laws are hard to implement, simple ones have a chance of success. This reinforces the rule of law and rebuild a lost trust. If laws are voluntarily obeyed, society benefits in many ways. With voluntarism, expenditure on maintaining deterrence decreases.

As social structures become simple, unproductive and parasitical activities give way to productive ones. Reduction in costs and greater efficiency follow. Society becomes more dynamic. With trust, a lot can be left to the judgment of people. This is not an issue of being pro or anti-state. Trust requires consensus over policies.

One complicating factor in all this is that the present society is undergoing rapid change. This coupled with alienation from society has caused a narrowing of horizons at all levels. Individuals are concerned more with the immediate and with self and less with society. Those who place their own interest above that of society are seen to be more successful so that there is the social selection of those who ignore the long term social interest. This needs to be rectified.

In these circumstances, is it futile to talk of the long run? Actually not, since with rapid change as systems become more unstable, the need for defining parameters within which society functions becomes greater and trust is one such parameter. It is not change which has led to loss of trust in society. As already argued, that is systemic and needs to be dealt with at that level. So, rapid change and mutual trust can co-exist and the latter can help the situation to remain stable hence enable change to take place. It is alienation which has led to individualism and needs to be dealt with. But this is again structural and trust works to reduce it.

Accountability of institutions and individuals and specially of the policy-makers would be an important step in restoring trust in society. Promises made need to be fulfilled or they should not be made. Words, deeds and things would have the meaning they are supposed to have. For instance, honesty cannot be redefined as not taking money personally but allowing the system to work as it is with corruption flourishing (as in the case of honest police officers who tolerate the hafta amongst their juniors). Instances like an honest finance minister in 1991 allocating Rs 100 crore to a private trust and giving Rs 450 crore of tax concession to benefit a big business house have to be seen to be what they are.

CONCLUSION

The system has become decrepit but the country does not lack well-intentioned people. As argued earlier, those *substantially* involved in the black economy are no more than 3% of the population. In other words, 97% are either not involved or marginally involved. The numbers of those who aspire to make illegal incomes may be substantially larger but they are at its fringe and if shown a way may never get involved in it. In essence, the vast majority of the people are honest or can give up their expectations of involvement in illegality. Hence countering the black economy is feasible.

What has been suggested in this chapter is to be seen as a package but none of it will happen by itself or because of someone's good intentions. Electoral reform will not take place since the vested interests would not allow it. Movements which change the consciousness of people and make them strong enough to resist the temptations are needed for a turn around. The hands of the vested interests would have to be forced before they give up.

In Bali, Ravana never dies, the struggle between good and evil continues. The players who enact the Ramayana wear a costume with black and white checks on it to symbolize the coexistence of the two tendencies in society. Movements by changing consciousness strengthen the positive. The nation is witnessing various small and localized movements all over but they do not yet add up to a decisive factor. They would have to aggregate to form a bigger one around a common theme, namely, the subversion of the popular will.

Social sciences cannot prove anything conclusively—they provide a guide to action. This book also does not prove things conclusively as in a theorem. It provides a framework to understand things as they are with the legal and the illegal coexisting. It shows that the black economy generates activity but it is akin to digging holes and filling them. It results in policy failure and destroys the vision of society by discrediting social action.

A lot has been left out, like black incomes generated in the film world, through lotteries, in transportation and restaurants, in jails, etc. What is left out is in essence similar to that which is presented. Conclusions have been drawn about the system (including the illegal) based on the idea that the systemic aspect presented here covers all that is essential. It has been pointed out that the critical problems before the country relate to the black economy (which represents illegality). While there is much that is good in the country, the elite which controls the systems has subverted them for their own narrow ends through the creation of the black economy. Interestingly, the elite is hurting its own long-term interest because the economy has become parasitical with the growth of unproductive activities. Many are busy digging holes and filling them.

It has been argued that there are no purely economic or technical solutions since the problem is all-encompassing. Given the shortcoming of methodology in social sciences, one needs judgments to work out solutions. Hopefully this book will help build a judgment to work out the solutions to the vast problems faced by India because in a critical way they are linked to the black economy.

The vision of India has to be a long run one in which the short run is integrated. It has to be all-inclusive and not sectarian. It has to be innovative and based on India's needs. The elite has to stop copying from other successful nations and give indigenous ideas a chance. The problems India faces are mostly the creation of the elite even though they portray a contrary picture. The black economy has discredited social action and reduced society's capacity to solve its problems. The nation is buffeted by a sequence of events and not governed by any well laid-out plan. Even if the black economy exists all over the world, given its repercussions that cannot be an excuse to tolerate it here. The attempt to contain/eliminate the black economy would be a fight to re-establish the rule of law and for enabling the citizens to live in dignity. In brief, it would be a fight to build a dynamic and civilized society.

Appendices

1.1 Important Corruption Cases in India Since the Mid-fifties

CASE NAME	YR OF DISCOVERY	APPROX. AMT	DESCRIPTION /PERSON IDENTIFIED
Mundra Scandal	1957	Rs 3 cr	LIC case
Kairon Case	1964		
Nagarwala Case	1971	Rs 60lakh	Indira Gandhi's name came up.
Tulmohan Rao Case	1974		
Antulay Case	1982		Cement Scandal
Churhat Lotteries	1982	Rs 5.4 cr	Arjun Singh accused.
Westland Helicopter			Obsolete helicopters purchase.
Fairfax case	1987		V P Singh sought to be fixed.
HDW Submarine deal	1987	Rs 10 cr	Rajiv Gandhi mentioned
Bofors Gun Deal	1987	Rs 65 cr	Rajiv Gandhi mentioned
Chez Pistol Deal	1987	Rs 10 cr	Arun Nehru mentioned
Kuo Oil Deal	1988	Rs 9-12 cr	Lalit Suri accused.
Rice Export	1987?	Rs 6 cr	Bacchan Brothers accused.
Zorawar Vanaspati	1989		Buta Singh Family accused.
Fodder Machines Case	1989		Balram Jhakhar accused.
Airbus Deal	1991	Rs 200 cr	Alleged kickback
Securities Scam	1992	Rs 132 cr	Money diverted from Oil India Development board to Syndicate Bank. Shankaranand accused
Securities Scam	1992	Rs 3,000 cr	Jankiraman Committee Estimate
ABB loco Deal	1993	$190 mill.	Ignored lower bid by BHEL.
Sugar Scam	1994	Rs 1,200 cr	
MS Shoes	1994	Rs 700 cr	Public Issue of shares and manipulation suspected.
Jain Havala Case	1995	Rs 65 cr	
Telecomm Scam	1995	Rs 3 cr	Sukhram and Ms Ghosh accused.

Reliance Case	1995		Duplicate 26500 shares by Reliance.
CJ A M Bhattacharjee	1995	$80,000	Accused for collecting money for Publication rights
abUrea Import	1995	Rs 133 cr	Rao's son and Turkish firm Karsan accused.
JMM Bribery case	1996	Rs 3.5 cr	Bribe to get Parliamentary votes. Congress
Bihar Fodder Scam	1996	Rs 1,200 cr	From the Eighties. Laloo Yadav, Jagannath Mishra and others accused of misappro- priation of funds.
Ayurveda Medicine Scam	1996		Mulayam Singh. UP. Misappropriation of funds
Indian Bank Scam	1996	Rs 1,200 cr	Chidambram accused.
Petrol Pump Allotment	1996	Rs 13 cr	Satish Sharma accused.
ITC Scam	1996	Rs 350 cr	Accusations by Chitalias of siphoning out money.

Allotment of land to Coop Societies. Abdul Ghafoor accused. 27 acres involved. HC strictures. 1987.

Kawas Gas Turbines Project allotted to French American combine CGEE Alsthom over nearest rival Krafts Werke Union (KWU). 1988.

St. Kitts Forgery Case.	1991		Mr. V P Singh sought to be implicated.

Fraud in PSU Disinvestment. Amount involved Rs 10,000 cr. 1993.

Overpricing of imported Omani gas. Satish Sharma's name mentioned in Rs 1000 cr contract. 1994.

BN Safaya accused Satish Sharma of getting money from Essar (7 cr), Videocon (5 cr) Reliance (4 cr), Jindal (0.5 cr), Bindal Agro (1 cr). Total recd. 17.5 cr. 1996.

Shaw Wallace alleged by E D to have siphoned off Rs 82 cr of money due to the Govt. 1996.

Sukh Ram accused of allotting Rs 80,000 cr worth of Telecomm Circles for consideration. 1996

Lakhu Bhai Pathak Cheating case. $ 1 lakh. Narasimha Rao accused. 1996.

Manu Chabbaria Liquor scam. Money involved Rs 1447 cr.

C R Bhansali case.

Snam Progetti.

Justice G Ramaswamy accused of various charges. Sought to be impeached in Parliament.

Source: The Times of India, The Telegraph, Indian Express, Tribune, Financial Express, Hindustan Tines, News Times, Deccan Herald, Blitz, The Statesman and *The Hindu.*

When the nineties are compared to the eighties, the amounts involved in the scams have grown exponentially. The biggest scam of the eighties was Bofors involving a sum of Rs 65 crores but there were at least a dozen scams involving larger sums in the nineties, the largest being the securities scam involving Rs 3,000 crore. The number of scams reported in the eighties was 13 while the number for the nineties till 1996 was 26.

2.1 Harassment of Businessmen

Problems faced in Conduct of a Small-Scale Industry/Business

SALES TAX: Problems begin from applying for the Sales Tax Number.

Step.1. Applying for Sales Tax No. At the start of a business one needs to apply for a Sales Tax No. After the form is submitted, an inspector visits at the address given. Even if everything is in order an okay is not easily forthcoming.

Step 2. After the report of the inspector, one has to go to the Sales Tax Office to get the S.T.No. Once again this does not come in the routine way.

Step 3. Sales Tax has to be deposited on a monthly or quarterly basis and there is an annual assessment. Even if the business is straight the clearance is not automatic. A simple thing like getting a C form or a ST form to carry on business becomes complicated.

INCOME TAX: To get the Income-tax Clearance Certificate (ITCC), which is required for various purposes, the businessmen face considerable harassment. Even the file is not easily traeable.

The phone goes out of order every two months and the linesman has to be kept in good humour. In business, non-functioning phones are a major problem. Reporting to higher authorities is asking for trouble. It may then remain dead for considerable periods of time.

Dealings in the electricity department in the normal way are very time-consuming. There maybe excess billing. Its rectification may take a couple of months and several visits.

BANKING: It is important for businesses to have timely flow of funds. This depends on the bank manager. There are possibilities of putting obstacles in the release of funds. According to businessmen, funds released late are like treating a patient when he is dead.

To manage all these agencies and their officials, businessmen develop equations with officials. This has a price. The extra costs incurred vary from tens of rupees to lakhs.

PROBLEMS FACED BY A SHOP KEEPER IN A MARKET

SALES TAX: The difficulties mentioned by the businessmen were also faced by the shopkeepers. Further, the shopkeepers mentioned that once every six months the sales tax authorities visited their market and visited every shop. He stated that to avoid harassment he has always maintained a good equation with the visiting inspectors. During these visits the officials seem to make a mental note of the size of the business and whether the shopkeeper is filing returns honestly or not. This information is useful at the time of assessment. Corrupt officers take advantage of this knowledge.

In various wholesale markets (steel, paper, auto parts, electrical goods, etc.) forms are available in the name of companies operated by politicians. Businessmen needing C or ST forms get them for a consideration. These firms are wound up in three years time before they come up for assessment and new firms are opened. The state loses revenue. This lost revenue is shared three ways between the firm of the politician, the businessman and the corrupt officers.

TAX DEPT: Survey department people come to each market once a year to check whether a return is being filed or not. According to the shopkeepers, there is little seriousness in the exercise as many dishonest businessmen get away without paying their taxes. According to them refunds are obtained by paying 10% of the amount. Scrutiny of business accounts is not done at random. It is a way of punishing those who may be difficult customers.

Policemen collect money. Some are charged daily, some monthly and some weekly. Those on the move are charged daily or weekly and those who have a fixed place are charged monthly. Those in legal pucca structures and not committing illegality pay less. Those spilling outside their shops on to pavements and roads are charged more based on a settlement. If payment is not made by those not committing an illegality, there is harassment. Shops on pavements and verandahs in the market are encouraged by the police so that they can charge a hafta. The municipal staff shares equally and collects its hafta/monthly.

According to a dealer in vehicles, transport vehicles have to pay money at every crossing. A monthly payment is made and each vehicle has a diary in which the officer supervising the crossing makes a noting/mark. After that any traffic violations committed do not matter.

Getting a connection and an increase or decrease of load sanctioned (permanent or temporary) often costs money. Likewise, for getting a meter fixed to show a lesser reading than actual consumption there was charge.

LABOUR DEPT.The labour inspector comes every six months and has to be kept satisfied.

SHOPS AND COMMERCE DEPT.Inspector comes monthly . Some establishments are kept open on off days. Usually, all those involved in this infringement in an area agree in turn to be prosecuted so that one establishment pays a fine and the others continue their business.

BUILDING DEPT. Sanction of a building plan if not handled properly can be time-consuming. The engineer visits the place of construction and advises what deviations can be made. Once construction incorporating these deviations begins, the citizen gets trapped in an illegality and has to pay for it.The police are also required to check illegal constructionas they become an interested party. 10% of the cost of additional construction has to be paid to avoid prosecution. Since the violation of building bye-laws is not shown on paper, property tax is saved and for this a bribe is paid to the tax department. In one well-known case where a basement was constructed under an existing structure, tens of lakhs were reported to be paid.

For most such jobs, middlemen like, brokers, CAs, lawyers and architects are available.

Misdeclared Personal Expenses of Managements

In the case of many small firms and those who are in the self-employed category, hardly any profits are shown since business expenditures are inflated on various counts including via misdeclaring personal expenditures. Some of them are:

Residential accommodation: Company guest house

Personal travel and transport: Company car and expense

Telephone: Company telephone

Help at home: Company employees

Entertainment: Company entertainment

In other words, only a small fraction of the household expenditure incurred is shown out of personal income.

Employees are kept temporary or ad hoc to avoid paying PF and insurance. It also helps avoiding registration of the unit and having to pay various taxes, etc.

Expenses are fudged. Corners are cut wherever possible, like, in worker safety, standards, quality of product, etc. Sales tax is evaded through false billing. Bribes are paid to get business. Free telephone lines are obtained to make long distance calls. Electricity meters are got manipulated.

Business becomes enormously complex requiring supervision by self and trusted staff which a family provides. Expansion is often then limited by the size of the family and capacity to attract people from wider family who would be loyal. There is need for extra manpower to run around various offices and for payments to get work done. It distracts from the routine work. Costs go up all around.

2.2 Undeclared Incomes in the Teaching Profession

It is also commonly believed that the influence of money has gained ground in the teaching profession resulting in malpractice at all levels. There is a loss of status for the teaching profession perhaps because the privileged sections feel education is not serving their interest. Post 1991, state support has declined resulting in a deepening of the crisis in the system of public education and to uncontrolled privatization. With it malpractices have been rapidly on the rise. Given here are select examples from Delhi and a few UP towns.

Tuition and Appointments

In the private sector, to keep costs low, permanent staff is rarely appointed Ad hoc appointments are the norm at salaries of between Rs 1,000 and Rs 2,000. This is roughly the minimum wage and less than what a peon or a domestic help would draw. Many girls waiting to get married, after completion of education, are willing to work on these terms. Typically, the management shows a much higher salary on paper. The difference between that which is paid and that which is shown in the records is taken in cash by the management. To manage these affairs, the critical staff, the principal, the manager, managing committee members and key accountants and clerks are often trusted people of the owner of the institution. The honest ones to stay on have to keep quiet.

An appointment as a teacher in a school opens an avenue for tuition so that the low salary offered may be ignored. In a small UP town, teachers were found to earn around Rs 5,000 per month from tutions. They coached two or three students together and charged them Rs 200 each. If the tutor was from a good school, the charge was Rs 500 per student. Science teachers earned more since they could influence marks in practicals. Many students did not take practicals seriously since their marks are often not dependent on the performance and learning. At times, money allotted for equipment and materials for laboratories was also siphoned off by the management and teachers making labs dysfunctional. In the case of 'difficult subjects', like maths, accountancy and statistics, tuition was necessary since only theory was taught in the class.

The percentage of teachers involved in tuition varies from subject to subject. Most male teachers are involved in this activity and many less well off married female teachers. Teachers considered to be good from the point of examinations command a high premium and prestige. Teachers most in demand are from science and commerce streams. Next are those from computers and English.

For the parents, success in entrance examinations for professional courses—medicine and engineering—has become important so that the costs are justified. In fact, nowadays even the 'good' students go in for coaching of various kinds—institutional, private at home and postal. This is also true for the public examinations, like civil services and banking.

In an innovative case that came to light, students of a private unrecognized school took admission to a government school in appear for exams. The school organized this for a payment of Rs 2,000. The money was equally shared. The money for the mid-day meal was also misappropriated in this case.

In the public sector, for an appointment, influence may no longer be enough and a bribe is required for getting an appointment. In one case that came to light for the appointment of a lecturer in Music, one year's salary was demanded but the appointment was not guaranteed. It depended on how much political pressure could be brought to bear on the selection board.

In some universities, teachers charge money for guiding research. More is charged for science subjects compared to arts and commerce. The deal between the faculty and students is negotiated by middlemen who are employees of the university/college. In such cases, the result is guaranteed by the supervisor. Examiners are suitably chosen. A quid pro quo exists amongst faculty of different universities— they oblige each other. The student has only to take care of the examiners by arranging for a comfortable stay and transportation. In case of students getting scholarships for research, some faculty members take the monthly stipend for guiding the student.

A research degree has become important since increments depend on having a degree.

Cheating
In Uttar Pradesh, this phenomenon is specific to examination centres. In some cases, it is almost like a contract. Money is charged for the invigilators putting up answers on the blackboard. It has come to light that there are professional examination takers where a person may appear on behalf of a candidate.

Leakage of question papers has become rampant and involves considerable sums of money. Parents of students are known to approach examiners for increasing the marks of their wards. Parents also find out who the moderators and tabulators of results are and approach them to get marks increased.

Capitation and New Centres

Good schools in UP charge a donation for granting admission. The amount varies from Rs 5,000 to Rs 20,000. In a city like, Delhi, the sum could run up to Rs 2 lakh.

Private professional institutions charge even higher sums of money. A whole host of such institutions have been set up since 1991. The universities have set them up in subjects, like, management, engineering and medicine. The fees for these courses are exorbitant (Rs 40,000 per semester) even when they lack adequate infrastructure and faculty. They are run on the basis of guest faculty and are displacing the more traditional courses. It is surprising that such institutions are getting recognition from the relevant authorities. It is suspected that these institutions pay money for recognition.

The directors of these institutions gain enormous clout by appointing teachers as guest faculty. Many teachers ignore their regular teaching and take lectures in these centres. Some are known to additionally earn upto Rs 15,000 per month from these institutions.

Second Jobs

Degree college lecturers and others who do not have the opportunity to earn through the above-mentioned mechanisms are indulging in various activities. They may open photostat shops, book and stationary stores, public-call booths or even general merchandise stores. Some obtain agencies of LIC, GIC, UTI, Postal Deposits, etc., in the name of their wives and assist them in the work. Vacations and leave come in handy in for this.

Corruption in Administration

There is widespread corruption in administration. In private colleges where this occurs, the matter is simple since the management is interested in diverting funds and does so in a centralized manner. In the case of public institutions, there is greater decentralization. Since many of the committees for overseeing work are headed by senior faculty, they either get involved in the corruption or ignore it. Vice-chancellors and principals build a coterie of their own people who assist them in doing the dirty work and get a share in the spoils. Some do not take money but get their personal work done and gain in influence which has other benefits. Money is made in purchases of equipment and materials and in construction and repairs.

Some heads of universities and institutions who are political appointees indulge in manipulating appointments, admissions etc.

There are many honest educationists and institutions left but corruption is now widespread at every level of our education system. For the dishonest, education is secondary and making money the primary goal. The amount of incomes either made or siphoned out of the system may equal the value added in education. Society is spending enormous sums of money on education but this has neither led to better education nor to better choice for citizens. There is increased activity to simply siphon out resources. Most educational institutions now run like a mafia. There is a conspiracy of silence about their corruption.

2.3 Medical Profession

This noble profession still has a large number of dedicated people. However, reports of malpractice have increased as it has become more and more commercialized. Considerations associated with the profession, like, cure regardless of other considerations, stand diluted. The decline of the public health system has aggravated these tendencies.

The medical profession consists of the private and the public sectors. There are different kinds of malpractice that prevail in these two sectors. In the private sector, the patients who are partially ignorant and partially under extreme stress specially in cases of grave illnesses may be duped by prescribing unnecessary tests, consultation with specialists, prolonged and unnecessary medication, use of placebos. In many cases, the doctors are in league with each other and the laboratories. These malpractice are hard to prove since they are supposedly done in the 'best interest' of the patient. It is always possible to attribute these activities to differences in the opinion and approach of doctors. Some may be characterized as conservative and old fashioned who do not like too much of testing or medication and others as modern believing in 'doing the best for the patients'.

However, there are clear money making rackets in the sale of blood, sale of organs and their transplant, sex determination tests and in pregnancy termination, vasectomy, procurement of children, unnecessary cesarean deliveries, etc. Some rackets have been reported. Cases of issuing of false certificates for various purposes is rampant as is the issue of false bills for claiming refund from the office or for obtaining money from insurance have come to light

As far as the public sector is concerned, malpractice may simply be that one hobnobs with those in power and gives them preferential treatment. In public hospitals there are two queues. One for the general public and another for the powerful (those with connections). Clearly, general patients get short changed.

However, often money is involved. Supplies (stores, medicines, food, etc.) are diverted, cuts taken on purchases and contracts, patients charged privately (by doctors, nurses, attendants, cleaners, etc.) for services rendered in the hospitals or clinics, etc. Hospital wastes are recycled rather than being properly disposed off. At times they are sold off to unscrupulous people who repackage them and sell them. One hears of contaminated IV fluids, untested blood and spurious drugs being administered in these institutions. Services have reached breaking point in many of these public institutions.

Many doctors who may not indulge in any malpractice but have high incomes do not declare their true incomes. Of course those who indulge in malpractice cannot declare their true income. According to Table VII.2 for the financial year 1993-94, income-tax assessees who declared their profession as Medical and Health Services numbered 2.1 lakh. Of these, companies were 1,282 and the balance were individuals. Companies declared an income of Rs 147 crore and individuals Rs 969 crore. On an average each individual declared an income of Rs 48,000. According to the Economic Survey, the total number of doctors as of December 31, 1993 was 4.28 lakh and of nurses 4.5 lakh. Thus, a small fraction of those who should be tax-payers from these categories are paying taxes. Further, the income they declared is very small. The per capita emoluments of public sector employees for that year was Rs 72,000. Can it be that the doctors on an average earned 2/3 of what the public sector employees did? In that year, tax was payable on incomes of around Rs 30,000 and there was a standard deduction of Rs 12,000. There were other exemptions available but even allowing for all that, the average income of Rs 48,000 is too low. All this suggests large scale evasion of taxes.

2.4 Army Canteen

In an interview with a major supplier to army canteen, the following facts emerged. Army procures goods from manufacturers for sales in their canteens. The goods range from soft drinks and liquor to consumer durables, like, washing machines. Sales are said to total about Rs 30,000 crores per annum. There are four stages at which money changes hand.

    a) Approval of the supplier and the product.
    b) Getting prices approved from the Price Approval
       Committee.
    c) Getting order placed. And
    d) Getting payments.

At the initial stage, the company and its product are to be registered after approval by a Board. The initial registration of a company apparently requires a payment depending on the business. Subsequently, for the acceptance of each of the products to be stocked in the Canteens, money is required to be paid. These are one time payments but payments are required to be made for each order and for collecting payments. At the base and area depots, different amounts are required to be paid of the value of order placed. Collection of the cheque is also not automatic. In addition to these payments, gifts are given to concerned officers at various social occasions.

The payments are reported to go right up to the top. Apparently, the percentage at each level is fixed. The sytem simply bypasses honest officers who are expected to keep quiet.

Those who have tried to get approval of their products without a payment have been unsuccessful. There are well known agents who get the approvals on payment of money

There is leakage of the goods to non-army sources. Either through the armed forces personnel procuring these goods for their friends and relations or the depot managers supplying the goods in the market. The goods sold through the Canteen are exempt from excise duty and pay a concessional sales tax. Hence the government loses considerable amount of taxes on these sales. Liquor has a heavy excise duty on it and is a major source of leakage.

It is better to eliminate the canteen system and increase the salaries of the defence personnel by 5%. In remote areas where there is a problem of supplies, regular army channels can be used to supply goods. Private sector channels of distribution are now available everywhere in the country. One could also put it that for the same amount of money, the fighting forces could have had more effective equipment, supplies and manpower. Corruption is a source of waste and sub-optimality.

2.5 Judiciary

In recent times, the judiciary has come in for adverse comments in the media. The impeachment proceedings against Justice Ramaswamy in parliament received wide coverage and many wondered whether this was only the tip of the iceberg. The case of a Bombay high court judge who accepted money from a publisher and of the Calcutta judge whose medical bill created controversy have added to public disquiet.

The public has been baffled by the groupism amongst the lawyer fraternity. This has even taken the shape of campaigning for or against the appointment of certain judges. It can only be hoped that such divisions do not spread to the wider community of legal functionaries because then it may lead to erosion of faith in the judicial independence. This needs to be avoided at all costs. There is nothing wrong with the association of groups of lawyers with political parties but such affiliations should not translate into taking positions within the judiciary.

The judiciary is overworked and the backlog of cases is immense. At the lower court, a judge may not have more than a few minutes for a case on a given date. This has created serious problems and the higher levels of judiciary have sometimes been forced to take note of judgements going contrary to pronouncements in the higher courts. His further adds to the backlog and delays. Justice delayed is justice denied but the legal fraternity is unable to do anything about it.

2.6 Police Hafta

Corruption in the police force is widely commented upon in the media. One aspect of it is known as the hafta. This system as it exists in two of India's important metropolises was described by some very senior officers who have had a reputation for honesty. A summary of what they narrated is presented below.

METROPOLIS A

Most of the police is involved in maintaining law and order and is based in the thanas. They are involved in the hafta system. Policemen in the licensing, armed or traffic or intelligence have no part of this system of collection. They have their own methods of generation of black incomes. Like, in granting licenses or through traffic violations. The following hierarchy in the police force in the city is relevant for the hafta system:

There are 10 constables to a Head constable.

There are 5 head constables to a sub inspector.

There are 4 to 5 sub-inspectors to an Inspector.

There are 3 inspectors to a Dy SP.

There are 3 Dy SP to one SP.

Above them are the Range DIG and then the IG.

The description given below is a simplified version of the actual system.

There are a large number of illegal activities going on in the area of jurisdiction of each thana, say, prostitution, encroachment for housing and for pavement stalls, auto thefts, pick pockets, black marketing, sale of smuggled and spurious goods, manufacture of illicit liquor among others.

Both the municipality and the police are supposed to prevent such activities from taking place.

These activities become points of generating 'extra' income for some of the municipal and police staff, depending on the profits being made. The collection is made weekly. Hence the name hafta.

The cuts go up the line and shared amongst the officers according to well defined criterion. Honest officers are bypassed. They hear complaints but cannot do much about the sharing going on.

Where commercial activity and illegality abound, there the pickings are greater. Hence, there are desirable police beats and thanas, postings to which are coveted. Political elements play an important role in postings since the local representatives are often involved in various illegal activities.

METROPOLIS B

In metropolis B the hafta system was found to be less well organized but of a similar nature to that in metropolis A. The sums mentioned were confirmed by shop keepers, pavement sellers and auto-rickshaw drivers.

The police force has 'dry' and 'wet' duties. Little money is made in the former case. The dry duties are say, Armed Police duties, security duty for VIPs and airport perimeter duty. Such duties constitute about 50% of the force of 56,000.

Money is made in police station duties, crime branch, licensing, traffic and investigation. Each has its own sources of making money. Some of them are weekly, daily or monthly.

The beat constable collects daily from pavement shops. But the pucca shops, cinemas, restaurants and industry pay protection money monthly. Places serving drinks pay well.

Unauthorized construction is touched once and pays lump sum. There is a construction mafia which keeps police happy.

Those who are arrested are harassed and money is extracted at every stage. The jhuggi-jhopri clusters are controlled by slum lords. They pay a monthly amount to the police. It is reported that one slum lord declared an income of Rs 30 crore under VDIS and paid the tax due mostly in small denomination currency notes (Rs 5, 10 and 20). According to the story, it took days for a team of income-tax people to count the amount paid.

Cases going before the Dowry cell (disputes) enable the police to charge money from both the parties.

The city has 123 police stations, each with an SHO in-charge and an additional SHO under him. There are 1,400 beats in the city each with two constables. Often, the constable works up to 16 hours to maximize his daily earning. There is also one head constable per beat. There are 500 sub inspectors above the head constable.

Above the SHO there are the ACP, DCP, Additional CP and then the Commissioner.

There are some very lucrative beats like where there are big markets or where prostitution goes on or where there is construction is on a big scale. Postings to these police stations, are sought after. Good beats are given to favoured policemen to maximize collections which may sometimes range between Rs 15,000/- to Rs 200,000/- per month.

The money is sent right up to the top at times. With some exceptions, honest officers are marginalized in the system and considered to be inefficient and given 'dry' postings. For prized posting, a lump sum may be paid and it is said that this money has at times gone right up to the top.

Today, the definition of an honest officer is that she/he does not interfere with the system and gets the work done when needed. Of course, the primary duty of maintaining law and order and checking crime becomes a casualty of the hafta. The goal changes to that things should not go out of control, a gradual deterioration is acceptable.

The licensing branch makes money on issue of licenses for various activities, like, guns, restaurants, cinemas, etc.

The traffic police make money from transporters, taxis and blue lines. Trucks entering the city pay a ceratin sum. Money is made when accidents are reported and traffic violations take place. Certification of Fitness of commercial vehicles is required annually and requires payment of money. The private transporters running buses in the city pay monthly. It was mentioned that the transport department and traffic police make Rs 1.25 crore a day.

The impact of all this on the morale of the police force is disastrous. As one senior officer stated, 'more police stations mean more crime'. In one incident, when a head constable came to demand money where construction was going on, he was told that the DIG had been talked to and'he had said that no money need be paid for such construction. His immediate response was, 'how much money did you pay? You would have had to pay me less'. The man could not have had much respect for his boss to have said what he did. Under the circumstances, the chain of command cannot be robust and orders issued may not be carried out. According to a DCP, an SHO has little respect for his DCP if he is directly posted by the Commissioner for reasons other than efficiency.

The police have developed a vested interest in illegality since that gets them the hafta. More the illegality, greater the earnings. Control of crime can only be in a limited sense.

Honest officers are marginalized and demoralized. One senior officer suggested that in the police stations, the treatment meted out to a criminal is often better than to a citizen. No wonder, people avoid going to the police to report crime. They also do not come forward to give witness to the police knowing that they would not get protection against criminals if needed.

In conclusion, the police while engaged in maintaining law and order also keep track of the illegal activities in their areas, a potential source of hafta collection. The reputation of the police as mixed up in illegality is encouraging individuals to take the law into their hands or go to the gangsters to settle scores. The chain of command is very weak as a consequence and orders issued may not be executed at lower levels.

2.7 Illegal Activites in the International Arena

A. DRUGS:

1.According to International Narcotics Control Strategy Report, 1989-USA, the estimates of production of drugs in 1988, on a conservative estimate, are:

Opium   2433 to 3308 MT

Coca leaf	173745 to 227055 MT
Cannabis	19870 to 25835 MT
Hashish	1185 to 1385 MT

2. Profits generated in the sale of drugs.

a. Return for 10 Kg of opium   US$ 400 to US$675

b. 10 kg of opium produces 1 kg. of
   pure heroin : on transportation return is   US$ 175000 (wholesale level)

c. Final product sold by cutting the heroin
   Thereafter it is diluted: return for the dose   US$ 45/unit

d. Rough value of the 1 kg of heroin   US$ 1mn

e. Global value of drug trade/annum   US$ 400bn

SOURCE : *UN Report (1987) quoted by Lok Sabha Secretariat.*

B. MISCELLANEOUS:

1.Gross Criminal Product $500 bn (2% of Global
(Illicit drug trade + Financialfraud +   Domestic product)
  Prostitution + Other crimes)

2. OVERINVOICING   On Paper   Average global price

a. Truck and bus tyres' import price $ 1000 $100

b. Export consignment   Rs 11.75 crore   Rs 2.5 lakh
  (bricks and used video cassettes)

c. Plastic buckets   Rs 750

d. Plastic ball-pen covers   Rs 55
   UNDERINVOICING

Exercise bicycle's export price   51 cents $ 100 approx.

3.

	Washed through	%age of dirty money recouped
a. Australia	$740mn to $3.3bn	1%

	Dubious Cases handled	%age of original suspects persecuted
b. Netherlands	14%	0.5%

4. Other information on the black economy in India.

a.   Money generated/stashed abroad
             $100bn
             (in defiance of FERA)

b.   Major source of leakage of FOREX
             Total(Suspected)   Havala Payments

1.1.97-31.8.98   Rs.3957 cr.   Rs.1111cr. (approx.)

SOURCES: *1 IMF Working paper. 1&2 Tribune, 22 Feb. 1998.*
3a & b Tribune 2 Feb.1998.
4a Tribune 22 Feb.1998. 4b Enforcement Directorate.

2.8 Stock Exchange Practices

Amongst the malpractice in the share markets, the following are important:

a) Manipulation of the profitability of the company

b) Floatation of new issues and their listing
c) Role of merchant bankers and underwriters
d) PSU disinvestment
e) Insider trading and speculation. And,
f) Conversion of black and white and vice-versa.

According to stock market analysts, companies cook up their balance sheets to show the profits they wish to. This is done to manipulate the share price and the taxes to be paid. To facilitate this, companies violate all the rules they can and use influence in the Ministry of Finance to get away with their manipulation.

The legal system is ineffective because even when the companies are caught manipulating, action is seldom taken since a settlement is arrived at and when action is taken, fines are negligible and delays endless. Stock market manipulations take place in this framework. Fraud in the stock markets has always existed but it has really taken off since the early eighties. Many companies (numbering in thousands) have simply disappeared after collecting money from the public.

A large gray market has developed for manipulating share prices. For the new shares trading begins before they are listed. The brokers and companies are involved in the rigging of prices so that they can dump some of the shares after listing takes place. The public is fooled by the rigged prices and the media plays a role in this. The high price quoted leads to a higher subscription and enables the company to command a higher premium than possible. From the mid-eighties to 1994 the most active share markets in manipulation were Jaipur, Rajkot and Surat.

Allotment of shares to employees was manipulated to allot shares to fictitious entities to keep control. Registrar of shares were appointed to facilitate manipulation of allotment.

After the share flotation, the share is listed in the secondary market. The first listing price is important since the price of shares needs to be maintained. This first listing price is manipulated. The funds needed for this purpose are obtained through financiers who provide their black funds. In this manner, without performance, companies got a premium. After the success of the first issue, often a second one followed and till such time the share price had to be maintained. At times, it is alleged rigging was aided by some government functionaries.

In 1992, Controller of Capital Issues (CCI) was abolished and SEBI emerged. Control over the price of the issue went.

DATA RELATED TO PERFORMANCE OF ED IN ITS KEY AREAS OF WORK

1. Enforcement Directorate's performance in the field of prosecutions launched under FERA, 1973

Year	No. of cases investigated	No. of persons arrested	% of arrest viz.-a-viz. Investigations	No. of cases in which persecution launched	% of persecution to investigation	No. of persecution cases disposed by the court	No. of cases resulting in conviction	% of conviction to disposal
1994	6601	365	5.52%	-	-	-	-	-
1995	5633	228	4.04%	-	-	-	-	-
1996	5486	213	3.88%	101	1.84%	75	13	17.33%
1997	5511	159	2.90%	92	1.66%	49	31	63.2%
1998 (8.98)	2496	60	2.40%	71	2.84%	64	33	51.5%
Total	25727	1025		264		192	79	

—ENFORCEMENT DIRECTORATE;FERA, 28.09.98

However, information disclosure was not implemented and there was no enforceability. According to experts, SEBI was clueless about capital markets and was a poor regulator. Merchant bankers encouraged a lot of dud issues in the period 1992-96. They were party to manipulations. 4000 issues came in this period. For instance, 'wave after wave of issues in granite, floriculture and finance came'. The GDR market also involved recycling of black money. It was returned back to the country through this route.

PSU disinvestment also involved fraud. There are hints of collusion between international bankers and financiers and government officials. This enabled the price to be kept low resulting in huge losses to the exchequer and opening the PSUs to the threat of foreign takeover at cheap prices.

FIIs and Mutual Funds have been involved in insider trading through obtaining advance information from companies. They also secure advance information from bureaucrats regarding policy changes, for a consideration.

Speculation in the price of shares is rampant in the stock market. Some operators spend the day watching which shares are rising or falling and where the activity is. They look at the trends and place orders for bying or selling. They do not take long positions and keep booking profits from times to time so that they are not exposed overly much. At the time of settlement, they typically square up, that is, if they had purchased, they sell and if they had sold, they buy, This was they either receive (profit) or pay (loss) the difference in the value of the two transactions.

The activity of these people is based on advance information about political and economic developments, impending company results and about what the big players are likely to do (in the present context the FIIs). This kind of information requires a network of contacts which only the large operators have.

Contacts are established in the political world, with journalists, bureaucrats, businessmen and analysts. In some cases the contact is with the topmost leaders or someone close to them. One has to belong to a high social circle which partly develops as a result of family connections and partly as a result of business.

This is another way that a nexus gets established amongst the politicians, businessmen and the bureaucrats.

Effectively, this is like insider trading where privileged information is used to make a profit before the public gets the information. If a company is doing badly, then the select people get to know and dump their shares to buy them back later at a lower price. The investing public gets duped.

The percentage of the population active in the stock markets is very small. Those investing (holding the shares) are more but still a tiny fraction of the population. While there may be many small holdersholding small odd lots here and there, many of the big investors hold shares in various portfolios some of which maybe benami. According to analysts, there may be no more than 20 lakh investors with significant holdings.

In mid-1999, the stock market capitalisation was around Rs 6 lakh crore. Reliance Industries Limited is supposed to have the largest base of investors. The number of folios may be 23 lakh but given the multiple holdings, this may amount to no more than 10 lakh households. These people hold 27% of the equity while the rest is held by a few, the Company promoters and the Financial institutions (Indian and foreign). Hindustan Levers has the largest market capitalizationn of around Rs 44, 000 crore. It has only 3.5 lakh share holders (folios) but the parent company holds over 50% of the shares. The big investors hold another 25% so that the 3.5 lakh hold around 25% of the equity. That is an average of Rs 3 lakh per folio or about 140 shares each.

If it is assumed that on an average the big holdings in the Indian companies account for 60% of the equity, then the public may be taken to hold Rs 2, 40, 000 cr worth of equity. With 20 lakh investors, the average holding of the public would be Rs 12 lakh which is small. Considering that these shares may be held in several names and also benami, each holding would be tiny not even enough to hold a small portfolio of a few blue chip companies. It is unlikely that there can be 10 million independent investors in the stock markets.

Finally, in the stock market, the Book Entry method is used for converting black to white and voice versa. If A needs to convert his black to white and B needs to do it the other way round, the stock market enables this to take place. A goes to a broker who gives him papers showing that he has made a profit in the sale and purchase of shares. A pays the broker his blank and gets a cheque for the same amount. B is shown to make a loss and makes a cheque payment to the broker and gets cash in return. Both A and B pay the broker not only his brokerage but also a commission for the conversion.

Speculation in the price of shares is rampant in the stock market. Some operators spend the day watching which shares are rising or falling and where the activity is. They look at the trends and place orders for buying or selling. They do not take long positions and keep booking profits from time to time so that they are not exposed overly much. At the time of settlement, they typically square up, that is, if they had purchased, they sell and if they had sold, they buy. This way they either receive (profit) or pay (loss) the difference in the value of the two transactions.

The activity of these people is based on advance information about political and economic developments, impending company results and about what the big players are likely to do (in the present context the FIIs). This kind of information requires a network of contacts which only the large operators have.

Contacts are established in the political world, with journalists, bureaucrats, businessmen and analysts. In some cases the contact is with the topmost leaders or someone close to them. One has to belong to a high social circle which partly develops as a result of family connections and partly as a result of business. This is another way that a nexus gets established amongst the politicians, businessmen and the bureaucrats.

Effectively, this is like insider trading where privileged information is used to make a profit before the public gets the information. If a company is doing badly, then the select people get to know and dump their shares to buy them back later at a lower price. The investing public gets duped.

The percentage of the population active in the stock markets is very small. Those investing (holding the shares) are more but still a tiny fraction of the population. While there may be many small holders holding small odd lots here and there, many of the big investors hold shares in various portfolios some of which maybe benami. According to analysts, there may be no more than 20 lakh investors with significant holdings.

In mid-1999, the stock market capitalisation was around Rs 6 lakh crore. Reliance Industries Limited is supposed to have the largest base of investors. The number of folios may be 23 lakh but given the multiple holdings, this may amount to no more than 10 lakh households. These people hold 27% of the equity while the rest is held by a few, the company promoters and the financial institutions (Indian and foreign). Hindustan Levers has the largest market capitalization of around Rs 44,000 crore. It has only 3.5 lakh share holders (folios) but the parent company holds over 50% of the shares. The big investors hold another 25% so that the 3.5 lakh hold around 25% of the equity. That is an average of Rs 3 lakh per folio or about 140 shares each.

If it is assumed that on an average the big holdings in the Indian companies account for 60% of the equity, then the public may be taken to hold Rs 2,40,000 cr worth of equity. With 20 lakh investors, the average holding of the public would be Rs 12 lakh which is small. Considering that these shares may be held in several names and also benami, each holding would be tiny not even enough to hold a small portfolio of a few blue chip companies. It is unlikely that there can be 10 million significant investors in the stock markets.

In the stock market, the Book Entry method is used for converting black to white and vice versa. If A needs to convert his black to white and B needs to do it the other way round, the stock market enables this to take place. Mr. A goes to a broker who gives him papers showing that he has made a profit in the sale and purchase of shares. A pays the broker his black and gets a cheque for the same amount. B is shown to make a loss and makes a cheque payment to the broker and gets cash in return. Both A and B pay the broker not only his brokerage but also a commission for the conversion.

2.9 Real Estate

Malpractices of Builders and Brokers
Usually, builders and brokers act in concert. Brokers are the go between in transactions and enable black money to be exchanged between the buyer and the seller. Typically, honesty is rare amongst them and they try to hoodwink both the buyer and the seller. If a deal is about to go through, they may intervene and offer to get a higher price. If a buyer approaches them for purchase, they quote a high price and if a seller approaches them, they quote a low price. Sometimes they act as an intermediary who advances a sum of money to a seller and holds him to a lower price and later make the full payment when they find a buyer from whom they extract a higher price. The difference is their profit over and above their brokerage.

In league with the builders, they try to create a demand for the builder's product using various kinds of falsehoods. They are the ones who enable the builder to sell more than what is available by doing multiple booking. The builders hope that some people drop out later and seek refund thus taking care of the over booking. Builders are known to resize the property in the end to overcome any remaining problem. Iin the books they may show a higher area than actually handed over. The buyer keeps quiet since she/he benefits from a higher value on the books and from a higher rent received.

The builders typically delay projects and do not pay interest on the delay in the handing over of the property. However, they charge a high interest on delayed payments. The money collected is diverted to other projects or other uses so that the projects typically get delayed. Almost all the building bye laws are violated during construction and bribes paid all around. The quality of construction is poorer than promised.

In Delhi, the builders set up their own maintenance societies whose accounts are not shown to the members of the societies. Typically these societies are not accountable to the owners of the property. The builders retain hold over the property in spite of having received the money from the buyers. Thus, all subsequent sales have to be routed through them and a hefty transfer charge levied on the seller and collected mostly in cash.

The brokers involve themselves in settling disputes and getting properties vacated. They maintain musclemen and other bad characters so that they can create a nuisance to have properties vacated. They keep a look out for disputed properties. They buy them cheap, get them vacated and make a hefty profit.

2.10 Tax Department

In the surveys conducted for the NIPFP report, in the early eighties, it was found that corruption is rampant in the income-tax department. Those in the department agreed with this perception. According to those who were interviewed now, corruption has increased and become more brazen. The help of CAs and tax lawyers is sought as the middlemen for businessmen in tax matters and in dealings with financial institutions. Cuts involved are from 33% to 50% of the amount of bribe to be paid for settling the case. According to some of the interviwees, 80-90 % of the professionals indulge in this activity.

Businessmen expect the CAs to sign on the dotted lines and give them advice on how to reduce the liability. They expect them to have links in the tax department to sort out matters if there are problems. In interviews with chartered accountants, the following rates of bribes were mentioned as payable to the officials:

1. Scrutiny of cases. 5 to 10% of cases are clean. No pay-off involved. In the other cases,
a. ITO deals with cases of upto Rs 2 lakh.
b. AC cases between Rs 2 to 10 lakh.
c. DC cases above Rs 10 lakh.
Bribes mentioned range from Rs 10,000 to Rs 5 lakh.
2. Form 34A. Intimation of sale of property above value of Rs 5 lakh.
Payment of Rs 5000 to Rs 50,000 are mentioned.
3. Survey. Payment of Rs 50,000 to 500,000
4. Raids. Payment of Rs 5 to 50 lakh.

Some refund cheques are automatically sent but where corrupt officials are involved, this requires payment of the 10% of the refund amount. Similarly, a consideration is needed for scrutiny of files, for getting orders etc.

3.1 Actual Investment, Savings, Exports And Import: Definition

Actual $I = (I_{priv} + I_{pub})_{white} + (I_{priv} + I_{pub})_{black}$

Actual $S = (S_{priv} + S_{pub})_{white} + (S_{priv} + S_{pub})_{black}$

Actual $X = X_{white} + X_{black}$.

Actual $M = M_{white} + M_{black}$.

The white components are already defined in the National Accounts Statistics. The black components above may be written in terms of their constituents as:

$I_{private,black}$ = incremental holding of gold, silver, gems and jewellery and balances in foreign accounts—over invoicing of investment + under invoiced inventories (including holding of commodities for speculation) + undeclared investments in the formal and informal sectors (including, for speculation) + increase in cash holding + investment in illegal activities.

$I_{public, black}$ = - over-invoicing of investments

$S_{private,black}$ = Black savings propensity x {over-invoicing of private investments + over-invoicing of public investments + over-invoicing of purchase of material (including, wages) + under-invoicing of sale price + value of undeclared production (legal and illegal) + cuts on contracts of public sector} + black savings of informal sector—Benami investments in banks and post offices.

$S_{public, black}$ = Cuts on contracts for sales and purchase of goods and services

X_{black}. = Under-invoiced exports + Export of drugs + under- invoicing of tourist expenditures + savings of Indian labour working abroad retained

$M_{black}.$ =Under-invoiced imports—Over-invoiced imports +
smuggling + Indians undeclared expenditure
abroad on education, health and tourism.

Gold, silver and gems and jewellery are included in I since they imply equal investments abroad through leakage.

3.2 Estimates of Elements of Black Investments and Savings

(As per cent of white GDP at market prices)

Given the definition of black incomes used in this paper, only factor incomes are considered. As such, investments in real estate, transactions in the secondary share markets, capital gains, bribes, etc., are not considered here. As far as possible, estimates are given for 1990-91.

1. Siphoning out of public sector savings through cuts on sales and purchases and over invoicing of investments. 6% of value   5.3%.

   Small projects may have 15% leakage and the large ones 6%. Additional activities, like, bank frauds, financial irregularities, electricity leakages need to be estimated. Hence this is like a minimum estimate.

2. Under invoiced inventories at 20% of increase in inventories.   0.3%

3. Over invoiced plant and equipment in the private sector.

   Assume that it equals the capital required to be put in by the private owners of the companies, i.e., 16.5% of the capital declared to have been invested   0.8%.

4. Smuggling in of gold, silver and gems and jewellery.   1.9%.

5. Flight of Capital through over and under-invoicing of exports
   and imports.   1.6%.

6. Transfer of funds through the havala route.   1.0%

7. Profits on drug traffic accruing to Indians   3.7%

3.3 Reassessment of NAS: What is Included and Excluded

Black Incomes and Underestimation of Output and Value Added

Let input be I at a declared price pi and let it be over-invoiced by a fraction β. Let undeclared output be a fraction of the declared output o and the declared price of the declared output be p_o which is a fraction σ lower than the true price.

The actual input cost is $I.p_i.(1-\beta)$

The actual revenue is $O.(1+\tau).p_o(1+\sigma)$

The true profit is the difference of these two terms.

The true profit is the difference of these two terms.

The declared profit is $O.p_o - I.p_i$

The undeclared profit is $p_o.O.[\sigma + \tau + \sigma.\tau + \beta.I.p_i/O.p_o]$

The ration in the last term is the ratio of over-invoiced input coast to declared gross revenue. The larger this is the greater is the undeclared profit.

The undeclared profit may turn out to be comparable to the declared profits even for small values of σ, τ and β, specially if the mark up on costs is low. Declared value added = wages W (included in I above) +

Assuming that the wages are over-invoiced by the same fraction as other costs, the true value added = W. $(1-\beta)$ + True profits.

It is higher than the declared value added by the extent of the undeclared profits but less by the amount of wage bill inflation (which is a part of the undeclared profits).

The input supplier does not show his output as $I.p_i (1-\beta)$ but less than this by false billing. Hence his value added is also lower than the true amount.

In the case of the unorganized sector the ration of undeclared profit to the declared profit is likely to be much larger because β, σ and τ are likely to be much lower than in the organized sector.

From the above formulae, it can be concluded that the evasion of output is smaller than the under-estimation of value added which is less than the generation of black incomes.

To conclude, depending on the numbers, a small amount of non-reporting of output may lead to a much larger under estimation of national income and to an even larger amount of generation of black incomes. Conversely, if the black economy is curbed, the increase in the recorded national income would not be so large and the increase in production would be even less.

A numerical example would help clarify the argument. If post tax margins on sales for a firm are 10%, then an output evasion of 10% would double the profit of the firm. The cost of production of the evaded output is already included in cost of manufacture of the declared output so that the entire sale proceed of the evaded output is profit. Consequently, while the profit shown on the balance sheet would be 10% of the total sales shown, the management would get another 10% of the sales through the sale of the undeclared goods. Another 5% increase in undeclared output increases the black income generated by 50%, etc.

If input costs are also inflated by 5%, and are 50% of the sale price then the black incomes are larger by another 2.5%. So that, the national income is underestimated by around 17%, correcting for the wages which are also inflated. However, the black incomes generated are 17.5% of the declared output.

Reassessing the NAS

The NAS as estimated currently needs to be reformed in four major directions to take into account the effect of the black economy so that the total social effort (goods and bads) are taken into account.

1. NAS is over-estimated in some sectors.
2. Where white incomes from legal sectors get excluded.
3. Where black incomes from legal activities are included.
4. Where black incomes from legal activities are included.
5. Where black incomes from illegal activities are included.

Finally, all transfer incomes, like capital gains need to be kept out of the NAS.

1. Public sector data needs revaluation where it is over-estimated.

a. Services are over estimated due to over staffing (not black) and due to harassment (due to black).

b.Private sector wages are over estimated due to inflation of wages.

2. White incomes from legal activities which get excluded are:

a. Under-estimation of incomes due to methodological deficiencies, especially in the case of the unorganized sector.

b. Under-estimation of incomes due to data inadequacies.

3. Black incomes from legal activities which get excluded are:

Under-estimation of incomes due to deliberate falsification of data.

4. Black incomes from legal activities which get included are those where the method of estimation is independent of tax reporting. Like, when input-output ratios are used:

a. From agriculture and construction. The amount from agriculture is not likely to be large since there is no direct tax on this activity. In the case of construction also, this is not likely to be large since the input-output ratio is likely to be from the white data alone.

b. Black incomes generated in the public sector which are based on diverting output which is siphoned out, like, in public distribution, electricity, water, railway reservation and ticketless travel, diversion of telephone connection for STD and ISD and misuse of government facilities for private purposes.

c. This is also the case with public sector contracts which are inflated or where work is performed below the specification in the contracts.

5. Black incomes from illegal activities get excluded.

Profits, from smuggling, drugs, prostitution, bootlegging, crime, extortion and illegal lotteries.

It excludes the leakage of savings from the economy.

Private sector wages in the illegal sector are under estimated.

5.1 1998 General Election Expenses of a Sample of Candidates

Elections represent the essence of India's political process. The subversion of the will of the people is visible in the malfunctionign of the electoral process. In it can be seen the formation of the triad in its embrionic form. The link between the politician on the one hand and the businessman and the bureaucrat on the other, gets established. Fourteen politicians were interviewed and their actual expenditure, not just what they formally reported to the Election Commission, was recorded. Ten of them fought 1998 election and eight of them won. They were aware that they had exceeded the limits set by the election commission. Some of them commented that their first act after winning elections was to tell a lie. All of them gave estimates of expenditure in their states. The remaining four politicians had fought other elections and gave their experiences of those elections. This helped the author make estimates of expenditure in their constituencies.

Many were not aware of their total expenses since there were indirect expenses which they do not count or where expenditures were made by others without their knowledge or resources were given in kind. Hence there was a need to estimate the direct (what the candidates counted as spending) and indirect (what was given in kind or spent without their knowledge) expenditure of the candidate.

In addition to expenditures by the candidates, society also spends resources at the time of elections which should be included in estimating how much a national election costs. In other words, the total resource cost to the nation needs to be estimated. Even if elections are expensive to society they are an essential part of our system—like, eating food may be expensive but is an essential expense.

The interviewees belonged to different parties and came from various parts of India were assured that what they revealed was in confidence. Each politician interviewed was treated as a data point, the actual name being irrelevant. Some others (separately or along with the candidates) who had either financed or organized elections on behalf of the candidates or parties were also interviewed. These were the people behind the scenes who were managing things for the candidates or were the big leaders in charge of party affairs.

It must be clarified that what is presented here is not based on a systematic sample, and, is therefore, not necessarily representative. There may be exaggerations and untruths on the part of those interviewed and there is no way of cross-checking this and unknown biases may be present. The detailed questions on the campaign and the activities of the candidate and supporters, it is hoped will provide some kind of counter-check. The candidates were also asked about their sources of finance and the possible quid-pro-quo.

REPRESENTATIVE EXPENDITURE PATTERN OF A CANDIDATE IN
THE 1998 GENERAL ELECTION

PRE-CAMPAIGN

Unspecified expenses were incurred for obtaining the ticket. It involves intensive lobbying with the leaders of the party. Candidates brought in their supporters and influential people to do the lobbying. Powerful moneyed people are also involved.

OFFICES AND COMMITTEES

1. Committees are set up by MPs for conducting the campaign. One MP set up 4 Level of committees. At the apex was the circle of trusted people who controlled the show. Under them there was a committee of 50 people each of whom controlled a designated area and they were paid Rs 15,000 each for organization. Under each of these people, there were 8 people (given Rs 5 to 10,000 each) and then there were the booth level committees. Booth level committees were set up for 10 days while other committees functioned for a month.

2. Generally, candidates needed a central office equipped with cars and telephones for the duration of the election period. In one case it was opened more than 21 days before the campaigning began. In most cases sub-offices were opened but worked from the homes of supporters.

3. In one case, campaigners in an urban constituency lived communally. Feedback and strategising took place at night.

MANPOWER

1. Huge manpower is required during campaigning. In one case about 5,000 workers were used daily. Rs. 100 per day per worker was paid.

2. Supervisory work is given only to the trusted core people, who brought their own money.

3. During campaigning musclemen maybe hired on contract. They were used to man booths along with volunteers and gave protection to the candidate during

the campaign. In one case, a sum of Rs. 2 lakh was spent. In one urban constituency, they were in cars so that they could move around quickly if trouble was created by the opponent.

MEETINGS

1. 15-20 small meetings were held daily. These cost between Rs 2-5,000 per meeting and were paid for locally.

2. There were a few large meetings in each constituency addressed by National leaders. These could cost between Rs 50,000 and Rs 2 lakh. A part of the expenditure on these meetings was borne by the State Campaign Committees. When the big leaders visited the constituency, they also gave some money for the local campaign.

PUBLICITY AND MEDIA

1. Advertisement in the papers are used. The rates charged were reported to be up to three times the normal rates. One candidate reported paying Rs 50,000 to Rs 1 lakh per advertisement.

2. Journalists were paid money for coverage. A sum of up to Rs. 20,000 was mentioned by one candidate.

3. Proprietors of local press were paid by column cm. (a sum of Rs 300 per cm. was mentioned) so as to avoid adverse publicity and get coverage. The maximum sum mentioned was Rs. 1.5 lakh.

4. In one case a candidate deployed a truck carrying a cultural troupe (with loudspeakers) to go around the constituency entertaining people at meetings. Loudspeakers on autos and rickshaws were also deployed.

5. In one campaign, local artists painted walls. This activity has considerably declined.

6. For independent candidates, familiarising the voter with the symbol is necessary. In one case, the candidate distributed the mock ballot paper.

TRANSPORT AND COMMUNICATION

1. Various forms of transport are used, like, cycles, boats, motor cycles, cars and helicopters. While helicopters were hired, cars came from several sources. No payments were made for scooters and motor cycles.

2. In urban areas, now cell phones and wireless sets are used for communication. In one case, 50 cell phones and 200 wireless sets were used. The cell phones were not returned. Those with own cell phones were given SIM cards. In one case, the expense mentioned on such communication was Rs 10 lakh.

AROUND POLLING DAY

1. Major expenses are incurred on election day and the day before. It came to between 10-20% of the total expenses.

2. The manpower requirement rises in the last three days since the preparations for the polling day have to be put . in place. Planning is required for counting, etc.

1. There is need to man each booth and there were generally 1500 booths per constituency. It was mentioned that between 10-20 workers per booth were required. Rs.1000 per booth was the minimum expense mentioned for a fair election. For an unfair election the sums needed were much more.

2. The night before polling, gifts were distributed in some urban pockets. Liquor, sarees, blankets , and food worth Rs 9 lakh were distributed in one case.

3. For bogus voting and booth capturing musclemen were employed. A sum of Rs. 3 lakh was mentioned in one case.

4. In the last three days intensive campaigning is needed . The numbers of campaigners may run upto 10-20000 people.

POST POLLING DAY

1. Counting may continue for two to three days. Large number of volunteers are needed. In one case 2 people per table were deployed for three days and 600

volunteers supported them from outside, relieving them and getting food.

2. Sometimes post election meetings (called thanks giving meeting) are held. One MP spent Rs. 5 lakh on this.

MISCELLANEOUS

1. Some candidates apart from the musclemen tried to manipulate religious leaders also to collect votes.

2. There is a practice of putting up dummy candidates. 8 candidates were supported and Rs.75 lakh was spent on them by one MP.

3. PMs and CMs had little idea of the expenditure in their constituency. They hardly visited their constituency because they were busy campaigning all over the State or the country. Their elections were managed by others. Local agents had a free hand and promises made to financiers on their behalf were not known to the leaders.

Most of the candidates did not know the full cost of their campaign. They tended to under-estimate it. The expenditure mentioned ranged from Rs 4 lakh to Rs 80 lakh with an average of Rs 37.4 lakh (Table V.11). However, the average of the total cost of election came to Rs 1.29 crore. This latter figure includes the voluntary contributions and expenses borne by the state and local committees. The average expense mentioned by the candidates for their own state or for those constituencies about which they had knowledge is given in Table V.12. The figure worked out to Rs 257.25 crore.

Those candidates who either had a base in their constituency or belonged to cadre based parties had low direct expenditures but a high component of voluntary contribution in manpower and other resources, like, transport and offices in individual homes. Local cadres also picked up the tab for the local meetings. For them, while the monetary outgo was small, the total cost was high because of voluntary contribution. Those who did not have much of a base in their constituency spent more cash to win elections.

Winning did not depend on expenditure alone. The same candidate may have lost at one point of time when the expenditure was higher because the wave was against his party while she/he won when the wave was in favour but money spent was less. This is a reflection of a weakness of our democracy where emotional issues matter more than the real ones.

The major candidates spent roughly equal amounts and other serious candidates also had to spend considerable amount to stay in the reckoning for the future. Parties poured in more money where the chances of winning were greater.

There was unanimity that expenses in urban constituencies were much more than in rural ones in the same state. Some mentioned that in certain urban constituencies, expenditure may have been as high as Rs 10 crore. However, this is not the norm. It was mentioned that region wise, the maximum expenditures are in the North East. They mentioned that the cost of elections was greater in the South than in the North.

5.2 Sources of Election Financing

The source of financing were:
1. Party funds. Central, State and local units.
2. Funds from important leaders.
3. Contributions from big business, local business and trade associations.
4. Contributions from friends, relatives and own resources.
5. Corrupt bureaucrats and policemen.

It was mentioned by some that while big businessmen give large sums to the Central and State party coffers, they also give smaller sums directly to candidates or their agents. When an issue of interest to big business comes up in the legislature there is direct pressure on the MP who may have been given the funds and also indirectly through senior leaders.

The figures for the various MPs are given in Table V.13.

5.3 Total Expenditures in 1998 Elections

According to data from CSDS Data Unit, there were a total of 4695 candidates for the 1998 elections. If one considers those polling less than 1% of the votes polled as non-viable candidates then the viable candidates turned out to be 2633. In other words, there were approx. 9 candidates per constituency and of them 5 were viable and 4 non-viable. Assuming three major candidates and two minor candidates to be viable one can try to work out the total expenditures by the candidates.

The non-viable candidates may be taken to be immaterial since either their expenditure is negligible or if they are put up by the major candidates then she/he bears their expenditure. Assume that the major candidates spend roughly the same amounts and the minor candidates spend 20% of what the major candidates do. Assuming further that the cost of election including voluntary contribution and party level expenditures is Rs 1.3 crore per candidate, the expense per constituency comes to Rs 4.4 crore. Hence for 2,633 candidates, the expense would turn out to be Rs 2317 crore. This would be the expense of the 1998 Lok Sabha elections for the political system.

If the guesses given the political leaders are used, the expenditure per candidate would be double at Rs 2.57 crore. Hence per constituency it comes to Rs 8.7 crore and for the entire election Rs 4601 crore. However, this figure is hard to confirm since no breakdown of expenditures was taken from the candidates.

To work out the total cost of the election to the nation, it would be necessary to add to the above figures the costs incurred in various other ways:

1. Expenditures by the party machinery. The process must be counted from the time the nomination process begins to the time that a government is installed.

2. Expenditures by the Election Commission. These figures are available from the budget. The figure mentioned over three budget documents comes to about Rs 650 crores.

3. The above figure may not include the normal expenditures on Law and Order agencies and Administration. Some movement of forces for elections may also not be included in the allocations for the

Election Commission. These are hard to estimate since these are spread out over a month.

4.Media spends considerable sums for coverage of elections and the announcement of results. However, these are resources which are diverted from normal coverage so only the additional funds spent need to be estimated.

5.During election time, there is lot of dislocation of work and without a political authority, policy decisions are held up. All this constitutes hidden costs which are hard to estimate. Due to the prevailing uncertainty, investments are also delayed and this may cause the economy to slow down. But as soon as the new government comes in, things may get speeded up so that in the net, it is not clear what the loss maybe, and, these costs are hard to estimate.

5.4 General Comments from Politicians

1. The two or three major parties spend roughly equal amounts on the campaign.

2. Mr. Sheshan did not succeed in curbing election expenses. They were driven underground.

3. Some politicians admitted to a strong nexus with big business and hinted that many leaders have close touch with Mafia. It was reported that all businessmen contribute to the politicians.

4. Since non-election time expenses of politicians have gone up sharply, businessmen have been contributing on a monthly basis also. Many receive money for asking questions in parliament, fixing appointments with ministers, giving advance information of developments, proposing favourable appointments, etc.

5. According to one former MP who has been a Minister and a former Speaker, some CMs have amassed wealth of the order of Rs 5,000 crore. He felt the nexus between the politician and the businessmen strengthened during Mrs. Indira Gandhi's time. The public has now come to

expect large expenditures by candidates. Simplicity is no more a virtue.

6. One MP who has fought elections as a party candidate, as an independent and has managed the elections of a former PM, felt, there was no relationship between winning and expenditures. The important things are the current wave, community solidarity and local alliances. Personal presence is not critical. Workers are the most important element of the campaign.

7. An MP who has been a key Minister and has been in charge of election campaigns of an important national party said that criminals earn during elections and they are used by politicians to fix things and protect themselves. According to him, increasingly, dishonest bureaucrats are being chosen for key positions to manipulate matters and some secretaries to the Government of India take cuts in deals. He stated that key postings of bureaucrats are often fixed from the top so that manipulation becomes possible. He also stated that the judiciaries are being interfered with. In his opinion, Prime Ministers are prisoners of many social and economic forces.

8. An ex-PM stated that as CM and PM or party president when he fought elections, he had no idea of expenditures since he hardly visited own constituency. He was busy campaigning generally. He felt, fund collectors have become more and more dishonest. He stated that the funds spent in the campaign did not determine whether he won or lost. He pointed to two trends, first, the politicians need more and more finance for elections and day to day functioning and secondly, the Corporate sector has high stakes in the economy and in controlling their economic climate. They need to control key politicians and bureaucrats. The two come together. He cited the example of the use of the promoter's quota to give money to bureaucrats and politicians. He felt the media is a part of the nexus. He gave the example of how events are created to subvert action against vested

interests and media is used to discredit the honest politician and the bureaucrat. In his opinion, the so called constraints on a PM are self-imposed. The PM is free to act, if honest. Bureaucracy cannot stop politicians if they are determined.

9. Another ex-PM stated that he had no idea of election expense incurred by his agents since he was busy. As PM, he was surrounded by day to day problems and had little time to think of the long run. He believed that State funding of elections would not work in India since this will only add to the funds already used. In the fifties, the elections were a celebration by the people and there was even communal langar in the villages to feed all the campaigners.

6.1.Increase in Costs of Production in Organized Industry

The black economy enhances three major items of costs for industry. Namely, transactions costs, indirect taxes and interest cost. It also increases the cost of production of the declared output.

1.Transactions costs.

A. Purchased input (material and labour) costs increase due to bribes and over invoicing.

B. Capital costs rise due to delays, bribes and over invoicing.

C. Costs sre higher due to the inferior quality of inputs and extra processing cost.

D. More working capital is required due to holding of larger inventories due to uncertainty and delays.

2.Indirect taxes.

A. Higher rates are needed to counter inadequate direct tax collections.

B. Higher effective rates follow due to cascading effects.

3.Interest costs rise.

A.Due to borrowings by industry from informal markets.

Bb.Due to government's (and public sector's) growing need for borrowed funds and increases in interest rates offered by it, raising the floor of interest rates.

4.The cost of production of the undeclared output is loaded on the declared output.

A.The increase in the transactions costs would be of the order of 40%, roughly the size of the black economy.

B. Assuming revenue neutrality, that is, if direct taxes were paid, how much would indirect taxes be less by [an exercise carried out in Kumar (1994)]? On this basis, indirect taxes add 25% to costs.

C. Assuming that, if direct tax collection was adequate, government's borrowing requirements would have been at the level in the seventies and interest rates would have been close to the LIBOR (say 10%) and assuming informal market rates to be at least 24% and the formal market rates to be 18%, the interest cost would be higher by 10%.

D. If the undeclared output in industry is 40% of the output, then the costs of declared output are higher by 40%.

In effect, the cost of production of organized industry in India in 1995 was higher by around 115% due to the existence of the black economy. These extra costs are a result of the waste involved in production and the extra profits accruing to the propertied classes.

7.1.Direct Tax Buoyancy Post 1991

There has been a consistent attempt by some to argue for the complete elimination of personal income-tax. The arguments advanced are a) it is expensive to collect, b) it collects very little and c) more could be collected through other taxes, like, corporate taxation. It is argued that earlier the tax rates were low and the same percentage of GDP was collected as today so why keep this tax on the statutes or at least the tax rates should be lowered and it should be levied only on high incomes.

The fact that the same percentage of GDP is collected now as earlier with higher current rates of taxes is precisely what proves that the black economy is much larger today than earlier. To collect more from the corporate sector in the present set up will be far more difficult given the resources for tax evasion at their command. The cost of collection of direct taxes is not high. Around 1% of the taxes collected. For the salaried class, tax is collected at source and there is little expense for the tax authority. Thus, most of the expense is on collecting taxes from businesses or from property.

Elimination of one more direct tax (earlier wealth tax, estate duty and gift taxes have been almost eliminated) will facilitate further generation of black incomes. The elimination of wealth tax facilitated evasion of income-tax by providing channels of evasion. With gift taxes non-functional, it is easy to split up capital, and, therefore, incomes thus facilitating tax evasion. If income-tax is eliminated, it would be hard to collect capital gains tax and interest tax.

Finally, to make up for lost direct taxes, indirect taxes would have to be increased and that will lead to both inflation and high cost of manufacture. VAT does not overcome these problems. If indirect taxes are not raised, revenue deficit would rise leading to fiscal crisis and more of borrowing with its attendant problems. Converting income-tax to Expenditure Tax will only aggravate the problems further since for revenue neutrality, tax rates will be in three digits. As suggested, in the main text, if some reform is instituted, a lot more can be collected.

Tables (VII.3 and 4) show that in spite of the introduction of taxes on services, presumptive taxes, reduction in tax rates, etc., the collection of direct taxes as a percentage of the tax base has not increased since 1991. It has fluctuated and remained at roughly the same level proving that more tax is *not* collected as tax rates are decreased.

Statistical Appendix

TABLE II.1

SIZE OF THE BLACK ECONOMY IN SELECT COUNTRIES

Country	Year	As % of GNP	Source
1. Australia	1978/9	10.7*	CBA, 1980
2. Belgium	1980	15	Mont (Pestieu,1985)
	1980	20.8	Geeroms (Pestieu,1985)
	1980	3.8-12.7	Geeroms (Pestieu,1985) #
3. France	1980	6.0-7.0	Contini,1982
4. W. Germany	1980	3.7-12.6	Langfeldt,1985
	1980	11	Kirchgassner,1983
5. Great Britain	1979	15	Feige,1981b
	1979	7.2*	Dilnot,Morris,1981
	1979	7.5	Contini,1982
6. Italy	1982	19**	Siesto,1987b
	1982	15.4	ISTAT,1987
7. Japan	1980	4.1	Weck,Frey,1985
8. Spain	1985	21.9***	CIS,1986
9. Sweden	NA	4.7	Central Statistical Office (Hansson, 1989)
10. Switzerland	1978	4.3	Weck,Frey,1985
11. United States	1980	4.5-6.1	Tanzi, 1983
	1980	8.1-14.3	Simon, Witte,1982
	1980	8.1-11.7	Tanzi, 1980

Notes:

* as % of GDP.

** in % of value added at producer's prices.

*** in % of total employment.

\# only activities not recorded in the national accounts.

Source: Brian Dallago, *The IrregularEconomy*, p. 21.

TABLE II.2

CORRECTED VALUES OF KEY MACRO VARIABLES
(1990-91)

(figures in Rs Crore)

		White comp.	Black comp.	Actual value
1.	GDP at market Prices	5,35,000	1,60,000	6,95,000
2.	Primary	31%	5%	25%
3.	Secondary	25%	25%	25%
4.	Tertiary	44%	70%	50%
5.	Gross Domestic Savings	24%	50%	30%
6.	Aggregate Investments	27.5%	17%	25%
7.	Incremental K/O ratio	5.0	1.9	4.4
8.	Exports (goods and services)	41,000	55,000	96,000
9.	Imports (")	49,000	13,000	62,000
10.	Tax revenue foregone		1,00,000	

Notes: 1. Figures presented under black component are indicative, based on
scattered evidence and a broad understanding of the black economy.
2. The % figures under actual value are the weighted average
of the black and the white components.
Item 10: refers to both direct and indirect taxes.
Item 7:The rate of growth of black economy is taken to be 9% and of the
white economy 5.5%. The increase in output of the black economy is not
only due to investments in the black economy but also due to the
misdeclared white output.

TABLE III.1

GROWING SHARE OF TERTIARY SECTOR AND NON-WAGE AND
SALARY INCOME (SURPLUS) IN NDP

Year	NDP at FC (Current Prices) (Rs crore)	Compensation of employees		Share of the rest (%)	Share of tertiary sector in NDP (%)
		Total (Rs crore)	% share in NDP		
1980-81	105506	42958.5	40.7	59.3	35.9
1981-82	120698	48511.9	40.2	59.8	36.4
1982-83	134138	55848.2	41.6	58.4	37.5
1983-84	158805	64599.6	40.7	59.3	36.3
1984-85	185697	NA	NA	NA	37.2
1985-86	207848	NA	NA	NA	38.0
1991-92	489689	NA	NA	NA	48.4
1992-93	557826	211777	38.0	62.0	48.9

(Contd.)

1993-94	651322	238057	36.5	63.5	49.2
1994-95	772680	276794	35.8	64.2	49.1
1995-96	894700	329150	36.8	63.2	50.5
1996-97	1022033	NA	NA	NA	51.8

Sources: National Accounts Statistics (1970-71—1983-84);1986 pp. 18, 142-43 ;
NAS (1980-81—1986-87); 1989 pp.40,42 and NAS 1998; pp. 28, 193

TABLE III.2

CALCULATION OF BLACK INCOME SHARES IN GDP IN 1995-96

	WHITE INCOMES		BLACK INCOMES (%)	
	1980-81	1995-96	1980-81	1995-96
Public Sector	21523	216033		
Public Administration & Defence	5414	46915	0	0
Public Sector Goods (PSG)	16109	169118		
Share of PSG	15	19		
Public Agriculture	583	4896	0	0
PSG less Agriculture (PSGNA)	15526	164222	4	6
Share of PSGNA	15	18		
Organized Private Sector	13484	144531		
Organized Private Agriculture	305	3969	0	0
Organized Pvt. Non-Agric. (OPNA)	13179	140563	12	40
Share of OPNA	12	16		
Unorganized Sector	70499	534136		
Unorganized Agriculture	38573	230717		
Unorganized Non-agriculture (UNA)	31926	303418	26	74
Share of UNA	30	34		
Agriculture	39461	239582	0	0
Public Administration .& Defence	5414	46915	0	0
Agri. + Pub. Ad. & Def. (APD)	44875	286497	0	0
Share of APD	43	32		
Black Inc. % of GDP (Basu mod.)	10		10	
Contribnution of PSG+OPNA	8	22		
Black Inc. Share (GDP)(Legal)				32
Black Inc. Share (GDP)(Illegal)			5	8
Total			15	40

Source: Economic Survey, 1997-98 and *National Accounts Statistics*, 1998.
Notes: 1. Where not mentioned, share means % of NDP.
   2. The size of the black economy in 1995-96 is lower than it may have been because of the legalization of gold flows and the conversion of a part of the formerly undeclared output by the corporate sector to dress up its balance sheet. That is why a 2% reduction in the size of the legal and the illegal sectors is taken into account.

TABLE III.3

NATIONAL ACCOUNTS STATISTICS: SECTORAL COMPOSITION FOR 1995-96

Sector	GDP at current prices in Rs crore					Contribution in NDP		Share of employees
	Total	Public Sector	Private Sector	% of Public Sector	% of Unorg. Sector	Comp. of employees	Total	
1.Primary	276852	8946	267906	3.23	95.9	48691	259088	0.19
1.1. Agriculture	255613	7434	248179	2.91	96.3	45328	239582	0.19
1.2. Forestry and Logging	11267	1503	9764	13.34	83.8	1557	10888	0.14
1.3. Fishing	9972	9	9963	0.09	99.9	1806	8618	0.21
2. Mining & Quarrying	20554	24598	-4044	119.68	8.4	6336	13288	0.48
3. Manufacturing	198348	29048	169300	14.64	38.2	55029	170117	0.32
3.1 Registered	126084	29048	97036	100	0	NA	105078	NA
3.2 Unregistered	72264	0	72264	0	100	NA	65039	NA
4. Elec., Gas & Water Supply	28021	28972	-951	103.39	2.2	8086	14398	0.56
5.Construction	58416	8678	49738	14.86	51.3	42730	55929	0.76
6 Trade, Hotels & Restaurants	142808	5972	136836	4.18	82.5	32976	139084	0.24
6.1 Trade	133529	5678	127851	4.25	83.4	30191	131049	0.23
6.2 Hotels & Restaurants	9279	294	8985	3.17	68.1	2785	8035	0.35
								(Contd.)
7. Transport, Storage & Comm.	75365	35814	39551	47.52	50.8	26116	57434	0.45

7.1.	Railways	12580	12580	0	100.00	0	6270	9133	0.69
7.2.	Transport by other means	48521	9463	39058	19.50	77.7	15959	37104	0.43
7.3.	Storage	815	322	493	39.51	45.9	275	751	0.37
7.4.	Communication	13449	13449	0	100.00	0	3612	10446	0.35
8.	Finance, insurance, real estate & business services	94475	44319	50156	46.91	29	20270	81237	0.25
8.1.	Banking & insurance	65314	43919	21395	67.24	8.3	18858	62430	0.30
8.2.	Real estate, ownership of dwellings & business services	29161	400	28761	1.37	97.8	1412	18807	0.08
9.	Community, Social & Pers. Services	111447	77610	33837	69.64	21.7	88916	104125	0.85
9.1	Public Admin. & Defence	52081	52081	0	100.00	0	46915	46915	1.00
9.2.	Other Services	59366	25529	33837	43.00	39.4	42001	57210	0.73

Source: National Accounts Statistics 1998, CSO, GOI, pp. 22, 80, 191, 199.

TABLE V.1

WHO PAID HOW MUCH INCOME TAX IN 1992-93?

Assessed Income Class ('000)	Individuals			Registered Firms			Companies			All Status		
	Number of returns ('000)	Income returned (Rs Cr.)	Tax payable (Rs Cr.)	Number of returns ('000)	Income returned (Rs Cr.)	Tax payable (Rs Cr.)	Number of returns ('000)	Income returned (Rs Cr.)	Tax payable (Rs Cr.)	Number Of returns ('000)	Income returned (Rs Cr.)	Tax payable (Rs Cr.)
L.T. 28	203.8	37.5	65.8	50.7	231.0	11.6	22.9	15.9	7.2	311.0	669.4	92.6
28-50	2363.8	8590.1	1118.0	171.2	756.3	45.4	10.8	34.4	15.6	2671.3	9983.0	1253.9
50-100	1597.6	11609.8	1311.4	336.5	2573.4	308.8	9.5	57.3	26.9	2017.4	14858.8	1816.9
100-200	104.9	1630.6	671.9	61.8	785.1	157.0	6.9	54.6	26.2	185.0	2689.7	915.7
200-300	25.3	678.5	271.2	14.4	368.4	62.6	3.9	117.9	58.5	46.4	1238.0	417.3
300-400	13.7	533.2	218.8	7.6	219.4	43.9	3.1	80.3	40.1	26.9	923.2	346.6
400-500	8.6	404.5	152.8	4.7	237.5	47.5	2.5	104.0	51.8	16.8	797.4	291.1
500-1000	2.4	177.5	88.1	2.5	3440.7	72.3	3.0	186.7	96.1	8.2	735.4	266.9
1000+	2.7	485.6	217.9	2.4	619.1	123.8	6.2	5792.1	3110.4	11.7	7112.7	3500.8
Total	4322.8	24484.9	4115.8	651.8	6134.3	872.8	68.7	6443.1	3432.7	5294.8	39007.5	8901.8

Source: All India Income Tax Statistics, Assessment year 1992-93, Directorate of Income tax, GOI, pp. 8-10

TABLE V.2.a

THE NUMBER OF ASSESSEES (OTHER THAN COMPANY) 1993-97

As on 31March of the following year	Number of assessees
1993	8232350
1994	10028974
1995	10108012
1996	10476940
1997	11416315

Source: Report of CAG of India for the year ended March 1997, Union Govt. (Direct Taxes) No. 12 of 1998, p.190

TABLE V.2.b

NUMBER OF RETURNS, GROSS INCOME AND GROSS TAX BY SOURCE OF INCOME ASSESSMENT YEAR: 1994-95

Source of Income	Number of Returns	Gross Income	Gross tax
1. Salaries	174.8491	10850.197	1962.7
2. Interest on securities	41.8287	2372.3508	930.03
3. House property	78.9623	2364.1199	811.75
4. Business and Profession	596.9953	58603.609	17425
5. Capital Gains	35.9739	1345.6581	456.85
6. Other Sources			
Dividends	227.4248	4229.7756	1035.8
Others	112.3716	5092.1056	1307.7
Total	227.4248	9321.8812	2343.2
Grand Total	804.391	84840.092	23930

TABLE V.3
CATEGORY WISE BREAK-UP OF INCOME TAX ASSESSEES AS ON 31ST MARCH 1997

('0,000)

Category	Individuals	Hindu Undivided Families	Firms	Companies	Others (incl.Trusts)	Total
(i) Category A	944.3293	39.2243	109.1502	12.8137	7.4953	1113.0135
(ii) Category B (Lower)	24.0262	1.2162	4.1946	4.3622	0.6545	34.4537
(iii) Category B (Higher)	4.0964	0.3696	1.2474	2.5277	0.0813	8.3224
(iv) Category C	1.9149	0.2321	0.7860	2.6951	0.1645	5.7926
(v) Category D	1.7758	0.2048	0.4537	0.3241	0.0144	2.7728
Total	976.1426	41.2470	115.8319	22.7228	8.4100	1164.3540

Explanation:

1. Category A - Company assessments with income/loss below Rs. 50,000 and non-Co. assessment with income/loss below Rs 2 lakh.

2. Category B (lower income group)- Company assessments with income/loss of Rs.50000 and above but below Rs.5 lakh and non-Company assessments with income/loss of Rs.2 lakh and above-but below Rs.5 lakh.

3. Category B (higher income group)- Company and non-Company assessments with income/loss of Rs.5 lakh and above but below Rs. 10 lakh

4. Category C- Company and non-Co. assessments with income/loss of Rs.10 lakh and above.

5. Category D- Search and Seizure assessments.

Source: Report of CAG of India for the year ending March 1997, p.20.
(For Table V.4 and Table V.5 see p. 305/306)

TABLE V.6

SIZE OF GOVERNMENT AND TAX-GDP RATIO OF SELECT COUNTRIES (% OF GDP)

Country	Tax Revenue		Non Tax Revenue		Total Expenditure	
	1980	1995	1980	1995	1980	1995
Kenya	19.1	19.6	8.5	10	25.3	27.4
India	9.8	9.6	5	4.1	13.3	16
Zambia	23.1	13.4	10.8	7	37	16.8
Sri Lanka	19.1	18	5.4	10.8	41.3	28.6
Egypt	28.9	26.3	4	5.6	45.6	42.8
Indonesia	20.2	16.4	1.8	6.2	22.1	16.2
Turkey	14.3	14.3	3.6	7.3	21.4	27
South Africa	20.5	25.2	5.6	10	22.1	33.2
Brazil	17.8	18.6	7.3	4.9	20.8	39
Korea, Rep.	15.3	17.7	8	6.5	17	17.8
Israel	43.3	33.4	12.4	13	70	45.2
Italy	29.1	38.4	7.7	11.2	39.8	49.9
Sweden	30.1	32.8	10.2	11.2	39.3	45
Netherlands	44.2	42.9	10.3	10.5	52.8	50.8
USA	18.5	19	0.9	0.8	22.1	22.9

Source: World Development Report 1997, pp. 240-41.
Note: Total expenditure is taken to represent the size of the government.

TABLE V.7

GOVERNMENT THE WORLD OVER HAS EXPANDED SINCE
1960
Central Government spending (% of GDP)

Group of countries	1960-64	1970-74	1980-84	1990-94
OECD countries	18	25	35	36
All developing countries	16	20	28	27
Sub-saharan Africa	19	19	26	27
East Asia and Pacific	16	18	26	26
South Asia	16	15	25	30
L. America & Caribbean	15	20	26	25
Mid.East and N. America	NA	35	38	35

Notes: Data are in current national prices.
Source: World Development Report 1997, p.22.

TABLE V.8

THE STATE HAS GROWN EVERYWHERE THIS CENTURY

Year	Total Govt. Exp. (% of GDP)	
	OECD Countries	Developing Countries
About 1870	9	NA
1913	9	NA
1920	14	NA
1937	21	NA
1960	16	15
1965	NA	17
1970	NA	18
1975	NA	24
1980	41	25
1985	NA	32
1990	43	25
1995	48	NA

Notes: Data for the OECD countries are for central and local government, including social security expenditures. Figures are approximate.
Source: World Development Report, 1997, p. 2

TABLE V.9

MANY COUNTRIES ARE LOOSENING RESTRAINTS ON INTERNATIONAL CAPITAL

Rules governing foreign capital transactions	Approximate No. of Countries		
	1975	1985	1994
Liberal	4	9	16
Mostly liberal	4	2	13
Partly Liberal	11	15	20
Restrictive	32	30	20
Very Restrictive	40	41	30

Notes: Data are for 102 industrial and developing countries. Liberal means no restrictions; Mostly liberal means a few restrictions by industry; Partly liberal means many restriction on the size and timing of transactions; Restrictive means that domestic investment by foreigners or foreign investment by domestic residents requires official approval; Very Restrictive means that all cross border transactions require official approval.
Source: *World Development Report* 1997, p. 135.

TABLE V.10

POLITICIANS WHO HAVE BENEFITTED FROM PROXIMITY TO LEADERS OR BECAUSE OF FAMILY

POLITICIAN	LEADER	LINK
Indira Gandhi	Jawaharlal Nehru	Daughter
Rajiv Gandhi	Indira Gandhi	Son
Sanjay Gandhi	Indira Gandhi	Son
Maneka Gandhi	Sanjay Gandhi	Widow
Sonia Gandhi	Rajiv Gandhi	Widow
M L Fotedar	Indira Gandhi	Secretary
R K Dhawan	Indira Gandhi	Secretary
K C Pant	Govind Ballabh Pant	Son
Ila Pan	K C Pant	Wife
Farooq Abdullah	Sheikh Abdullah	Son
Omar Abdullah	Farooq Abdullah	Son
Rabri Devi	Laloo Prasad Yadav	Wife
Ajit Singh	Charan Singh	Son
Lakshmi Parvati	N T Rama Rao	Wife
N Chandrababu Naidu	N T Rama Rao	Son-in Law
J Jayalalitha	M G Ramachandran	Secretary

Navin Patnaik	Biju Patnaik	Son
S. S. Badal	Prakash S Badal	Son
Madhav Rao Scindia	Royal Family.	
Vasundhra Raje Scindia	Royal Family.	
Murasoli Maran	M Karunanidhi	Nephew
Shiela Dixit	Uma Shankar Dixit	Daughter-in-law
P R Kumaramanglam	Mohan Kumaramanglam	Son
Om Prakash Chautala	Devi Lal	Son
Meira Kumar	Jagjivan Ram	Daughter
Prakash Ambedkar	B R Ambedkar	Son

This is a partial list and there are many other leaders who have benefited from links with important leaders or have had important family links. The Left parties and the BJP are not so widely afflicted by such a tendency since most leaders of these parties have to come up from the grass roots. However, in these parties also, family connections have mattered.

TABLE V.13

CALCULATION OF THE AVERAGE ELECTION EXPENDITURE BASED ON ESTIMATES GIVEN BY THE POLITICAL LEADERS

Region mentioned	Expenditure per constituency	No. of constituencies relevant	Weighted average Estimated Expenditure	
			region	country
1 Maharashtra	165	18		
	750	45		
	1000	10		
	1000	1		
	1000	1	649.6	
2 South	110	120		
South	500	120		
Coastal Andhra Pradesh	175	10		
Urban	325	20	301.667	
3 Garo Hills	200	1	200	
4 MP	85	45	85	
5 East	50	55	50	
				257.25

Source: Interviews of 14 MPs conducted for the purpose of this book.
Note: Expenditure is in Rs lakh.

TABLE V.11

ELECTION EXPENSES OF SELECT CANDIDATES IN 1998 ELECTION

	Part of India	Rural/ Urban	Elec.Day & day before	Manpower	Meetings	Office expense	Vehicles	Publicity & Journ.	Misc.	Total	Mentioned by cand.	Indirect / Voluntary
MP1	West	R	22	16@	4	..	10	2	..	54	30	24
MP2	East	R	27	100	26	2	8	6	..	169	54	115
MP3	South	R-U	25	30	8	..	6	30	5*	104	80	24
MP4	South	..	30	3	..	..	15	..	100	148	70	78
MP5	Central	R	20	38	4	..	24	11	..	97	50	47
MP6	West	..	..	90	25	..	3	2	..	120^^	12	108
MP7	East	..	15	22	..	..	5.5**	15***	..	57.5^^	26	31.5
MP8	South	..	..	63	..	..	3	15	..	81	30	51
MP9	East		Rajya Sabha Member									
MP10	North	R-U	No idea of expenses									
MP11	North	U(metro)	32	163.7#	1	3.5	30^	25	75$	329.2	40	289.2
MP12	East	R-U	..	240	2.5	8.7	6	2	1##	260.2	4	256.2
MP13	South	R	No idea of expenses CM and party presidents took care of funds									
MP14	North	R-U	..	..	..	..	..	..	..	15	15	..

Legend:
* Post Election Expenses.   ** 3.5 on vehicle and 2 on helicopter.   *** Includes publicity and meetings both.
# 3.7 lakh was spent on muscle men   ## Cultural troupe and wall writers.   @ Includes payment to leaders with vote banks.
$ Expense on opponents.   ^ 30 lakhs on communications.   ^^ Projected figure from earlier elections.

TABLE V.12

SOURCES OF FINANCING OF EXPENDITURE IN 1998 ELECTION

(In Rs. Lakh)

Part.	Calculated Expenditure	Mentioned by the candidate	Party	Big leaders	Friends/ Relatives	Corr. Bureau. and police	Business	Indirect/ Voluntary
MP1	54	30	5 to 10	1	..	..	..	24
MP2	169	54	10	2	10	2	30	115
MP3	104	80	10	4	NA	NA	NA	24
MP4	148	70	..	..	70	..	..	78
MP5	97	50	10	1	..	..	36	47
MP6	120	12	..	..	..	..	108	108
MP7	57.5	26	2	..	..	..	29.5$$	31.5
MP8	81	30	..	..	..	..	51$$	51
MP11	329.2	40	25	..	..	75^$	55^^	159.2
MP12	262.2	4						256.2
MP14	15	15	2		13			

Notes: ^^ 50 lakh from trade associations and 5 lakh from big business

^$ From local businessmen and corrupt bureaucrat.

NA money was collected but exact breakup not available.

$$ From friends, relatives and businessmen.

Source for Tables V.11 and V.12: Interviews of 14 political leader, conducted for this book.

TABLE VII.1

EMPLOYMENT AND COMPENSATION OF EMPLOYEES IN THE PUBLIC AND THE PRIVATE SECTORS IN THE MID-NINETIES

		1992-93	1995-96	% Growth over 1992-93
1	Compensation of Employees in Organised Sector	137785	216049	
	1.a.Public Sector	100852	151020	
	1.a.1. Departmental Enterprises	15153	20968	
	1.a.2. Other Enterprises	85699	130052	
	1.b.Private Secor	36933	65029	
2	Employment in Organised Sector	27.1	27.94	
	2.a.Public Sector	19.25	19.4	
	2.a.1.Departmental Enterprises	2.15	2.05	
	2.a.2. Other Enterprises.	17.1	17.35	
	2.b.Private Sector	7.85	8.54	
3	Per capita emolument			
	3.a.Public Sector			
	3.a.1.Departmental Enterprises	70479	102282	45.12
	3.a.2.Other Enterprises.	50116	74957	49.57
	3.b.Private Sector	47048	78348	66.53
	3.c.Total	50843	77323	52.08
4	Per Capita Income	6262	9578	52.95

Source: National Accounts Statistics 1998 and Economic Survey 1997-98

TABLE VII.6

THOSE PAYING DIRECT TAXES ON 31ST MARCH 1997

	Income Tax	Wealth Tax	Gift Tax
Individuals	9761426	255136	45777
HUF	41247	33141	01246
Firms	1158319	NA	18
Companies	227228	11631	124
Trusts	49629	NA	NA
Others	34471	NA	199
Total	11643543	299908	47364

Source: Report of CAG of India for the year ending March 1997, p. 9

TABLE VII.2

NUMBER OF RETURNS, GROSS INCOME AND GROSS TAX FROM BUSINESS AND PROFESSION BY NATURE OF BUSINESS

Nature of business	Status	Number of Returns	Gross Income (Rs'000)	Gross Tax (Rs'000)	Income declared per return (Gross inc/No. of ret)
1.Business Services	Non-Company	470706	28477080	7098535	60.50
	Company	11361	11058452	2472068	973.37
	Total	482067	39535532	9570603	82.01
2. Real Estate	Non-Company	46588	1493837	459483	32.06
	Company	1822	1216837	429717	667.86
	Total	48410	2710674	88920	55.99
3. Legal services	Non-Company	64005	2252573	678339	35.19
	Company	365	1230598	402775	3371.50
	Total	64370	3483171	1081114	54.11
4.Medical & Health Services	Non-Company	208948	9686449	2964148	46.36
	Company	1282	1467226	421278	1144.48
	Total	210230	11153675	3385426	53.05
5.Recreational & Cultural Services	Non-Company	19082	1756265	318049	92.04
	Company	605	347909	122841	575.06
	Total	19687	2104174	440890	106.88
6.Personal Services	Non-Company	70684	3518872	552814	49.78
	Company	376	523861	188426	1393.25
	Total	71060	4042733	741240	56.89
7.Services not elsewhere classified	Non-Company	360237	17351619	29994216	48.17
	Company	1913	2460376	785257	1286.13
	Total	362150	19811995	3779473	54.71

Source: Statistical Abstract, 1997, Page 540

TABLE VII.3

DIRECT TAXES AND THEIR TAX BASE: HAS COMPLIANCE IMPROVED?

(In Rs. Crore)

Particulars	1990-91	1991-92	1992-93	1993-94	1994-95	1995-96	1996-97	1997-98	1998-99	1999-00
1 Income Tax	5371	6731	7888	9123	12025	15592	18231	17097	21430	24910
2 Corporation Tax	5335	7853	8899	10060	13822	16487	18567	20016	27050	29750
3 Interest Tax	(-)1	305	716	727	801	1170	1712	1205	920	1000
4 Other taxes on income and exp.	82	...	151	229	197	228	293	9834	300	330
5 Aggregate Tax (Income+Corp.+Interest+Other)	10788	14889	17654	20139	26845	33477	38803	48152	49700	55990
6 NDP at factor cost (Cur. prices)	425619	489689	557826	651322	772680	894700	1022033	NA	NA	NA
7 Share of Unorg. in NDP at FC (Cur. Prices)	63.8	63.3	63.5	62.3	61.7	59.7	NA	NA	NA	NA
8 Unorg. Seg. Contr. to NDP at FC (Cur. Prices)(7*6/100)	271544.9	309973	354219.5	405773.6	476744	534135.9	NA	NA	NA	NA
9 Org. Sect. Contr. to NDP at FC (Cur. Prices)(6-8)	154074.1	179716	203606.5	245548.4	295936	360564.1	NA	NA	NA	NA
10 Agr. Contr. to NDP at FC (Cur. Prices)	127259	149824	166949	194316	225396	239582	NA	NA	NA	NA
11 Share of Org. Sec. in Agr.	3.2	3	3	3.2	3.1	3.7	NA	NA	NA	NA
12 Total Org. Sect in Agr. (10*11/100)	4072.3	4494.7	5008.5	6218.1	6987.3	8864.5	NA	NA	NA	NA

13	Org.Sect.NonAgr Contr to NDPat FC(Cur. Prices)(9-12)	150001.8	175221	198598.0	239330.3	288949	351699.6	NA	NA	NA	NA
14	Non-Wage and Salary Income in Org Sect NDP	48749	59017	66046	92655	118220	144927	NA	NA	NA	NA
15	Direct Tax Base (13*14/9)	47460.5	57541	64421.3	90308.7	115429	141363.9	NA	NA	NA	NA
16	Ratio of income tax to Org Sect NDP (1/13*100)	3.58	3.84	3.97	3.81	4.16	4.43	NA	NA	NA	NA
17	Ratio of Corp. Tax to Org Sect NDP (2/13*100)	3.56	4.48	4.48	4.20	4.78	4.69	NA	NA	NA	NA
18	Ratio of Direct Taxes to Org Sect. NDP (5/13*100)	7.19	8.50	8.89	8.41	9.29	9.52	NA	NA	NA	NA
19	Ratio of Direct Taxes to NDP(5/6)	0.03	0.03	0.03	0.03	0.03	0.04	NA	NA	NA	NA
20	Ratio of Direct Taxes to Direct Tax Base (5/15)	0.23	0.26	0.27	0.22	0.23	0.24	NA	NA	NA	NA

Source: 1. Receipts Budget 1999-2000, GOI; p. 64.
2. National Accounts Statistics, CSO,GOI 1998 and 1997.

TABLE VII.4

GROSS PROFIT AND TAXES PAID BY PUBLIC LIMITED COMPANIES: ARE THEY PAYING THESE TAXES

(Rs. Crore)

Particulars	1990-91	1991-92	1992-93	1993-94	1994-95	1995-96	1996-97	1997-98
1 No. of companies surveyed	1802	1802	1802	700	756	807	807	807
2 % of paid up capital represented in the sample	42.2	42.2	42.2	20.7	17.8	21.1	21.1	21.1
3 Sales	89912	107026	120120	78031	106096	149420	166037	175200
4 Gross Profit	10407	12721	13218	9588	15727	23284	22964	22102
5 Tax Provision	1742	2425	1998	1473	2099	3206	3666	3307
6 Gross Profit as % of Sales (4/3*100)	11.57	11.89	11.00	12.29	14.82	15.58	13.83	12.62
7 Tax Provision as % of Gross Profit (5/4*100)	16.74	19.06	15.12	15.36	13.35	13.77	15.96	14.96

Notes: * For 1993-94 to 1997-98 Surveyed Pub.Ltd.Co. are nongovernmental nonfinancial large pub.ltd.co. each with paid up capital of Rs.1 crore and above.

Source: RBI Bulletin ; Jan 1997, p. 9; Mar.1998 p. 221; Sept.1998 p. 702; Apr.1999, p. 519.

TABLE VII.5

AMNESTY SCHEMES OF GOVERNMENT OF INDIA SINCE INDEPENDENCE

		Year	No. of Cases	Income declared	Tax Collected
1	Income Tax Investigation Commission	1946-47	..	48	30
2	VDS	May-Oct 1951	20912	70.2	10.89
3	Detected by the deptt.	1963-64 to 66-67	..	81	31
4	VDS I	Mar-May 1965	2001	52.18	30.8
5	VDS II	Aug 65-Mar 66	114226	145	19.45
6	Under Section 271 (4A) of income tax act of 1961	1965-68	..	22	NA
7	VD of income and wealth Act 1976	Oct-75	(W) 245570 (I) 13422	(W) 746.08 (I) 841.72	(W) 249 (I) 7.7
8	Special Bearer Bond Scheme (1981)	1980	..	400	160
9	Voluntary deposits (immunities and exemptions)	1991	NA	NA	984
10	Finance Act (1985)	1985-86	1,53,990	2940.37	388.03
11	VDIS	1997	4,70,000	33,000	10,100

Notes: i) (W) Wealth, (I) Income.

ii) There were four amnesty schemes in 1991 three for domestic evaders (under Voluntary Deposits (Immunities and exemptions)), (Gold Bond, Deposits with National Housing Bank and Amended Section 273A of the Income Tax Act) and remittances of FOREX and investment in FOREX bond.

iii) Resurgent India Bond in 1998 collected approx. Rs. 4 billion It is not listed in the table because it was only partly like an amnesty scheme.

Source: Various Economic Surveys, GOI and Kabra (1982), p44.

TABLE V.4

MAXIMUM MARGINAL TAX RATE AND THE LEVEL OF PERSONAL INCOME AT WHICH IT BECOMES EFFECTIVE IN 1984-85

Multiples of per capita GDP and the level of personal income at which it became effective in 1984-85

Maximum MTR (%)	<30	30-50	>50
>70	Portugal	Rep. of Korea Zambia	Burma Morocco Cote d'Ivore Niger Egypt Tanzania Ethiopia Tunisia Liberia
50-70	Ghana Mali Greece Pakistan Jamaica Sri lanka Malaysia Sudan	Argentina Zaire Brazil Zimbabwe India Sierra Leone	Benin Mexico Chile Nigeria Chad Peru Kenya Senegal Madagaskar Thailand Malawi Turkey
<50	Hong Kong Yemen Arab Republic	Burkina Faso Ecuador	Colombia Jordan Gutemala Indonesia Philippines Singapore

TABLE V.5

INCOME LEVEL AT WHICH PERSONAL INCOME TAX LIABILITY BEGINS AND SUBSEQUENT STRUCTURE OF THE MARGINAL TAX RATES DURING 1984-85

Category A	Category B
Brazil	Bangladesh
Colombia	Burma
Ghana	Chile
Jamaica	Guatemala
Malaysia	India
Mexico	Indonesia

Sierra Leone	Kenya
Sri Lanka	Niger
Tunisia	Peru
Turkey	Zaire
	Zambia

Source: World Development Report, p.96.

Notes: Category A - The Lowest Marginal Tax Rate is around 10% at 1.5 times per capita GDP. It rises very steeply till 4 times GDP per capita to between 30% and 50%. It then rises slowly to between 45% to 70%.

Category B - The Lowest Marginal Rate is 5% at per capita GDP. It remains constant for some countries at that level while for some it rises steeply to 30% at 10 times GDP per capita. It rises to 40% at 15 times GDP per capita.

Glossary of Technical Terms

1. Activity - Legal and Illegal: Economic work which is in conformity with the law of the land constitutes legal activity (other wise, illegal). Even if an activity is legal, black income may be generated in it by not declaring the income. An illegal activity at one point of time may become an illegal activity (or vice-versa) at another point of time.

2. Balance of Payment (BOP): Depicts the position of an economy vis-a-vis the rest of the world whether it can meet its payments obligations or not.

3. BOP Current Account: BOP consists of two parts called the current and the capital Accounts. The current account represents all the transactions with the rest of the world which do not create future obligations, like, trade in goods and services and payment of interest. The capital account as the name suggests deals with flows of capital.

4. BR- Bankers Receipts: As the name suggests, these are the papers issued by the banks for the securities kept by them on behalf of their clients. In the financial scam these were misused by the brokers to get or transfer funds without touching the underlying securities.

5. Deficits: Generally speaking deficit is the difference between expenditure and income. Various concepts are used for theoretical purposes. Budget deficit is the difference between total expenditure and total inflow into the government account, including the borrowings. Revenue deficit is the difference between revenue expenditure and revenue receipt. Fiscal deficit is the difference between total expenditure and revenue receipt. Primary deficit is the fiscal deficit less the interest payment.

6. Externality: When goods are produced or consumed by economic agents and this affects at least one other economic agent (positively or negatively) directly and not thorough the price changes in the market then there is said to be an externality. Playing music loudly, which disturbs the peace of the neighbourhood or cars polluting the air and someone getting asthama as a result of it are examples of this from consumption. A factory discharging effluent into the river and affecting drinking water and the catch of fish is another example of this but in production and consumption.

7. Factor incomes: There are two basic factors of production, namely, labour and capital. The incomes received by the owners of these factors for their use are called factor incomes. They are: wages and salaries to labour and profits to capital.

8. Investment: Addition to the stocks of capital in a given fiscal year. It is a very complex process involving the future. Hence it is always

characterized by uncertainty of the future. There is always a chance that plans set out may fail.

9. Macro variables: National income, General price level, Employment, Investment, Savings, Exports and Imports are some of the macro variables. They have an overarching impact on the various economic activities and do not refer to specific activities though they are obtained by some form of aggregation and affect them.

10. Multiplier: When investment is made in an economy, the national income increases by a multiple of it. This is called the multiplier. Similarly, there is a Money Multiplier which gives the multiple by which the money released by the RBI is multipled in the economy through the banking channels.

11. Near Money Forms: There are different kinds of assets in an economy. Some can be quickly sold to get money but others either take time or there is a loss in disposing them off. Those assets which cannot be used in transactions by themselves but can be easily disposed off to get money are near money forms.

12. National Accounts Statistics Refers to the account of the total flow of income and output of an economy during the year. The sum total of the incomes gives the national income. Crudely speaking, the total of the output gives the GDP. The accounts are divided into major activites in the economy called the sectors.

13. P/E ratio: It is the ratio between price of the share and the earning on it (not counting capital gains) in a financial year.

14. Price Index: In an economy there are many goods each having its own price in the market. The price index gives the representative price in the market. It may be thought of as the composite price. Consumer Price Index (CPI) gives the price relevant to the consumer. But it depends on what the consumer consumes. Hence there are different CPI for different areas and for different class of people. The Wholesale Price Index gives the composite price prevailing in the wholesale market.

15. Prime cost: The cost which are used by the manufacturer to fix the price of a commodity. Overhead cost are not included in them. A mark up on prime cost gives the price set by the manufacturer.

16. Government Revenue: Government revenue is made up of Tax and Non-tax sources. For details on tax revenue see Tax, types of. Non-tax revenue comprises interest payment, revenue from the sale of public assets, etc.

17. Savings propensity: It indicates that part of income which an individual saves. Average propensity to save is total saving divided by total income. While marginal propensity is the addition to saving consequent to an increase in income. The consumption propensity is one minus the savings propensity.

18. Stagflation: It is a state of the economy in which the inflation occurs simultaneously with stagnant output.

19. Supply side response: When incentives are given to economic activity and increased activity follows. For instance, if taxes are cut it is hoped profits will rise and lead to increased economic activity.

20. Tax, types of:

Direct Tax: It is a kind of tax which falls directly on the income of the individual. Indirect Tax: as the name suggests, the tax falls on the incomes indirectly. Say through the consumption. When an excise duty is levied on a good, the consumer pays the tax when she/he purchases the good. At the first stage it is paid by the manufacturer. Like sales tax is levied on the wholesale dealer seller but she/he passes it on to the consumer through the price of the commodity.

21. Taxation, criterion for: There is a debate as to who should pay tax and how much of it. It is believed that every citizen should contribute their fair share, that is, the tax system must be equitable. Usually there are two principals of taxation: the Ability to Pay and Benefits Received. The first criterion is supposed to contribute to equity while the second is like a payment for the services received hence independent of equity considerations.

22. Terms of Trade: It is the ratio between the price index of two sectors. Say between agriculture and industry or between the national and the external sectors. It is like saying how much of my output will buy the output of others with whom I do trade. Adverse terms of trade mean I am worse off.

23. Transfer activity: It is an activity which does not generate factor incomes. Assets simply change hands. Like, the purchase and sale of shares in the secondary markets.

24. Value addition: A good is produced using different raw materials and factors of production. The total value of any commodity produced is called gross output. The purchased raw materials are not the result of the effort of the producer so they do not constitute the output of that producer. Hence value added in production is obtained by subtracting the value of purchased raw materials from the gross output.

25. Velocity of Circulation: Money moves from transaction to transaction and goes around several times each year. It is the totality of the annual transactions which result in the generation of national income. Thus it can be said that money circulates the income in the economy. How fast or slow it circulates incomes is called the velocity of circulation. There two concepts of velocity of money. The first is income velocity of money which gives the number of times a unit of money circulates in the transaction of final goods and services. The second is the transaction velocity of money which gives the number of times money circulates in the transaction of all the goods and services (including intermediate goods).

Bibliography

1. Allingham, M.G. and Sandmo, A. 1972. Income Tax Evasion: A Theoretical Analysis. *Journal of Public Economics*, Vol. 27, No. 3-4, November.
2. Cagan, P. 1958. The Demand for Currency Relating to the Total Money Supply. *Journal of Political Economy,* Vol. 66.
3. Dallago, B. 1990. *The Irregular Economy.* Dartmouth Publishing Co., Dartmouth.
4. George, S. 1997. The Capitalist Threat. *The Atlantic Monthly.* February.
5. Gupta, S.B. 1992. *Black Economy in India.* Sage Publications, New Delhi.
6. Hansson, I. 1982. The Underground Economy in the High Tax Country: The Case of Sweden, in Tanzi, V. (ed.), *The Underground Economy the United States and Abroad,* D.C. Heath and Co., Toronto, pp. 233-243.
7. Hubberman, L. 1937. *Man's Worldly Goods: The Story of the Wealth of Nations.* Reprinted in India by People's Publishing House, N Delhi.
8. Kabra, K. N. 1982. *The Black Economy in India: Problems and Policies.* Chanakya Publications, Delhi.
9. Kaldor, N. 1956. *Indian Tax Reform: Report of a Survey.* Ministry of Finance, Department of Economic Affairs, New Delhi.
10. Kalecki, M. 1971. *Selected Essays on the Dynamics of the Capitalist Economy.* Cambridge University Press, Cambridge.
11. Kumar, A. 1983. *Inflation in the Indian Economy: Effect on the Terms of Trade and Incomes.* Mimeo. Unpublished Ph.D. Dissertation.
12. ———— 1985a. The Chequered Economy in Black and White, *Economic and Political Weekly.* March 30.
13. ———— 1985b. Sizing up the Black Economy: Some Issues Raised by the NIPFP Methodology. *Economic & Political Weekly.* Aug 31.
14. ———— 1986. 1986-87 Budget: Signs of Growth Pains Without Growth. *Economic & Political Weekly.* April 12.

15. ——— 1987. A Perspective on Urbanisation and Urban Land Policy. *Nagarlok*. January-March.

16. ——— 1988a. Diminishing Returns of an Unchanged Fiscal Policy Regime. *Economic and Political Weekly*. April.

17.. ——— 1988b. The Black Economy, Services and Surplus: The Growing Triad.

18. ——— 1990. Some Economic Aspects of the Growing Social Tensions in India. In S. C. Tewari (ed.) *Terrorism in India*. New Delhi: South Asia Publishers.

19. ——— 1993. The Missing Dimension of Macro-Economic Policy Making in India. The Black Economy. Mimeo. *Working Paper of the DSA*, Centre for Economic Studies and Planning, School of Social Sciences, JNU, New Delhi.

20. ——— 1994. Corruption as a Source of Black Income in India. Review of S. B. Gupta
1992, *Black Income in India*, Sage Publications, New Delhi.
The Indian Economic Review, July-December.

21. ——— 1994. Proposals for a Citizens' Union Budget for the Nation for 1994-95. An Alternative to the Fund Bank Dictated Union Budget for 1994-95. Mimeo. Presented to the Citizen's Committee on February 12, 1994 at GPF, New Delhi. Organized by Preparatory Committee for Alternative Economic Policies.

22. ——— 1995. Reinterpreting Retreat of State In Second Best Environment, *Economic and Political Weekly*, May, 6-13.

23. ——— 1996. The Black Economy in India. *Lokayan Bulletin*. January-February.

24. ——— 1999. The Black Economy: Missing Dimension of Macro Policy-Making in India. *Economic & Political Weekly*. March 20. Pp. 681-694.

25. Lal, A. 1995. *India: Enough is Enough*. Virgo Publications, New Delhi.

26. National Institute of Pubic Finance and Policy (NIPFP) 1985. *Aspects of the Black Economy*.

27. Rowthorn, R. 1977. Conflict Inflation and Money Illusion, *Cambridge Journal of Economics*, September.

28. Singh, B. 1973. Making Honesty the Best Policy, *Journal of Public Economics*, Vol.2, No. 3.

29. Tanzi, V. 1982. (ed.) *The Underground Economy in the United States and Abroad*. D. C.

30. World Development Report, Various Years. Oxford University Press. Oxford.

31. Zdanowicz, et.al. 1996. Capital Flight from India to the United States Through Abnormal Pricing in International Trade. *Finance India*. December.

LIST OF GOVERNMENT REPORTS

1. Government of India, Ministry of Finance. 1971. *Report of the Study Team on Leakages of Foreign Exchange Through Invoice Manipulation.* (Chairman: Mr. M G Kau*l*).

2. ———— Ministry of Finance. *1971. Direct Taxes Enquiry Committee. Final Report.* December. (Chairman: Justice Wanchoo).

3. ———— *Report of the Central Excise (Self Removal Procedure) Review Committee.*

4. ———— Ministry of Commerce. 1978. *Report of the Committee on Import-Export Policies and Procedures.* January. (Chairman: Mr. Alexander.)

5. ———— Ministry of Finance. 1978. *Report of the Indirect Taxation Enquiry Committee.* (Chairman: Mr. L K Jha).

6. ———— Ministry of Finance. 1979. *Report of the Committee on Controls and Subsidies.* May. (Chairman: Mr Dagli).

7. ———— Central Statistical Organization. 1980. *National Accounts Statistics: Sources and Methods.*

8. ———— Ministry of Finance. 1983. Economic Administration Reforms Commission, *Reports on Tax Administration, 1981-83.* December. (Chairman: L K Jha).

9. ———— Ministry of Finance. 1992. *Report of the Tax Reforms Committee.* (Chairman: Mr R J Chelliah).

10. ———— Ministry of Planning and Programme Implementation, Department of Statistics, Central Statistical Organization. 1998. *Statistical Abstract, 1997.*

11. ———— 1998. *Report of the Comptroller and Auditor General of India for the Year ending 1997.* Union Government (Civil). Revenue Receipts, Vol. II, Direct Taxes. No. 12.

12. ———— Ministry of Finance. 1999. *Receipt Budget, 1999-2000.*

13. ———— Central Statistical Organization. *National Accounts Statistics, Various Issues.*

14. ———— Ministry of Finance. *Economic Survey, Various Issues.*

15. ———— Ministry of Finance. Directorate of Inspection. *All India Income Tax Statistics (AIITS), Various Issues.*

16. ———— Reserve Bank of India. *RBI Bulletin, Various Issues.*

OTHER RELEVANT WRITINGS ON THE SUBJECT BY THE AUTHOR

1. Kumar, A. 1982. Real Estate Boom in Delhi: Has the Bubble Burst? *Financial Express.* April 29 and 30.

2. ———— 1983. Complexity and Essence. (Review of *Promise and Performance* by Praxy Fernandes). *Hindustan Times.* November 6.

3. ——— 1984. Black is Bountiful. *Herald Review*. November 14.
4. ——— 1985. Sugar Pricing: Accounting for Unaccounted Accounts. *Business Standard*. February 22 and 23.
5. ——— 1985. Black Money Menace: Lower Taxes No Solution. *Business Standard*. May 7 and 8.
6. ——— 1985. Black Money Phenomenon. *Frontline*. June 1-14.
7. ——— 1985. The Black Economy Report: A Critical Review. (Review of *Aspects of Black Economy in India* by Acharya, S N & Associates). *Social Scientist*. Sept.
8. ——— 1987. State Funding of Elections No Solution to Black Money in Politics. *Economic Times*. December 9.
9. ——— 1988. Real Estate and Stocks: Speculators in Command. *Financial Express*. July 25.
10. ——— 1988. The Harm Black Money does to the Economy. *Deccan Herald*. November 22
11. ——— 1988. Taxation and the Black Economy. *Deccan Herald*. November 29.
12. ——— 1989. The Case for High Property Taxes. *Financial Express*. May 30.
13. ——— 1990. Tax Reforms: Making the Desirable Possible. *Economic Times*. February 22.
14. ——— 1990. Tax Reforms: Steps to be Taken. *Economic Times*. February 23.
15. ——— 1991. Rising Surplus, Stagnant Savings. Review of Roy Chowdhury, U.D. and Bagchi, A. (ed) Domestic Savings in India: Trends and Issues. *Economic Times*. August 4.
16. ——— 1991. Black Money Schemes: Catch 22 Situation. *Hindustan Times*. October 2.
17. ——— 1992. Speculation and the Union Budget 1992-93. *Hindustan Times*. April.
18. ——— 1992. Finance Scam and the JPC. *Hindu*. October 12 & 13.
19. ——— 1992. Economic Reforms : For Whose Benefit? *Hindustan Times*. October 14.
20. ——— 1994. The New Invaders: Pitfalls of Globalization Designed Abroad. *Indian Express*. August 8
21. ———. 1994. Plague: Reason for Introspection. *The Hindu*. October 13
22. ——— 1994. Electoral Reform: Treat the Voter as King. *Indian Express*. December 7.
23. ——— 1995. The Real Reform Checking Illegality. *The Economic Times*. February 2.
24. ——— 1995. The Real Emergency . *The Hindu*. August 24 and 25.
25. ——— 1996. The Creamy Layer Havala. *The Hindu*. January 24.

26. ——— 1996. Is it the Silly Season Again? *The Economic Times.* January 27.
27. ——— 1996. The Real Rate of Industrial Growth. *The Hindu.* February 28.
28. ——— 1998. Case for Strengthening Democracy in India. *Politics India.* January.
29. ——— 1998. VDIS or VDWS: Does it matter? *The Economic Times.* March 3.